Ministers of Propaganda

# Ministers of Propaganda

*Truth, Power, and the Ideology of the Religious Right*

Scott M. Coley

WILLIAM B. EERDMANS PUBLISHING COMPANY

GRAND RAPIDS, MICHIGAN

Wm. B. Eerdmans Publishing Co.
4035 Park East Court SE, Grand Rapids, Michigan 49546
www.eerdmans.com

Book design by Lydia Hall

Printed in the United States of America

30 29 28 27 26 25 24     1 2 3 4 5 6 7

ISBN 978-0-8028-8281-3

**Library of Congress Cataloging-in-Publication Data**

A catalog record for this book is available from the Library of Congress.

Unless otherwise noted, Scripture quotations are taken from the Christian Standard Bible.

*For Melissa*

# Contents

# INTRODUCTION

# *The Scandals of Evangelicalism*

A merican evangelicalism is beset by two distinct yet related scandals, one intellectual and the other social. In the decades since Mark Noll published *The Scandal of the Evangelical Mind*, evangelical anti-intellectualism has only grown more pronounced: white evangelicals are overrepresented among skeptics of public health officials and scientific experts; and white evangelicals are more likely than other Americans to embrace conspiracy theories that threaten public health and weaken our nation's democratic institutions. According to a 2021 poll from the Public Religion Research Institute (PRRI), a majority (60 percent) of white evangelicals believe that the 2020 presidential election was stolen, and white evangelicals are more likely than any other demographic to embrace QAnon (nearly one in four).[1] A 2015 study by Pew Research Center found that only 28 percent of white evangelicals believe that climate change is caused by human activity, while 37 percent believe there's no solid evidence for climate change at all.[2]

Meanwhile, a large and growing number of evangelicals are dismayed by the social agenda that has come to define American evangelicalism: for over fifty years, a majority of white evangelicals have consistently opposed political efforts to rectify race and gender inequalities. White evangelicals were among the last Americans

1

to abandon their commitment to laws imposing racial segregation, and white evangelical leaders continue to express skepticism about the impact of systemic racism. Thus many white evangelicals attribute racial disparities in wealth and income not to systemic racism or centuries of oppression but to vices that disproportionately afflict people of color. The same white evangelicals are likely to view gender inequality not as an expression of human iniquity but as evidence of God's design. Indeed, white evangelicals were instrumental in halting the Equal Rights Amendment in the 1970s. And some prominent evangelical institutions still promote an overtly patriarchal vision of gender roles, according to which women shouldn't be permitted to speak in church or exercise authority over men under any circumstances, and the ideal domestic arrangement is one in which a husband provides income while his wife keeps house and raises children. Experts who interrogate these evangelical social preferences—sociologists, historians, philosophers, and race or gender theorists—are routinely dismissed by evangelical gatekeepers as "Marxists" or "secular humanists," whose methods of analysis are "incompatible with a Christian worldview."

## Ideology, Propaganda, and "Deconstruction"

I argue that American evangelicalism's social and intellectual infirmities are mutually reinforcing: social practices shape beliefs about what others deserve and which authorities are legitimate; those beliefs, in turn, shape social practices. By way of illustration, a striking historical example of such a feedback loop is found in the cooperation between white supremacy and racial segregation in the Jim Crow South: racial segregation (a social practice) normalizes white supremacy (a belief), which in turn reinforces racial segregation, which perpetuates white supremacy, and so on. I'll use the term *ideology* to describe this kind of feedback loop between beliefs and social practices.

Ideology is facilitated by *propaganda* that manipulates political, intellectual, or religious ideals in order to preempt dissent and silence perspectives that threaten an ideology's legitimacy. In what follows, I will give special attention to one form of propaganda in particular: rhetoric that appropriates an ideal in order to perpetuate intellectual or social practices that contradict that very ideal. Those who defended the institution of slavery in the antebellum South, for instance, often appealed to the political ideal of *liberty* in alleging their right to own other human beings—maintaining that they should have the liberty to practice slavery if they wished.[3] Thus, they argued, efforts to end slavery constituted a violation of their liberty. Of course, the principal argument *against* the institution of slavery is that it violates enslaved persons' right to liberty. But that appeal to liberty is neutralized if, as antebellum southerners alleged, the ideal of liberty is more fully realized in the freedom to enslave than in freedom from slavery. So antebellum enslavers' appeal to liberty is an example of exactly the kind of propaganda I have in mind: it invokes a political ideal (liberty) in defense of an institution (slavery) that undermines that very ideal (by depriving people of liberty). What makes this form of propaganda especially potent is that it forecloses the possibility of dissent by appropriating the very ideals that animate dissenting arguments: liberty cannot serve as the basis for outlawing slavery if true liberty consists in the freedom to own slaves.

I contend that much of what's described as evangelical *deconstruction* is essentially an effort to decode propaganda that's embedded in the ideology of the religious right. As we'll see, ideology and propaganda don't operate in a vacuum: they are part of a broader ecosystem that involves social practices, the stories we tell ourselves about the legitimacy of our own social practices, and modes of reasoning that dispose us to find those stories credible. In presenting the argument of the book, I'll need a framework for organizing the salient features of such an ecosystem. And as I lay out the details of that framework, a concrete example will enhance clarity. So before turning to more recent developments in American evangelicalism, let us dwell on the example of white supremacy in the antebellum South and unpack its internal logic—particularly the role of white evangelical theology in legitimizing the entire system.

## White Supremacy and Evangelical Theology

We've observed that the defenders of American slavery believed the political ideal of liberty to be expressed more fully in freedom to enslave than in freedom from enslavement. The absurdity of this appeal was obscured by the social hierarchy on which American slavery was based: liberty was the birthright of those at the top of the hierarchy, while those at the bottom of the hierarchy were regarded as property. According to the logic of that hierarchy, abolishing slavery was tantamount to depriving those atop the hierarchy of their liberty to hold a particular form of property, namely slaves.[4] So defending slavery in the name of liberty seemed plausible to antebellum southerners because they were enculturated into a social hierarchy in which some people *owned* property and some people *were* property.

Still, it's not as though it just hadn't occurred to anyone that race-based chattel slavery was problematic: by the middle of the nineteenth century, all of America's North Atlantic peers had abolished chattel slavery. Within the United States, attitudes toward slavery were bitterly divided, prompting denominational splits among Baptists, Methodists, and Presbyterians.[5] So it's worth asking how the defenders of slavery maintained the legitimacy of a social hierarchy that classified some human beings as property, and how they justified basing this hierarchy on race.

The answer to both questions is *biblical prooftexting*. In keeping with a pattern that we'll have occasion to revisit throughout the book, when white evangelicals in the antebellum South needed to defend the indefensible, they appealed to theological narratives based on dubious interpretations of isolated passages of Scripture. The primary text used to defend American slavery is found in the ninth chapter of Genesis, to which we'll return in a moment. Lesser prooftexts included verses like Leviticus 25:45–46, according to which the Israelites may purchase and take possession of strangers who sojourn among them. (Of course, antebellum southerners weren't ancient Israelites; and the people they enslaved were only "sojourning" in the American South by virtue of their ancestors' having been abducted and sold into slavery. Conveniently, theological defenses of slavery often overlook Exodus 21:16, according to which anyone who abducts and sells a person into slavery shall be put to death.) In Genesis 17:12, God instructs Abraham to circumcise slaves; and God commands Israel in Deuteronomy 20:10–11 to take captive those they've defeated in battle. (Again, these instructions were issued to Abraham and the Israelites, respectively, under circumstances very different from those that obtained in the antebellum South.) In the New Testament, Paul repeatedly (see Rom. 13; Col. 3:22; 1 Tim. 6:1–2) instructs slaves to obey their masters, even when slave and master are fellow believers.[6] (Never mind that Paul was writing letters to specific people in a context that presupposed slavery as a feature of the social order, not a political treatise on the question that confronted antebellum southerners—namely, whether slavery *should be* a feature of their own social order.)

Even more dubious was the theological justification for a system of chattel slavery based on race in particular. It derives from a puzzling episode in the ninth chapter of Genesis, often called *the curse of Canaan* (or, alternatively, *the curse of Ham*). Following the flood, Noah exits the ark and plants a vineyard. He then ferments wine and gets drunk, gets naked, and passes out in his tent (vv. 20–21). Ham, the youngest of Noah's three sons, discovers Noah in this state and alerts his older brothers, Shem and Japheth (v. 22). The two older brothers then walk backward into Noah's tent (to avoid seeing their father naked) and cover him with a cloak (v. 23). The text is a bit ambiguous about who did what, but the reader is left to infer that Shem and Japheth reacted appropriately to the revelation that their father was drunk, naked, and unconscious, while Ham did not. When Noah awakens and realizes what Ham has done, he curses Ham's son, Canaan, along with all of Canaan's descendants. Why Noah cursed Ham's descendants rather than Ham himself, the text doesn't say. Nor does the text indicate what led Noah to curse Canaan rather than one (or all) of Ham's other three sons. The text does report that Noah was approximately six hundred years old at the time (vv. 28–29), and context suggests that he may have been suffering from a formidable headache on the morning in question. So we can't rule out the possibility that Noah was just confused. In any event, according to Noah's curse, the descendants of Canaan were destined to be enslaved by the descendants of Shem and Japheth.

Despite the fact that Canaan and his descendants were cursed by Noah, *not God*, evangelicals in the antebellum South cited this episode in Genesis 9 as divine sanction for enslaving the descendants of Canaan in perpetuity. And for essentially no reason at all, those same evangelicals asserted that Black people were descended from Canaan.[7] Hence, according to this line of theological reflection, the institution of race-based chattel slavery in nineteenth-century America enjoyed God's blessing because, one morning roughly four thousand years ago, for reasons that aren't entirely clear, a probably hungover six-hundred-year-old man cursed the descendants of his grandson, Canaan—who might, for all anyone knows, be a distant ancestor of people who were later kidnapped from the continent of Africa and sold into slavery in the American South. The proslavery theology of Iveson L. Brookes, a founding trustee of the Southern Baptist Theological Seminary (1859–1861), features a typical appeal to Genesis 9:

> God himself instituted human slavery, when he authorized Noah to doom the posterity of Ham, through his youngest son Canaan (see Genesis ix.) to perpetual servitude: and the perpetuity of that doom rests, not merely upon the authority of Bible prophecy, but upon the unalterable stamp of inferiority of intellect, which characterizes the descendants of Canaan, and must make them in some form or shape, servants of Shem and Japhet, as well as servants of one another.[8]

Presbyterian minister and theologian Robert Lewis Dabney shared Brookes's assessment of Genesis 9 and his views on racial hierarchy—which views, in turn, reinforce his exegesis of the text. In view of upcoming concerns about ideology and biblical interpretation, Dabney's reasoning on this point is worth quoting at length:

> In explanation of [Genesis 9], the following remarks may be made; on which the majority of sound expositors are agreed. In

this transaction, Noah acts as an inspired prophet, and also as the divinely chosen, patriarchal head of church and state, which were then confined to his one family. God's approbation attended his verdict, as is proved by the fact that the divine Providence has been executing it for many ages since Noah's death. Canaan probably concurred in the indecent and unnatural sin of Ham. As these early men were extremely ambitious of a numerous and prosperous posterity, Ham's punishment, and Canaan's, consisted in the mortification of hearing their descendants doomed to a degraded lot. These descendants were included in the punishment of their wicked progenitors on that well-known principle of God's providence, which "visits the sin of the fathers upon the children," and this again is explained by the fact, that depraved parents will naturally rear depraved children . . . so that not only punishment, but the sinfulness, becomes hereditary. Doubtless God's sentence, here pronounced by Noah, was based on his foresight of the fact, that Ham's posterity, like their father, would be peculiarly degraded in morals; as actual history testifies of them, so far as its voice extends.[9]

It's worth underscoring the fact that Genesis 9 says nothing about God's having "authorized" or "inspired" Noah to curse Canaan. Nor does the text report that Canaan or his descendants were morally or intellectually inferior to anyone else. And there's no evidence of any kind—biblical or otherwise—that persons enslaved in the American South were among the descendants of Canaan.

Given that the reasoning of Confederate theologians like Dabney and Brookes was so obviously and fatally flawed, we might wonder why so many white evangelicals in the antebellum South found their arguments compelling. The Southern Baptist Theological Seminary's *Report on Slavery and Racism in the History of the Southern Baptist Theological Seminary* provides some insight on this point:

> Slaveholding affected the shape of nearly all aspects of experience in most parts of the South and formed the basis of plans for securing prosperity for wives and children. Throughout the na-

tion the slave economy was fundamental to prosperity of a large swath of American business and finance. In consequence, slavery perverted the social conscience of most southern and many northern whites.[10]

White evangelicals in the antebellum South benefitted tremendously from the institution of slavery. Thus they believed biblical defenses of slavery to be compelling at least in part because they *wanted* to believe that biblical defenses of slavery were compelling. Psychologists call this *motivated reasoning*: reasoning that's motivated by self-interest. (This is why, for example, we expect referees to be impartial, and we ask judges to recuse themselves when their own interests may be affected by the outcome of a given case.) As we'll see, motivated reasoning predisposes us to accept narratives that legitimize social practices which serve our own interests—even when the practices in question are clearly illegitimate (like slavery) and the legitimizing narrative is obviously flawed (like the use of Genesis 9 to justify slavery).[11]

Our account of white supremacy in the antebellum South suggests the following heuristic—a general, working model—for analyzing ideology and propaganda. Ideology begins with some form of *social hierarchy* that requires moral justification: why think it's acceptable for these people to possess wealth, liberty, and power while others are impoverished, subjugated, or disenfranchised? That justification comes in the form of a *legitimizing narrative*: a story meant to explain the moral legitimacy of the social hierarchy in question. Legitimizing narratives are facilitated by *motivated reasoning*, which inclines us to accept even poor, unreasonable justifications for social arrangements that we prefer. (As we'll see, one needn't occupy a position of privilege within a given hierarchy in order for motivated reasoning to have this effect: even those whose status within the hierarchy is relatively low might be motivated to defend the established social order, for fear that they might fare worse under some other arrangement.) Finally, *propaganda* insulates our legitimizing narratives from arguments against the established hierarchy by manipulating and appropriating the ideals on which opposing arguments are based.

A recurring theme throughout the book will be legitimizing narratives that draw on the resources of religion—specifically, Christian theology as it is practiced within the power centers of American evangelicalism. Because regard for the authority of Scripture is core to evangelical identity, legitimizing narratives that claim biblical provenance are especially potent. Thus evangelicalism's intellectual marketplace is inundated with a theological practice that I will call the *hermeneutics of legitimization*. (Hermeneutics is the study of interpretation, especially methods for interpreting sacred texts like the Bible.) The hermeneutics of legitimization is an approach to biblical interpretation that consistently produces moral justifications for social practices and institutional arrangements that benefit oneself. In addition to biblical prooftexting, two habits of mind are essential to the hermeneutics of legitimization. The first is a practice that I'll call *motivated literalism*, which is a tendency to interpret Scripture literally, but *only* when it doesn't undermine one's material interests. Motivated literalism allows evangelicals to insist that the earth and all its contents were created in six twenty-four-hour days (Gen. 1:1–2:3) while maintaining that Jesus didn't really intend to say that a wealthy man will have more difficulty entering heaven than a camel passing through the eye of a needle (Matt. 19:24), or that Jesus didn't really expect his followers to emulate the conduct of the Good Samaritan (Luke 10:30–37).[12]

The second habit of mind that's essential to the hermeneutics of legitimization is the theological paradigm of authority and submission. According to this paradigm, "Who has authority and who must submit?" is one of the principal questions the Bible sets out to answer, and it should be front of mind as we seek to understand and apply Scripture. Predictably, evangelicals who embrace this paradigm—who believe that instituting human hierarchies of authority and submission is one of Scripture's overriding concerns—believe the Bible to be littered with prooftexts that confirm the moral legitimacy of institutions that preserve the power and privilege of evangelicals like themselves.[13] As we'll see, the hermeneutics of legitimization renders Scripture both useful for legitimizing and useless for critiquing the social practices and political objectives of American evangelicals—especially evangelical leaders.

Before moving on, I should take a moment to acknowledge and discard a few potential concerns about my characterization of white supremacy and the role of white evangelicals in defending race-based chattel slavery. The first is that evangelicals weren't the only Americans who defended the institution of slavery. I concede the point. In fact, this is consistent with a pattern we find in contemporary politics: so-called cobelligerents who are happy to patronize conservative evangelicals as long as their political interests are aligned. This phenomenon does nothing to mitigate the fact that white evangelicals used biblical prooftexts to legitimize American slavery. Another worry might be that my analysis is potentially misleading, since there were also evangelicals who condemned slavery. This is accurate: many evangelicals in the United States and abroad condemned slavery. And those evangelicals were denounced by other evangelicals who were desperate to preserve the institution of slavery. This book isn't about evangelicals who claim that their faith inspires them to seek justice for the oppressed—it's about those whose faith is a perennial source of justification for social arrangements that benefit themselves, often to the detriment of marginalized groups. A final concern is that it's difficult to judge the merits of my argument thus far, or the promise of what's to come, since I have yet to indicate what I mean by *evangelical* or *religious right*, or how I conceive of the relationship between the two. I'll address this now.

## Evangelicalism and Ideology

Religious affiliation involves both personal belief and social context, and accounts of evangelicalism often emphasize one or the other. The National Association of Evangelicals (NAE) offers a characteristic example of the emphasis on evangelicalism as a system of personal beliefs, defining an evangelical as one who embraces the following four theological commitments:

- *conversionism*—the belief that lives need to be transformed through a "born-again" experience and a lifelong process of following Jesus;

- *biblicism*—a high regard for and obedience to the Bible as the ultimate authority;
- *activism*—the expression and demonstration of the gospel in missionary and social reform efforts;
- *crucicentrism*—a stress on the sacrifice of Jesus Christ on the cross as making possible the redemption of humanity.[14]

The NAE maintains that "these distinctives and theological convictions define us—not political, social or cultural trends." Nevertheless, social scientists, historians, and scholars of religion have observed that evangelicalism can be fruitfully described in terms of evangelical social practices, political commitments, and institutional networks.[15]

For the purposes of my argument, it's not important to settle the question of whether evangelicalism is best understood as a set of shared theological convictions, a social movement, a collection of institutional networks, or some combination thereof. My project concerns evangelicals but not evangelicalism as such. Regardless of how we define *evangelical* or where we draw the line of demarcation between evangelicals and nonevangelicals, the fact remains that we can identify prevailing patterns of thought and practice within American evangelical theology, politics, and institutions.[16] I'm interested in analyzing these identifiable patterns in order to expose the ways in which evangelical theology *shapes and is shaped by* the objectives of political conservatism in the United States. This dynamic, I argue, is key to understanding the moral and intellectual scandals that now plague American evangelicalism. So, for my purposes, it doesn't matter whether this or that individual counts as an evangelical, or why. Nor does it matter whether every single evangelical embraces a given belief or practice featured in my account. As far as evangelicalism is concerned, all that matters to my argument is that we can identify prevailing norms of belief and practice among evangelicals.[17]

For roughly half a century, conservative politicians have courted evangelical leaders as a means of winning elections; and evangelical leaders, in turn, have framed winning elections as a means of shaping American culture in their own image. A by-product of this

transaction is an ideology that brings religion into conversation with
right-wing politics—hence the ideology of the religious right. In particular, the religious right is presently under the sway of an ideology
that I will call *Christo-authoritarianism*, since it presses the resources
of Christian theology into the service of authoritarian social and
political objectives.

I should emphasize that not all evangelicals embrace the ideology
of the religious right. Some actively oppose it. Others reject the ideology of the religious right in principle while simultaneously promoting
theological doctrines—for example, gender hierarchy—that further
the social and political objectives of the religious right in practice.
Conversely, not all who promote the ideology of the religious right
are evangelical Protestants: some are Roman Catholic, Eastern Orthodox, or mainline Protestant.[18] Indeed, some public figures who
wield considerable influence on the religious right—such as Jordan
Peterson, Ben Shapiro, Dave Rubin—don't identify themselves as
Christians at all, let alone evangelical Protestants.

## Christo-Authoritarianism

In tracing the genealogy of Christo-authoritarianism, I'll draw on
a number of threads—historical, political, theological, scientific,
economic, and philosophical—the connections among which may
not be immediately obvious until the full picture comes into view.
So it will be helpful to highlight some defining elements of Christo-
authoritarianism and indicate how each element features in the arguments of the chapters to follow.

Christo-authoritarianism, as its name suggests, is a species of
authoritarian ideology that incorporates elements of the Christian
tradition. Christo-authoritarian ideology is "Christian" only in the
sense that it uses the resources of Christian theology to underwrite
its authoritarianism—not unlike Islamofascism uses the teachings
of Islam to underwrite fascism. There's nothing inherently fascist
about the teachings of Islam, and there's nothing inherently Islamic
about fascist ideology; Islamofascism emerges when the teachings of
Islam are pressed into the service of fascist politics. Similarly, there's

nothing inherently authoritarian about the teachings of Christianity, and there's nothing inherently Christian about authoritarianism. The prevalence of Christo-authoritarianism among American evangelicals is the product of a decades-long effort to legitimize the increasingly authoritarian political project of American conservatism using the theological resources of evangelical Protestantism. This effort has been advanced, wittingly or unwittingly, by ministers of propaganda: celebrity preachers, entrepreneurial theologians, parachurch leaders, and conservative pundits and politicians.

In describing the political ideology in question as "authoritarian," I mean to indicate that it meets all the classic criteria that political theorists ascribe to authoritarian political movements, namely:

- rigid commitment to social hierarchy as a source of moral order;
- propaganda that manipulates moral and intellectual ideals;
- a social identity rooted in nostalgia for a mythic past;
- conspiracy theories that delegitimize conventional sources of authority;
- anti-intellectualism;
- a sense of victimhood that engenders populist resentment of "cultural elites";
- emphasis on "law and order" as a means of preserving the status quo through violence; and
- sexual anxiety that finds expression in patriarchal masculinity and fetishization of racial or ethnic purity.[19]

For the sake of clarity, I'll occasionally pause to highlight these features of authoritarianism throughout the book, drawing attention to the ways in which evangelical Protestants have deployed Christian theology to legitimize the features of authoritarianism at hand in a given case.

Finally, in the interest of continuity, it will be helpful to anticipate the point of contact between the foregoing features of authoritarianism and the arguments of the chapters to follow. Chapter 1 develops a framework for analyzing ideology and propaganda, with emphasis on prevailing social practices, legitimizing narratives, and theological commitments rooted in so-called common sense. I then turn to theological propaganda that aims to justify rigid gender hierarchy using the hermeneutics of legitimization. We'll also consider propagandistic appeals to biblical authority that in fact serve to subordinate the authority of Scripture to the sovereign "common sense" of ecclesial authorities. The argument of the first chapter thus highlights sexual anxiety, social hierarchy, and an important precursor to anti-intellectualism (namely, common sense).

Chapter 2 examines evangelical attempts to legitimize racial hierarchy—and related anxieties around sexuality and racial purity—using the very methods of biblical interpretation deployed in legitimizing gender hierarchy. We'll then consider the propaganda of colorblindness, which furnishes white evangelicals with intellectual resources to decry racism while actively perpetuating racialized socioeconomic disparities rooted in white supremacy.

Chapters 3 and 4 focus on the creation science industry and its pivotal role in legitimizing the social objectives of political conservatism, along with skepticism of experts who call those objectives into question. Evangelical skepticism of mainstream science has accelerated in recent decades. Most evangelicals in the middle of the twentieth century endorsed "day-age" or "gap" interpretations of Genesis 1–2, which can accommodate the insights of modern science. But by the 1980s, "creationism" was largely synonymous with the proposition that all life on earth was created in six twenty-four-hour days roughly ten thousand years ago. By 1991, according to Gallup, just under 47 percent of Americans believed that humans were created no more than ten thousand years ago.[20] And a 2015 survey by Pew Research Center found that 60 percent of white evangelicals believe that God created all living things in their current form.[21] These developments track with the growth of the creation science industry, from the Institute for Creation Research to the Creation Museum and the Ark Encounter. Moreover, the creation science industry has proven to be a model for alternative evangelical gatekeeping institutions with their own "experts" and "peer-reviewed journals" that legitimize the aims of cultural conservatism. I argue that creation science is itself a form of propaganda, insofar as it appeals to the intellectual ideal of rigorous scientific inquiry in service to an agenda that promotes pseudoscience over and against the consensus of actual scientific experts.

I do not argue that evangelicals reject all deliverances of modern science. (I'd wager that most evangelicals have no special reservations about taking their cholesterol medication, using GPS technology on their smartphones, or tracking their heart rate with an Apple watch.) The point, rather, is that the creation science industry has engendered habits of mind that enable a majority of evangelicals to reject the consensus of scientific experts whenever that consensus is in tension with the social, economic, or political objectives of the religious right. Thus, in addition to deploying propaganda and legitimizing social hierarchies favored by social conservatives, the creation science movement promotes anti-intellectualism, conspiratorial ideation, and a sense of victimization by mainstream "secular" elites—all important features of authoritarian ideology.

Chapter 4 examines the social and political context that engendered the rise of the creation science movement in the middle of the twentieth century. The identity of the modern religious right was forged in reaction to demands for equal rights on the part of women and people of color. The religious right has long alleged that gender parity violates the domestic arrangement prescribed by God in the third chapter of Genesis, featuring man as breadwinner and woman as homemaker. It's worth noting that this legitimizing narrative, like the curse of Canaan, is based on an interpretive approach to Genesis that's facilitated by the creation science industry. We'll examine this connection in chapters 2 and 3. Meanwhile, white supremacist tropes about the curse of Canaan remain in circulation today.[22] (In keeping with my assessment of the creation science industry, the Ark Encounter renders Ham's wife—the mother of Canaan—with an unambiguously darker complexion than any other character depicted in the exhibit.) The persistence of this legitimizing myth enables white evangelical resistance to the reality of structural racism, insofar as it furnishes an explanation for racial disparities in wealth and income apart from America's history of racial discrimination, oppression, and disenfranchisement. Consistent denial of the role that structural racism plays in perpetuating racial disparities is integral to the persistence of racial hierarchy—which hierarchy is a core feature of authoritarian politics.

Together, the arguments of chapters 1 through 4 document a process of intellectual and cultural ghettoization that has accelerated since the middle of the twentieth century. As a result, the social and cognitive (un)reality that a majority of white evangelicals inhabit is one in which the conventional gatekeepers of knowledge—so-called cultural elites in the scientific establishment, higher education, and mainstream media—routinely disseminate misinformation designed to undermine "traditional" (white) Christian, American values. These conventional gatekeepers have been supplanted by an evangelical culture war machine that privileges the "biblical" common sense of celebrity preachers and enterprising theologians over genuine expertise. Unreality, conspiracy, the imminent threat from "cultural elites," and social hierarchies founded on race, gender, and sexual anxiety are integral features of authoritarian politics, all of which are actively perpetuated by ministers of propaganda under the auspices of a "biblical" worldview.

Building on our analysis of racial hierarchy and white supremacist propaganda, chapters 5 and 6 examine the prevailing evangelical fondness for antidemocratic politics—from the birth of the New Right in the latter half of the twentieth century to the religious right's current embrace of soft authoritarianism. Chapter 5 argues that conservative politicians since Reagan have leveraged racial resentment to give middle- and working-class (white) voters the false impression that their economic interests are served by cuts to government programs that benefit undeserving (Black) welfare recipients. (The politics of racial resentment hardly began with Reagan—he was merely the first modern conservative to successfully couch the argument for economic austerity within the politics of racial resentment.) Thus the religious right since Reagan has encouraged middle- and working-class (white) voters to pull themselves up by their bootstraps, clutch their pocketbooks, and eye people of color with suspicion. Meanwhile, economic elites have robbed the rest of America blind. Thus, with the indispensable support of the religious right, conservative politicians in the United States have engineered staggering levels of economic inequality, eroding democratic institutions and inviting the rise of authoritarian populism. As downward mobility breeds victimhood, resentment, and nativism, members of traditionally privileged groups—those who perceive themselves as "real Americans"—take refuge in the politics of "law and order," which promises to preserve the established order through violence.

Chapter 6 highlights the growing affinity between authoritarian political tactics and a form of religious ethnonationalism according to which "real Americans" are (white) Christians.[23] For example, much of the present controversy around the alleged influence of "critical race theory" in public education has nothing to do with critical race theory. Rather, it's a manifestation of the religious right's anxiety over basic facts of American history that call into question the social, political, and economic axioms of Christian nationalist mythology. While it's natural to see this dispute as a disagreement over competing visions of America's history, on a more fundamental level it is in fact a disagreement over competing visions of history as an enterprise. Cultural conservatives see US history as an exercise in corporate nostalgia, meant to inform our collective understanding of who we are as a nation. Whether or to what extent this nostalgia corresponds to any actual moment in our nation's past is irrelevant. Indeed, insofar as genuine insights into the actual people, events, or material conditions of our national past threaten to problematize conservatives' sense of our national identity, genuine historical inquiry is at cross-purposes with the function that conservatives call upon history to perform—namely, promoting a national myth that confers legitimacy on their understanding of America as *their* nation, rooted in *their* values. This founding myth is a key element in the religious right's embrace of authoritarianism, insofar as it justifies the use of violence and antidemocratic tactics as a means of reclaiming the nation that they believe to be rightfully theirs.

Finally, chapter 7 argues that Christianity itself provides resources for disrupting the ecosystem in which Christo-authoritarianism thrives. Ideology, propaganda, and motivated reasoning are powerful forces that afflict all human beings. But Christians can and should resist these forces by actively questioning the legitimacy of social hierarchies that privilege our own interests above those of our neighbors, which is precisely what Christ calls us to do. When we divest ourselves of our own interests in defending the established order, we are free to abandon theological narratives that the religious right uses to legitimize that order—along with any antagonism toward expertise that poses a threat to those theological narratives. For example, when I am no longer invested in defending the way that resources are allocated in the United States, I'm free to admit that racial disparities in wealth and income are wrought by centuries of racial injustice. Then I no longer need to rely on a particular reading of Genesis for a narrative that legitimizes these disparities. And then I'm free to look dispassionately at the creation science industry and admit that it's unscientific. When we focus on giving others their due instead of legitimizing our own privilege, flawed ideology loses its intellectual purchase and we can see propaganda for what it is. Thus evangelicals can subvert Christo-authoritarianism by pursuing justice rather than pouring their energy into maintaining social arrangements that work to their own advantage.

# 1

## *Ideology, Propaganda, and Gender Hierarchy*

B efore expanding on our model of ideology and propaganda, it will be helpful to examine some longstanding evangelical assumptions about the nature of truth and human knowledge that make evangelical theology an effective conduit for ideology and propaganda.

### Common Sense

For roughly two centuries, *common sensism* has been the prevailing evangelical view of the relationship between reality and human perception.[1] In this view, all ordinary humans have some cognitive faculty that gives us direct access to reality. And by virtue of that faculty, we are well equipped to ascertain the truth about morality, Scripture, and the natural world. George Marsden observes that in the eighteenth century and following, evangelicals regarded common sensism as

> a sure base for the rational and scientific confirmation of the truths
> of the Bible and the Christian faith. The Bible, it was constantly
> asserted, was the highest and all-sufficient source of authority. . . .
> The Protestant doctrine of the perspicuity of Scripture provided a
> further basis for the belief that the common person could readily

understand Biblical teaching. Common Sense paralleled this doctrine with its insistence on the perspicuity of nature.[2]

In keeping with that general outlook, evangelicals held that

> the Bible . . . revealed the moral law; but the faculty of common
> sense, which agreed with Scripture, was a universal standard. Ac-
> cording to Common Sense philosophy, one can intuitively know
> the first principles of morality as certainly as one can apprehend
> other essential aspects of reality.[3]

Referring to the persistence of common sensism in the popular evangelical imagination, Mark Noll observes:

> The same conviction continues as a prominent feature of
> twentieth-century evangelical thought, where it appears not so
> much as a philosophical argument as a premise of mind. With the
> exception of a small group of philosophers and a smaller number
> of theologians, popular evangelical leaders have been content
> with a pragmatic, common-sensical acceptance of the reality of
> the external world, and have not been troubled by the arguments
> of idealists, historicists, or sociologists of knowledge.[4]

The salient feature of common sensism, for our purposes, is its
emphasis on the universality of common sense: the notion that *all*
ordinary humans have a cognitive faculty that allows us to directly
perceive moral, scientific, and biblical truth.[5]

The principal difficulty with common sensism is that all available
evidence indicates that no such faculty exists. Consider human perceptions of moral truth. (We'll return to biblical and scientific truth
in due course.) Assuming that moral truth is objective, if there were
some feature of human cognition that allows us to *just see* moral
truth, then we would expect most humans to agree on most questions of basic morality. But in fact, human beliefs about morality vary
widely across time and cultural context. Here are some examples of
this phenomenon, which ethicists call *moral disagreement.*

## Common Sensism and Moral Disagreement

We've already observed that the founding faculty and trustees of the Southern Baptist Theological Seminary were enthusiastic white supremacists who insisted on the moral legitimacy of race-based chattel slavery. Nearly two centuries later, the same seminary officially rejects white supremacy and acknowledges the moral illegitimacy of American slavery. The Southern Baptist Convention (SBC) has followed the same trajectory. The SBC was formed in 1845 by Baptists in the South who maintained the moral legitimacy of slavery—and, more specifically, the appropriateness of ordaining slaveholders to serve on the mission field. In 1995, the Southern Baptist Convention formally renounced and apologized for its founders' embrace of slavery. So even within a single evangelical denomination, and within a single academic institution within that denomination, we find stark examples of moral disagreement over time. If there were a universal human capacity to *just see* moral truth, we wouldn't expect to see such stark disagreement over a basic moral question like the legitimacy of race-based chattel slavery—especially within a single theological tradition, whose adherents share most of the background assumptions that are important to moral deliberation.[6]

On the issue of abortion, prevailing evangelical attitudes have been comparatively nimble, reversing course in a matter of decades rather than centuries. The Baptist Press (the SBC's official news service) observes that

> the SBC adopted a resolution at its 1971 meeting that supported legislation permitting abortion for reasons nearly as expansive as those the Supreme Court eventually allowed in Roe v. Wade and its companion ruling, Doe v. Bolton. Resolutions in 1974 and 1976 did little, if anything, to move the SBC beyond that statement.[7]

Less than ten years later, in 1980, the SBC adopted a resolution calling for a constitutional amendment that would outlaw abortion (except for threats to the mother's life). The overwhelming majority of

Southern Baptist leaders thereafter categorically affirmed efforts to overturn *Roe v. Wade*.

Moral beliefs also vary widely across cultural context, even within a single historical moment. In 1987, anthropologists at the University of Chicago surveyed six hundred subjects across two locations: the Hyde Park region of Chicago and the town of Bhubaneswar in Orissa, India. Researchers presented subjects with a variety of scenarios in which someone does something that violates prevailing moral norms either in the United States or in India, and then asked subjects to rate the rightness or wrongness of the actions described. As Jonathan Haidt recounts in his book *The Righteous Mind*, the study found that American respondents and Indian respondents disagreed sharply about the moral permissibility of the conduct described in the following situations:

> *Scenario 1.* A young married woman went alone to see a movie without informing her husband. When she returned home her husband said, "If you do it again, I will beat you black and blue." She did it again; he beat her black and blue.

> *Scenario 2.* A man had a married son and a married daughter. After his death his son claimed most of the property. His daughter got little.

> *Scenario 3.* In a family, a twenty-five-year-old son addresses his father by his first name.

> *Scenario 4.* A woman cooked rice and wanted to eat with her husband and his elder brother. Then she ate with them.[8]

American respondents regarded the conduct of the husband in scenario 1 as immoral, while Indian respondents viewed the husband's conduct as acceptable. Similarly, American respondents viewed the son's conduct in scenario 2 as wrong, while Indian respondents regarded the son's actions as acceptable. In scenario 3 and scenario 4, responses flipped: Indian respondents regarded the conduct of the son in scenario 3 and the wife in scenario 4 as wrong; and the Americans surveyed said that the behavior described in both scenarios was morally acceptable.

Examples of moral disagreement across time and culture are legion.[9] So either moral truth changes across time and culture, or a lot of people are (or have been) badly mistaken about morality. Neither option is good for the common-sense account of moral cognition. If moral truth is subject to change across time and culture, then moral relativism is true.[10] But moral relativism is totally at odds with basic tenets of Christian theology.[11] Since our central focus is the ideology of the religious right, and openly embracing moral relativism isn't an option for evangelicals, we'll just assume that moral relativism is false. It follows that a lot of people are (or have been) badly mistaken about moral truth. And if a lot of people are badly mistaken about moral truth, then there's no universal human faculty that gives us direct access to moral truth. So, at least with respect to morality, common sensism appears to be false.

I would expect those who espouse common sensism to defend their position in the following way. "Common sensism holds that all ordinary humans have the cognitive capacity to directly perceive moral truth. But this capacity can, of course, be corrupted through enculturation into morally illegitimate social practices, motivated reasoning, ideology, and propaganda. It is therefore unsurprising that we find moral disagreement across time and culture, since the influences that corrupt our moral perception also change across time and culture. So common sensism offers an accurate account of the way humans perceive moral truth, provided that their moral perception hasn't been corrupted in this way."[12]

I'm prepared to concede that moral disagreement is a result of corrupting influences. But this strikes me as a pyrrhic victory for common sensism. The fact remains that many human beings suffer from extremely unreliable moral cognition. And we have no reason to suppose that our own ability to ascertain moral truth is more reliable than that of those whose moral beliefs differ from ours. So, without some special reason for thinking that our perception is accurate, we shouldn't think that we can observe some or other human behavior and *just know*, by virtue of common sense, whether it's right or wrong.

Common-sense evangelicals are likely to respond that they *do* have a special reason for believing that their moral beliefs are true: the Bible. "I know that my beliefs about morality are true," the reasoning goes, "because I know that the Bible is true; and the Bible confirms my beliefs about morality." The logic of this reply is pristine: if Scripture is true and Scripture confirms my moral beliefs, it follows that my moral beliefs are true. Moreover, if my moral beliefs track the truth, then anyone whose moral beliefs are incompatible with mine must be mistaken. So *their* moral perception is unreliable, not mine. Thus the problem of moral disagreement isn't a problem after all—at least not for those of us who embrace biblical morality.[13]

In order to highlight the point of contact with upcoming concerns, we should dwell for a moment on this line of reasoning. For clarity, here's the argument:

1. The Bible is true.
2. The Bible confirms my moral beliefs.
3. Therefore, my moral beliefs are true.

As we've observed, the reasoning is valid: if the premises are true, then the conclusion follows. So, are the premises true?

The first premise is essentially a corollary of biblicism, which is a core theological tenet of evangelicalism (see the introduction). So we'll assume, if only for the sake of argument, that the first premise is true. Thus the evangelical's case for common-sense morality hangs on the second premise, which claims that the Bible confirms her moral beliefs. And the truth of *that* claim hinges on questions of biblical interpretation, to which we now turn.

### Common Sensism and the Science of Biblical Interpretation

In keeping with their approach to moral knowledge, evangelicals have long maintained that biblical interpretation is governed by common sense. According to Noll, "Evangelicals assumed that when they

applied scientific common sense to Scripture and God-given experience more generally, they could derive a fixed, universally valid
theology."[14] Citing the remarks of televangelist Jerry Falwell Sr. in a
1981 interview, Noll observes that

> the long-term effects . . . are visible perhaps most especially at the
> popular level, as in the recent words of a well-known television
> preacher on the growth of his own theological understanding:
> "I was studying mechanical engineering before I even became a
> Christian. . . . You come to exact, simplistic answers if you follow
> the proper equations, and the proper processes. . . . Theology, to
> me, is an exact science. God is God. The Bible is the inspired,
> [inerrant] word of God. And if everyone accepts the same theses
> and the same equations, they will arrive at the same answer."[15]

Yet the history of disagreement over biblical interpretation seems
to indicate that concurrence on "exact, simplistic answers" is less
forthcoming than Falwell suggests.

For example, over the course of roughly two decades preceding
this interview, Falwell engaged in several high-profile disagreements
with himself over the Bible's counsel on such momentous questions
as racial segregation and the role of religion in politics. Falwell is
hardly the only evangelical to have reversed course on these issues
during the 1960s and '70s. But the contrasts in his personal views
are both stark and well documented, and therefore instructive.

In a 1958 sermon on the subject of racial segregation, replete with
prooftexts from Genesis 9, Falwell asserts that

> we have left God out of decisions altogether. If Chief Justice War-
> ren and his associates had known God's Word and had desired
> to do the Lord's will, I am quite confident that the 1954 decision
> [in *Brown v. Board of Education*] would never have been made. . . .
> If we persist in tearing down God's barriers, God must punish us
> for it. The theory of communism is social equality—but there is
> no such thing. Souls are of equal value and importance, but that
> is as far as we can go. The true negro does not want integration.

He realizes his potential is far better among his own race. Who
then is propagating this terrible thing? . . . Finally, we see the Devil
himself behind it. What will integration of the races do to us? It
will destroy our race eventually.[16]

In March 1965, as civil rights leaders marched from Selma to Montgomery, Falwell remarked from his pulpit in Virginia, "I do question the sincerity and non-violent intentions of some civil rights
leaders such as Dr. Martin Luther King, Jr., Mr. James Farmer,
and others, who are known to have left-wing associations."[17] Falwell explicitly appealed to Scripture as the basis for his policy of
political separatism:

> Believing the Bible as I do, I would find it impossible to stop
> preaching the pure saving gospel of Jesus Christ, and begin doing
> anything else—including fighting communism, or participating in
> civil rights reforms. As a God-called preacher, I find that there is
> no time left after I give the proper time and attention to winning
> people for Christ. Preachers are not called to be politicians but
> soul winners.[18]

In particular, he cites Jesus's encounter with the woman at the well
as grounds for ignoring racial injustice:

> This woman was saying to Jesus that the Jews were segregated
> from the Samaritans. It was much like many of the situations ex-
> isting today in America and in other countries between different
> nations and races. But as we read the rest of the account, we see
> that Jesus totally ignored her attempt to involve Him in a discus-
> sion about segregation. He immediately began to tell her that her
> need was spiritual water.[19]

Between 1958 and the 1981 interview quoted above, Falwell reversed
his position on racial segregation and political separatism.

In or around 1970, Falwell recalled all copies of his previous sermons (many of which had been widely distributed as pamphlets) and
went on to issue a series of public apologies for the views espoused

therein. For example, in 1979, at Court Street Baptist Church in his hometown of Lynchburg, Virginia, Falwell admitted that he had been wrong to advocate for racial segregation. According to Elmer Towns, Falwell's longtime friend and colleague, Falwell told the congregation, "I'm sorry—I was wrong. I was prejudiced. I'm a product of Campbell County here. I believed what I was always told, but I was wrong."[20] And in 1980, he retracted his criticism of ministers who engage in political activism, explaining, "I was saying to pastors that we should not be involved politically; we should not be out leading marches, we should not be out demonstrating. . . . I was wrong, and later, of course, became very involved."[21]

Falwell's views on abortion also appear to have changed over time. *Listen, America!*, Falwell's Christian nationalist jeremiad published in 1981, lists abortion first among the five major sins for which America is subject to God's judgment, lamenting, "Every year millions of babies are murdered in America. . . . The Nazis murdered six million Jews, and certainly the Nazis fell under the hand of the judgment of God for these atrocities. So-called Christian America has murdered more unborn innocents than that."[22] And yet,

> according to his associate Elmer Towns, he wrote his first full-length sermon on abortion in 1978 at Towns's behest. In 1980, when journalists asked him what made him change his mind about preachers in politics, he usually responded with a list of four or five events such as the Supreme Court's school prayer decision and the "pornography explosion," and the list was always changing. In June he said that the 1973 abortion decision had been a turning point for him, but the following January he said that evangelicals (among whom he included himself) had not paid much attention to the issue until three to five years ago—that is, until 1976 or 1978.[23]

An evolving perspective on abortion would hardly have made Falwell an outlier among evangelicals of his vintage. In response to the Supreme Court's decision in *Roe v. Wade*, W. A. Criswell—former president of the Southern Baptist Convention and pastor of First Baptist Church of Dallas (where Billy Graham was a member)—

commented, "I have always felt that it was only after a child was born and had a life separate from its mother that it became an individual person, and it has always, therefore, seemed to me that what is best for the mother and for the future should be allowed." On the subject of regulating abortion, none other than Carl F. H. Henry—founding editor of *Christianity Today*, whose name adorns the Institute for Evangelical Engagement at the Southern Baptist Theological Seminary—remarked that "a woman's body is not the domain and property of others," which seems to suggest that it would be inappropriate for the state to intervene on behalf of fetal life. And at least as late as 1973, James Dobson held that since the Bible doesn't speak directly to the issue of abortion, it wouldn't be unreasonable for an evangelical to believe that a fetus isn't a full human being.[24]

Perhaps the clearest indication of how far evangelical moral sentiment has migrated on the issue of abortion is this. In November 1968, *Christianity Today* published a statement that it described as the "Consensus of 25 evangelical scholars who participated in 'A Protestant Symposium on the Control of Human Reproduction,' Aug. 27-31, 1968." The statement's prologue declares its authors' embrace of biblicism: "We affirm that ultimate values come from God through biblical revelation rather than from the human situation alone."[25] So, on the common-sense account of biblical interpretation, we'd expect to find in this statement a uniformity of opinion on the ethics of abortion—not only among the authors themselves, but between the authors and present-day evangelicals who share their regard for the authority of Scripture. Yet we find neither.

The authors note that "as to whether or not the performance of an induced abortion is always sinful we are not agreed, but about the necessity and permissibility for it under certain circumstances we are in accord." The statement continues,

The physician, in making a decision regarding abortion, should take into account the following principles:

1.    The human fetus is not merely a mass of cells or an organic growth. At the most, it is an actual human life or at the

least, a potential and developing human life. For this reason the physician with a regard for the value and sacred-
ness of human life will exercise great caution in advising
abortion.

2. The Christian physician will advise induced abortion only
to safeguard greater values sanctioned by Scripture. These
values should include individual health, family welfare,
and social responsibility.

It's difficult to imagine a single prominent evangelical today—or at
any point after, say, the mid-1980s—issuing a statement to the effect that *family welfare* or *social responsibility* might conceivably be
relevant to the moral permissibility of abortion. Yet in 1968, this was
the consensus of twenty-five evangelical scholars enlisted to issue a
statement on the evangelical view of abortion. Thus the prevailing
evangelical stance on abortion has shifted considerably since the end
of the 1960s.

Citing a range of biblical prooftexts, an overwhelming majority
of evangelicals now claim that human life begins at conception (see,
e.g., Exod. 21:22-25; Ps. 139; Isa. 44:2; Jer. 1:5; Luke 1:31, 36, 41, 44).
The difficulty this position raises for the common-sense notion of
biblical interpretation is that the Bible contained each of these prooftexts in the 1960s. All that's changed is the way that evangelicals
understand and apply these verses. If biblical interpretation were
a matter of common sense, then Christians everywhere and at all
times would agree on the essence of Scripture's counsel regarding
grave moral questions that implicate major biblical themes—for
example, the treatment of human persons as bearers of God's image. But this isn't at all what we find. In the United States alone, just
among evangelicals, the Bible's authority has been invoked on either
side of debates around slavery, segregation, abortion, gender equality, and the place of politics in Christian life. So the common-sense
notion of biblical interpretation suffers from the same prevalence of
disagreement as common-sense morality.

Even if he does so unwittingly, Falwell himself acknowledges that
common sensism is problematic when he observes that his under-

standing of morality and Scripture was heavily inflected by the social norms into which he was enculturated in Campbell County, Virginia. If common sensism were correct, then social context would be irrelevant to our grasp of morality and Scripture. But social context is clearly relevant to our understanding of morality and Scripture. So common sensism is plainly false. (Or it's at best badly misleading, if we allow that humans have some innate capacity to directly perceive moral and biblical truth but that this capacity is subject to rampant corruption.) What remains to be seen is why, given the prevalence of disagreement about morality and Scripture, common sensism continues to be the dominant evangelical view of how human beings come to know truth.

*Common Sensism as Propaganda*

As it pertains to evangelical thinking around theology and morality, common sensism is a form of propaganda that gives those in power the authority to decide what constitutes truth.

Common sensism invokes the ideal of universal human reason in service to an agenda that effectively denies the universality of human reason in order to silence dissenting viewpoints. Here's what I mean. According to common sensism, my intuitions about morality aren't merely *my intuitions*, subject to the limits of my own perspective.[26] Rather, my moral intuitions arise from a universal human capacity to directly perceive moral truth. Likewise, my reading of Scripture isn't constrained by my own interpretive horizon, which may be tethered to self-interest, personal ambition, or the limits of my own experience. Rather, my understanding of Scripture issues from the universal human capacity to directly observe biblical truth. It follows that any claim about morality or biblical interpretation that is at odds with my perception must be the product of a defective intellect. Thus common sensism appeals to universal human reason in service to an agenda that effectively denies that human reason is universal: since *my* moral beliefs and *my* understanding of Scripture are based on universal common sense, anyone who disagrees with me lacks common sense—at least with respect to any subject about which we disagree. And if anyone who disagrees with me lacks common sense, then common sense isn't universal—it's limited to me and those who agree with me.

We've already established that intuitions about morality and biblical interpretation are heavily influenced by the patterns of thought and social practice into which we've been enculturated. Consider once more Falwell's confession that "I was prejudiced. I'm a product of Campbell County here. I believed what I was always told." Falwell admits that his erstwhile insistence on the legitimacy of racial segregation was informed by his enculturation into white supremacy: in the context of the segregated South, racial segregation normalized white supremacy; and white supremacy, in turn, reinforced racial segregation, which served to perpetuate white supremacy. And given that white supremacy was woven into the background beliefs that informed his thinking about morality and Scripture, the notion that Genesis 9 was a narrative about white supremacy would have seemed to Falwell a matter of basic common sense. In other words, what we regard as a matter of common-sense morality or biblical interpretation is informed by the social and intellectual patterns into which we've been enculturated—that is, ideology. By ignoring the way that common sense is informed by social context, common sensism relegates marginalized perspectives to the domain of irrationality without so much as an argument.

Moreover, given the organizational structure of most evangelical institutions, common sensism effectively allows those in positions of influence to dictate truth by fiat: if truth comes to us through the deliverances of common sense, then those with the authority to decide what claims are consistent with common sense have the power to decide what is true. Thus propagandistic appeals to common sense culminate in a feedback loop in which institutional authority reinforces and is reinforced by epistemic authority. When those in power have the institutional authority to decide which truth claims are epistemically legitimate, they can reinforce their institutional authority by recognizing as legitimate only those truth claims that confirm the legitimacy of their own authority.

Nowhere is this dynamic more evident than in the context of ongoing evangelical debates around gender hierarchy, sometimes called

*biblical patriarchy* or *male headship* or *biblical manhood and womanhood*. Because evangelicals who advocate for gender hierarchy tend
to state their social objectives in explicit terms, arguments for biblical
patriarchy offer an uncommonly clear vantage point from which to
observe the interplay of hierarchy, ideology, and propaganda. So it will
be instructive to dwell at some length on the constellation of issues
surrounding gender hierarchy in American evangelicalism. Against
that backdrop, we'll return to questions of truth and power.

## Gender Hierarchy

Briefly, by way of background, evangelical disputes over so-called
biblical manhood and womanhood revolve around the question of
whether and to what extent Scripture prescribes a gender-based social hierarchy in which men exercise authority over women.[27] Views
on the matter fall along a spectrum that can be helpfully divided into
two general camps:

- *complementarianism*—the view that Scripture prescribes gender
  hierarchy; and
- *egalitarianism*—the view that Scripture prescribes gender
  equality.[28]

Complementarians base their position on a handful of prooftexts
that appear to commend male headship and female submission—
including, for example, Genesis 3:16, in which God declares that
Adam will rule over Eve, and 1 Timothy 2:11-12, which admonishes
women to be quiet and submissive, and forbids women from teaching or exercising authority over men. Egalitarians disagree among
themselves about how best to account for these and other complementarian prooftexts. But prooftexts notwithstanding, egalitarians
generally agree that the whole of Scripture's counsel favors gender
parity rather than patriarchy.

Most of the men who wield power within evangelical institutions
share both a fondness for complementarianism and an enthusiasm
for defending complementarianism by appeal to common sense. And

their rhetoric provides a concrete illustration of the way that common sensism allows men in positions of power to dictate truth by fiat.

A characteristic example of this dynamic appears in the spring 2008 issue of the *Journal for Biblical Manhood and Womanhood* in an essay by J. Ligon Duncan III, chancellor of Reformed Theological Seminary, former president of the Alliance of Confessing Evangelicals, and cofounder of Together for the Gospel (T4G). (It's worth noting that Duncan's essay is written on behalf of the founders of T4G: himself, Albert Mohler, C. J. Mahaney, and Mark Dever.) In a celebrated passage that prominent complementarians recite with the cadence and frequency of a ritual incantation, Duncan reasons that evangelicals must reject egalitarianism because

> the denial of complementarianism undermines the church's practical embrace of the authority of Scripture. . . . The gymnastics required to get from "I *do not* allow a woman to teach or to exercise authority over a man," in the Bible, to "I *do* allow a woman to teach and to exercise authority over a man" in the actual practice of the local church, are devastating to the functional authority of the Scripture in the life of the people of God. By the way, this is one reason why I think we just don't see many strongly inerrantist-egalitarians. . . . Inerrancy or egalitarianism, one or the other, eventually wins out.[29]

(*Inerrancy* is common shorthand for *biblical inerrancy*—the doctrine that Scripture is without error.) Without elaborating on the causal mechanism that links egalitarianism to lost esteem for Scripture's authority or inerrancy, Duncan offers a second reason why evangelicals must reject egalitarianism:

> Following on the [previous] point, the church's confidence in the clarity of Scripture is undermined [by egalitarianism], because if you can get egalitarianism from the Bible, you can get anything from the Bible. Paul may be excruciating to read aloud and hear read aloud in a dominant feminist culture, but he's not obscure in his position![30]

Citing prooftexts from 1 Timothy 2:11–12 and 1 Corinthians 14:34–35—
according to which women are to remain silent in church and direct questions or comments to their husbands in the privacy of their
homes—Duncan contends that

> these verses (and many others) are uncomfortably clear and
> certainly politically incorrect, and though some of us may be
> consoled by "exegesis" that shows that they don't really mean
> that women can't preach, teach, rule in the church, yet [sic] there
> remains this nagging feeling that such interpretive moves are
> the victory of present opinion over clear but unpopular biblical
> teaching.[31]

These arguments, according to prominent complementarians,
provide us with two compelling reasons to reject egalitarianism—
namely, that egalitarianism subverts the authority of Scripture
and it's inconsistent with the clarity of Scripture.[32] Both claims
are propaganda.

Consider the notion that egalitarianism is inconsistent with confidence in the clarity of Scripture. Duncan reasons that the Bible
clearly and unambiguously endorses gender hierarchy—and thus,
in an effort to avoid that fact, egalitarians must adopt methods of biblical interpretation that obscure the clear meaning of the text. Note
that Duncan's whole line of reasoning is predicated on the notion
that complementarians are obviously correct about the meaning and
significance of Paul's remarks on gender. But egalitarians deny this.
Rather than engaging egalitarians in good faith—as spiritual and intellectual equals who sincerely disagree—Duncan's reasoning simply
assumes, without argument, that egalitarians are wrong. Assuming
that at least some egalitarians are Christians who sincerely believe
that egalitarianism is consistent with Scripture, it follows that those
egalitarians simply lack the ability to perceive the clear meaning of
Scripture (at least with respect to the subject at hand). This is pure
common sensism. And for precisely the reasons outlined above,
it's propaganda: Duncan invokes the universal human capacity to
directly perceive the meaning of Scripture in order to advance an

argument from which it follows that the capacity to perceive the meaning of Scripture is not, in fact, universal.

Before moving on, I should mention three additional flaws in Duncan's line of argument. One is that his appeal to the clarity of Scripture is hopelessly question-begging. The notion that egalitarianism is inconsistent with the clarity of Scripture presupposes that Scripture clearly mandates gender hierarchy. But that's precisely the point at issue in the debate: complementarians say that the Bible prescribes gender hierarchy, and egalitarians say that it doesn't. So unless I've already accepted the argument's conclusion that I should reject egalitarianism, I have no reason to accept its premise that egalitarianism is at odds with the clarity of Scripture. But that's not how arguing works. An argument doesn't ask us to assume its conclusion in order to find its reasoning persuasive—it compels us to accept its conclusion with persuasive reasoning. So the appeal to the clarity of Scripture can't be a good argument for complementarianism, because it isn't an argument.

A second problem with the appeal to the clarity of Scripture is that it emphasizes isolated prooftexts over and against the whole of Scripture. Favorite complementarian prooftexts include:

- 1 Timothy 2:11-12: "A woman is to learn quietly with full submission. I do not allow a woman to teach or to have authority over a man; instead, she is to remain quiet."
- 1 Corinthians 14:34-35: "As in all the churches of the saints, the women should be silent in the churches, for they are not permitted to speak, but are to submit themselves, as the law also says. If they want to learn something, let them ask their own husbands at home, since it is disgraceful for a woman to speak in the church."
- Titus 2:3-5: "In the same way, older women are to be reverent in behavior, not slanderers, not slaves to excessive drinking. They are to teach what is good, so that they may encourage the young women to love their husbands and to love their children, to be self-controlled, pure, workers at home, kind, and in submission to their husbands, so that God's word will not be slandered."
- Ephesians 5:22-24: "Wives, submit to your husbands as to the

Lord, because the husband is the head of the wife as Christ is
the head of the church. He is the Savior of the body. Now as the
church submits to Christ, so also wives are to submit to their husbands in everything."

Complementarians like Duncan argue that in light of these verses,
no reasonable person can doubt that the Bible prescribes a gender
hierarchy in which women submit to the authority of men.[33]

Note the way that this reasoning conflates *the contents of a few
decontextualized Bible verses* with *the import of the entire Bible*. This is
a tacit acknowledgment that the debate around gender doesn't really
turn on complementarian prooftexts. The point at issue isn't whether
we can locate a few Bible verses that seem to support patriarchy—it's
fairly obvious that we can. The point, rather, is whether the Bible
as a whole counsels us to pursue gender hierarchy or gender parity.
Prooftexts are relevant to the debate only insofar as they constitute
part of the Bible (albeit a rather small part). So the question that egalitarians must answer is whether it's possible to integrate the message
of complementarian prooftexts with the assertion that the Bible as a
whole encourages us to seek gender parity.[34]

Here's a plausible story that an egalitarian might tell about why
we should think that *the Bible as a whole* encourages us to pursue
gender parity (prooftexts included).[35] Throughout Scripture, God
demands justice—it's one of the Bible's major themes. Specifically,
God commands his people to give a voice to the voiceless, to take
up the cause of the dispossessed, and to give the disenfranchised
their due. As Beth Allison Barr notes, "As soon as humans forged an
agricultural society and began to build structured communities, they
also began to build hierarchies of power, designating some people
as more worthy to rule than others."[36] In many places, for much of
human history, these social hierarchies have taken the form of patriarchy. And patriarchal social arrangements, by their very nature,
leave women vulnerable to financial, emotional, spiritual, and physical abuse. This is manifestly unjust. So part of what it means to fear
God and keep his commandments is to resist the kinds of patriarchal
social arrangements that leave women vulnerable to exploitation.

This attitude is borne out in the life and teachings of Jesus, the author and perfecter of our faith. In his interactions with women, Jesus consistently flouts patriarchal norms. He chooses a woman as the apostle to the apostles. And the Gospels recount *not one instance* of Jesus having said a single word in favor of patriarchal social arrangements.[37] If anything, the Gospels leave the opposite impression. According to the tenth chapter of Luke, for instance, when Martha wants Jesus to send Mary to the kitchen to help with women's work, Jesus passes on the opportunity to lecture Mary about the sacred female calling to domestic service. Instead, Jesus commends Mary for her decision to forgo cooking and cleaning in favor of furthering her education. So Jesus doesn't seem at all anxious to instill in his followers a special appreciation for patriarchal gender norms. Given that the word of God is most faithfully interpreted by the word of God, and Jesus is the Word become flesh, Christ's complete and utter lack of interest in promoting gender hierarchy is an important feature of the background information with which I approach the rest of Scripture.

With all of this in view, by the time I arrive at the Epistles, the notion that Paul would direct me to institute patriarchal gender norms in my church or in my home is simply out of the question. Given my understanding of the Bible as a whole, and my conviction that the Bible must be consistent with itself, I'm convinced that whatever Paul is saying, he isn't saying *that*. Maybe his apparent endorsement of patriarchy is contingent on cultural factors that no longer obtain—or biblical principles that resemble gender hierarchy when practiced under certain cultural conditions that are remote from my own.[38] Or perhaps Paul is addressing very specific circumstances in the churches to which he's writing, and he has no intention of laying down universal norms.[39] Regardless, my overall understanding of Scripture is that the Christian life isn't about instituting or maintaining a social hierarchy that reinforces the position of those who already enjoy the privileges of power—in this case, men. So, for reasons that have nothing to do with secular culture and everything to do with my understanding of Scripture, a handful of decontextualized prooftexts will not suffice to persuade me that Paul—let alone the

Bible as a whole—mandates patriarchy. And I categorically reject the proposition that gender hierarchy is in any sense integral to Christian faith or practice.

No doubt complementarians will object that this reading of Scripture is influenced by my own ideological commitment to prioritizing justice, which prevents me from reading Paul in the way that complementarians do. I plead guilty, with the important caveat that my regard for justice is a natural by-product of my Christian faith. I'll postpone my argument for this claim until the final chapter of the book, where I propose an antidote to Christo-authoritarianism. For present purposes, I needn't persuade anyone that they should reject complementarianism: all that matters is that I've presented a coherent vision of biblical interpretation and Christian practice, according to which it makes perfect sense to reject complementarianism. In light of this alternative paradigm, the notion that egalitarianism entails a low view of Scripture or a commitment to byzantine methods of exegesis is patently false.

Albert Mohler, who founded T4G with Duncan, understands this—or at least he did at one time. By his own testimony, he was a committed egalitarian until as late as 1984. In a chapel message delivered at the Southern Baptist Theological Seminary on September 14, 2010, Mohler recalls his leading role in an organized effort to oppose a 1984 resolution by the Southern Baptist Convention that declared the office of pastor to be reserved for men: "We bought an ad in the *Courier-Journal* and made a statement about God as an equal opportunity employer. By the way, I did this while affirming biblical inerrancy, absolutely sure that the Bible was the infallible, inerrant Word of God."[40] Furthermore, Mohler's remarks during a Q&A session with students at the Southern Baptist Theological Seminary in 1993 demonstrate an awareness that the Bible's counsel on the subject of gender isn't reducible to a handful of prooftexts. In answer to a question about his position on the ordination of women, Mohler maintains that

> any of us are responsible to have as comprehensive and consistent
> a hermeneutical method as possible. On any number of issues,

one must do everything possible to interpret Scripture on the basis of what it intends to say—what God reveals through the text. And that is a weighty responsibility. And for any of us, there are passages one must read within the totality of the biblical revelation, and understand it. I do not believe Scripture contradicts itself; it is not internally conflicted. But we must do everything we can to understand scriptural principles and teachings, and to understand the harmony that is there within Scripture—*unity* is perhaps a better word than *harmony*. Again, this is not the forum for a lengthy exegetical discussion. But I would reject the notion that the position [that Scripture forbids the ordination of women] that I articulate here is wanting in scriptural support. Indeed, I was driven there, in terms of my own internal conflict on this issue . . . a comprehensive presentation and exegesis of the texts that deal with this issue drove me to the conclusion I articulated.[41]

Thus Mohler acknowledges that the question of whether the Bible commends gender hierarchy turns not on prooftexts but on the whole of Scripture. And he admits to having been internally conflicted over the issue—despite his commitment to the inerrancy and authority of Scripture—presumably because the biblical case for gender hierarchy isn't nearly as clear as Duncan's essay suggests.

Here I'd expect a complementarian to say that my argument for egalitarianism hinges on a conception of justice that is deeply flawed— not because it's wrong to emphasize justice but because I've totally misunderstood the nature of justice. According to complementarians, justice is achieved when we inhabit our place in the social hierarchy ordained by God. For some of us, that means exercising authority in certain contexts. For others, it means practicing submission. In the words of one former president of the Council on Biblical Manhood and Womanhood, "The interplay of authority and submission extends even to the Godhead. Christ submits to the will of His Father, His head (1 Cor. 11:3). We see from this and other texts that submission is not damaging, problematic, or unkind. It is the just response to proper authority."[42] Since God has ordained that men exercise authority over women, they reason, *biblical justice* is achieved through gender hierarchy. (More below on the modifier *biblical*.) And how could a concern for biblical justice give us reason to reject gender hierarchy, when gender hierarchy is precisely what biblical justice requires?

This question brings us to a third problem with the complementarian assertion that Scripture clearly prescribes patriarchy: it's grounded in a theological paradigm that places *authority and submission* at the center of Christian faith and practice. According to the authority and submission paradigm, one of the principal questions that Scripture sets out to answer is "Who has authority, and who must submit?" But when we treat Scripture as a collection of decontextualized prooftexts, and then read those prooftexts through the theological lens of authority and submission, Scripture can equally be used to legitimize other forms of social hierarchy that we have good reason to reject—such as the institution of slavery.

*Patriarchy and Slavery*

Those who argue that the Bible legitimizes slavery can match, if not exceed, the apostles of biblical patriarchy for prooftexts. (Yes, the main verb in the previous sentence is present tense. And yes, we're going to talk about it.) Here are just a few examples from the New Testament:

- Ephesians 6:5: "Slaves, obey your human masters with fear and trembling, in the sincerity of your heart, as you would Christ."
- Colossians 3:22: "Slaves, obey your human masters in everything. Don't work only while being watched, as people-pleasers, but work wholeheartedly, fearing the Lord."
- 1 Timothy 6:1: "All who are under the yoke as slaves should regard their own masters as worthy of all respect, so that God's name and his teaching will not be blasphemed."
- Titus 2:9-10: "Slaves are to submit to their masters in everything, and to be well-pleasing, not talking back or stealing, but demonstrating utter faithfulness, so that they may adorn the teaching of God our Savior in everything."

Given complementarians' commitment to the paradigm of authority and submission and their habit of using isolated prooftexts to legitimize social hierarchy, it's not altogether surprising that several prominent complementarians defend the institution of slavery.

Consider John MacArthur, the Southern California megachurch pastor and Bible college chancellor who made headlines in 2020 for refusing to submit to public health authorities in Los Angeles County. In a 2019 sermon, MacArthur declared that "women are to maintain submission to men in all churches in all times."[43] And in a 2012 interview, MacArthur offered the following thoughts on the subject of slavery:

> It is a little strange that we have such an aversion to slavery because historically there have been abuses. There have been abuses in marriage—we don't have an aversion to marriage particularly because there have been abuses. There are parents who abuse their children—we don't have an aversion to having children because some parents have been abusive. Of course it can have any kind of situation where abuse can be involved [*sic*]. . . . So to throw out slavery as a concept simply because there have been abuses I think is to miss the point. In any kind of human relationship there can be abuses. There can also be benefits. For many people—poor people, perhaps people who weren't educated, perhaps people who had no other opportunity—working for a gentle, caring, loving master was the best of all possible worlds. . . . So we have to go back and take a more honest look at slavery, and understand that God has, in a sense, legitimized it when it's handled correctly.[44]

Elsewhere MacArthur gives us some indication of who, in his view, might be in a position to benefit from the oversight of a benevolent enslaver. In a 2001 sermon on—you guessed it—the ninth chapter of Genesis, MacArthur claims that

> the curse falls on Canaan. And the curse is that he would be a servant of servants, and he would wind up enslaved under the

dominant rulership of others. . . . The Canaanites here, then, are doomed to perpetual slavery because they followed the moral turpitude of their ancestors, Ham and Canaan. It isn't that God punished them by making them evil; it is that they followed the evil of their fathers, and thus in the providence of God were to be cursed.[45]

(Note the resemblance between MacArthur's speculative logic and that of Confederate theologians quoted in this book's introduction, particularly around the alleged moral inferiority of Canaan and his descendants.) And in case there's any doubt about who MacArthur has in mind when he refers to the descendants of Ham and Canaan, his 2010 remarks on the subject leave not a drop of ambiguity: "it seems that Ham became a more servile people and may have moved south and wound up in Africa."[46]

Given that he actively promotes a theological narrative that has been used for centuries to legitimize racial hierarchy, it's worth noting that MacArthur is at the forefront of the religious right's latest wave of opposition to racial justice.[47] This is no accident: it's easy to dismiss structural racism as a myth when your theology legitimizes racial disparities in wealth, income, and opportunity by reference to the intergenerational "moral turpitude" of those whose ancestors "became a more servile people and may have moved south and wound up in Africa." More on this dynamic in the chapters to follow.

MacArthur is hardly the only influential complementarian with a history of indefensible comments on the subject of slavery. Consider, once again, Albert Mohler, president of the Southern Baptist Theological Seminary since 1993, member of the Council on Biblical Manhood and Womanhood since 2000, and second runner-up in the race for Southern Baptist Convention president in 2021. Mohler is described in an April 2003 interview with *Time* magazine as "the reigning intellectual of the evangelical movement in the U.S."[48] Five years prior, in June 1998, Mohler appeared on *Larry King Live* to make the biblical case for wifely submission.[49] When the subject turned to slavery—as it inevitably does when excerpts from Paul's letters are used to legitimize social hierarchy—Mohler denied that Scripture "endorses" slavery but allowed that the Bible "does say, if you're a slave, there's a way to behave." King asked if Mohler condemned runaway slaves such as Harriet Tubman. "Well," Mohler replied, "I want to look at this text seriously, and it says submit to the master. And I really don't see any loophole here, as much as, in terms of popular culture, we'd want to see one."

In a May 2020 interview with Religion News Service, Mohler offered the following assessment of his 1998 comments on slavery. "It sounds like an incredibly stupid comment, and it was. I fell into a trap I should have avoided, and I don't stand by those comments. I repudiate the statements I made."[50] It's unclear what Mohler means by *trap*. Perhaps he's referring to the unpleasant experience of being ensnared by a line of questioning that forced him to concede a morally repugnant consequence of his argument for gender hierarchy. In any event, it's difficult to imagine what sorts of interpretive "gymnastics" might enable Mohler to sever his case for biblical patriarchy from proslavery hermeneutics. He shares MacArthur's theology of authority and submission, as well as his fondness for motivated literalism.

Moreover, in fortifying his biblical defense of gender hierarchy, Mohler appears to have no qualms about appealing to the interpretive acumen of proslavery theologians. On May 9, 2021—Mother's Day, incidentally—Mohler took to Twitter to express his enthusiasm for the following quote from John A. Broadus (slaveholder, Confederate chaplain, and second president of the Southern Baptist Theological Seminary): "Now it does not need to be urged that these two passages [1 Tim. 2:11-15 and 2 Cor. 14:34] from the Apostle Paul do definitely and strongly forbid that women shall speak in mixed public assemblies. No one can afford to question that such is the most obvious meaning of the apostle's commands."[51] Evidently, Mohler is either unaware or unconcerned that the same was said of slavery, for effectively identical reasons, and indeed by the very same John Broadus. So if Mohler has theological resources to maintain his argument for complementarianism while reversing his 1998 position on obeisance to enslavers, those resources are not in evidence.

For clarity, I should emphasize that my purpose here is *not* to comment on whether Mohler and MacArthur harbor racist attitudes or beliefs. The salient point is that the theological narratives that men like Mohler and MacArthur use to justify biblical patriarchy are inextricably bound up in those that legitimize white supremacy. Below we'll examine how the ideology of the religious right obscures the contradiction inherent in disavowing racism while embracing white supremacist legitimizing narratives. For now, we need only note that the biblical case for patriarchy is inseparable from the biblical case for slavery.

At least one prominent complementarian explicitly asserts that the biblical case for patriarchy cannot be severed from proslavery hermeneutics. Douglas Wilson, who identifies as a "paleo-Confederate," maintains that "Christians who apologize for what the Bible teaches on slavery will soon be apologizing for what it teaches on marriage."[52] Unlike Mohler, Wilson seems to relish the tether between theological justifications for patriarchy and slavery. In *Black and Tan*, Wilson's second book defending the virtues of the antebellum South, he opines that

> one of the things that racial harmony propaganda has done for us is make us think that racism never has any raw material to work with. In other words, we ... scratch our heads in amazement that intelligent people once thought that whites were superior to blacks. Of course we know they were wrong for thinking this, but they were not *stupid* for thinking this. They were dealing with objective facts, which (they assumed) could only have one explanation. It was this latter assumption that tripped them up so badly, and not the objective realities they were trying to account for.... All men exhibit the image of God equally, but all cultures are *not* equal. As we look at all the tribes of men, we see some that have landed a man on the moon, and some that have not yet worked out the concept of the wheel. We have some with one whole row in the supermarket dedicated to shampoo, while in another tribe hair is washed in cow urine. We have orchestras playing *The Brandenburg Concertos* compared to someone beating on a hollow log with a couple of sticks.[53]

According to Wilson, Robert E. Lee was "a gracious Christian gentleman," and "Christians who owned slaves in the South were on firm scriptural ground." He insists that "by the time of the war, the intellectual leadership of the South was conservative, orthodox, and Christian." And though he acknowledges that there were perhaps some Christians in the North, Wilson maintains that "on the slavery issue the drums of war were being beaten by the abolitionists, who were in turn driven by a zealous hatred of the Word of God."[54]

Wilson's views on gender hierarchy are roughly as palatable as his reflections on slavery and "culture." In a 2014 blog post defending patriarchy, Wilson describes those who advocate for gender parity as "small-breasted biddies who want to make sure nobody is using too much hot water in the shower."[55] And in an August 2022 episode of his podcast titled "The Kill Switch and the Steering Wheel," Wilson explains that an ideal dating relationship is one in which men control the "steering wheel" and women control the "kill switch." According to Wilson, a woman may turn away a male suitor or potential suitor whenever she pleases (the kill switch). But the men in a woman's life should control the direction of her romantic relationships (the steering wheel). By this Wilson means that a woman should "just sit in the passenger seat, looking cute," while her male suitor and her father define the relationship and negotiate future plans. (In Wilson's mind, it would be untoward for a woman to ask a man where their relationship stands. That's her father's responsibility.) In Wilson's view, this approach to courtship sets an appropriate tone for marriage, since "a marriage is a little kingdom and the husband is a little king. Once married, he is the king of that little kingdom, and his decisions have real authority."[56]

It would be a mistake to dismiss Wilson as nothing more than a racist, misogynistic carnival barker on the margins of American evangelicalism: thanks to a network of prominent evangelical personages and institutions, he no longer resides on evangelicalism's fringe. As Kristin Kobes Du Mez observes,

> When he published *Future Men* in 2001, Wilson certainly wouldn't have located himself at the center of evangelicalism. In fact, he

was a stalwart critic of mainstream evangelicalism. Although his views on gender and authority aligned in many ways with those of other conservative evangelicals at the time, Wilson often carried those views to extreme, or perhaps logical, conclusions. A woman wearing a man's clothing was "an abomination." If a wife was not properly submissive, it was a husband's duty to correct her. For instance, if dirty dishes lingered in the sink, he must immediately sit her down and remind her of her duty; if she rebelled, he was to call the elders of the church to intervene. . . . But by the 2000s, with the rise of New Calvinism, the growing popularity of "biblical patriarchy," and the turn toward increasingly militant models of masculinity, Wilson found himself within shouting distance of the evangelical mainstream.[57]

In 2007, *Christianity Today* featured Wilson in a series of articles about his debates with Christopher Hitchens; and in 2013, Wilson's novel *Evangellyfish*—published by Canon Press, the publishing house Wilson founded in 1988—won *Christianity Today*'s Book Award for Fiction. Thus, despite his overt racism and misogyny, Wilson is hardly a marginal voice. His views on race and gender hierarchy are promulgated from the power centers of evangelicalism, and, by Wilson's own account, biblical justifications for patriarchy are inseparable from biblical justifications for slavery.

So we have at least three reasons to reject Ligon Duncan's appeal to the clarity of Scripture. First, it's hopelessly question-begging. Second, it conflates the content of decontextualized prooftexts with the counsel of the entire Bible. And third, it's based on a theological paradigm that's inextricable from theological justifications for racial hierarchy and the institution of slavery. Moreover, it's propaganda: it invokes the common-sense ideal of a universal capacity to understand the Bible's meaning while effectively denying that those who sincerely disagree possess such a capacity.

This brings us to the first reason that Duncan and other prominent complementarians offer for rejecting egalitarianism—namely, that it subverts the authority of Scripture. In passing, it's worth observing that this appeal to Scripture's authority is no less question-begging than the appeal to Scripture's clarity: egalitarianism subverts the Bible's authority only if the Bible prescribes gender hierarchy. But that's precisely the point at issue: complementarians say the Bible prescribes gender hierarchy, and egalitarians say it doesn't. So unless I've already accepted Duncan's conclusion that I should embrace complementarianism, I have no reason to accept his premise that egalitarianism subverts the Bible's authority. Again, that's just not how an argument works.

But beyond the fact that this appeal to the Bible's authority is unpersuasive, it highlights a broader problem with the way that Scripture's authority is invoked in the context of evangelical debates around biblical interpretation. Such appeals take a variety of forms, like affixing the modifier *biblical* to a particular position—for example, "biblical" manhood and womanhood, or "biblical" patriarchy—as a cheap way to frame opposing viewpoints as unbiblical and therefore wrong. It's also a pervasive form of propaganda within American evangelicalism.

## Propaganda

Appeals to the authority of Scripture evoke the Reformation ideal of *sola scriptura*, "Scripture alone." According to this principle, the Bible is the only infallible authority on matters of Christian faith and practice. It follows that Scripture, as the only infallible authority, is the *highest* authority. This doesn't mean that there is no authority outside of Scripture—merely that Scripture is sovereign over lesser sources of authority, such as church tradition, ecumenical creeds, doctrinal statements, or ecclesial officials (e.g., pastors or denominational leaders). Thus, in theory, the Reformation ideal of *sola scriptura* subordinates the conventions, institutions, and opinions of men to the word of God. In practice, however, appeals to biblical authority often serve to amplify rather than attenuate ecclesial authority. And in such cases, appeals to biblical authority constitute propaganda. Let's unpack this point.

Denominational leaders like Mohler and Duncan claim that we should reject egalitarianism on the grounds that "egalitarianism undermines the authority of Scripture." There's a trick of language here that deserves close attention. Philosophers of language distinguish between features of a statement that invite further discussion, and features of a statement that furnish the factual backdrop that must be assumed in order to engage in further discussion:

- *at-issue content*—the parts of a statement that are up for discussion; and
- *not-at-issue content*—the factual backdrop on which at-issue content is predicated.[58]

For instance, suppose I said, "Hey Bill, when did you stop drinking and driving?" My question contains both at-issue content and not-at-issue content. The at-issue content concerns the matter of when Bill stopped drinking and driving. The not-at-issue content asserts that Bill has a history of drinking and driving. (Unless Bill adopted the practice of drinking and driving at some point, how could Bill have *stopped* drinking and driving?) So if Bill has no history of drunk driving, then there's no honest way for Bill to answer the question. In order to speak truthfully, Bill would need to point out that the question is predicated on a bad assumption about his driving history.

Similarly, the claim that "egalitarianism undermines the authority of Scripture" involves both at-issue content and not-at-issue content. The at-issue content asserts that egalitarianism erodes the authority of Scripture. Of course, that claim presupposes that the Bible in fact prescribes gender hierarchy. (Unless the Bible prescribes gender hierarchy, why would rejecting gender hierarchy undermine the authority of Scripture?) Thus, embedded within the claim that egalitarianism undermines the authority of Scripture, there's a not-at-issue assertion to the effect that Scripture prescribes gender hierarchy. And as we've established, that assertion rests on nothing more than the common-sense reading of biblical prooftexts dictated by ecclesial authorities like Mohler and Duncan. So the complementarian appeal to biblical authority rests, ultimately, on an assertion of ecclesial authority.

The Reformation ideal of *sola scriptura* is meant to attenuate ecclesial authority. Yet the opposite is achieved when ecclesial authorities like Mohler and Duncan dictate the meaning of Scripture and then invoke the authority of that same Scripture in order to silence dissent. So the complementarian appeal to biblical authority is propaganda: rather than attenuating ecclesial authority, it amplifies it by permitting ecclesial authorities to speak on behalf of God.[59]

We see the same basic pattern in conservative evangelicals' profligate use of the modifier *biblical* to describe any number of their own pet theological viewpoints: "biblical manhood and womanhood," "biblical justice," "biblical worldview," "biblical patriarchy," "biblical anthropology," and so on. If the Bible's authority is sovereign and mine is the biblical worldview, then anything that's in tension with my own worldview must be wrong. If my conception of justice is biblical, then all competing visions of justice are, by definition, unbiblical. And if "biblical manhood and womanhood" entails gender hierarchy, then egalitarians fail to appreciate the authority of Scripture. In each case, the modifier *biblical* provides a veneer of divine sanction that enables ecclesial authorities to amplify their own power—which is antithetic to the Reformation ideal of biblical sovereignty.

But perhaps the most remarkable piece of complementarian propaganda is the term *complementarianism* itself—a euphemism popularized by John Piper and Wayne Grudem in their 1991 book, *Recovering Biblical Manhood and Womanhood: A Response to Evangelical Feminism.* (Observe the modifier *biblical* in the title, and its juxtaposition with evangelical feminism—i.e., egalitarianism.)[60] Piper's body of work includes detailed reflections on feminine versus masculine professions, and general guidance for women on the delicate subject of providing turn-by-turn directions to a man without compromising her biblical womanhood or his biblical manhood. In a June 2023 episode of his podcast, "Ask Pastor John," Piper reflects on the question of whether women are eligible for positions of leadership in parachurch organizations. Piper laments that "the world today is in a free fall of denial that nature teaches us anything about what maleness and femaleness are for." According to Piper, "the argument that the biblical teachings on manhood and womanhood don't have any bearing on roles outside the home and church is both naïve and culturally compromised." Piper holds that God designed men and women to live in a hierarchical relationship in which it is "a peculiar responsibility of men to bear the burden of leadership and care." Citing standard prooftexts from Genesis and Paul's epistles, Piper concludes that "nature teaches that it goes against man's and woman's truest, God-given nature to place a woman in a role of regular, direct, personal leadership over men."[61] Piper's coeditor, Wayne Grudem, has published his views on an incredible array of subjects, ranging from anthropology and gender to systematic theology, economics, political philosophy, and international affairs. He has also distinguished himself as one of the religious right's most strident defenders of former president Donald J. Trump. In a September 2020 interview with *World* magazine, when asked to comment on the perception that Trump is aggressively indifferent to truth, Grudem declared that Trump "is given to exaggeration. Sometimes he's made a statement after being given inaccurate information. I'm not sure he's ever intentionally affirmed something he knows to be false, which is how I define a lie. As you know, I have written an ethics textbook."[62]

In *Recovering Biblical Manhood and Womanhood*, Grudem and Piper indicate that they chose to call their position *complementarianism* in an effort to elide negative associations attached to the term *patriarchy*. As they explain, "the term *complementarian* . . . suggests both equality and beneficial differences between men and women."[63] *Complementarianism* therefore conveys the sense that men and women are *different* but *equal*. And yet, apart from the demands of pregnancy and childbirth, the tasks that complementarians ordinarily assign to women—cooking, cleaning, supervising small children, and so on—can all be accomplished by men. Nature, it turns out, has endowed men and women with an equal measure of all the capacities required for folding laundry, changing diapers, and preparing refreshments in the church fellowship hall. So it seems that *redundancy* is rather a more apt term to describe the complementarian vision of gender, since it presents women as redundant men whose lot in life is attending to chores that actual men find unpleasant. Thus the term *complementarian* is propaganda, insofar as it invokes an ideal of gender according to which women are both equal to and different from men, in order to perpetuate social arrangements that effectively regard women as lesser men.

In exchange for enduring second-class status in most aspects of daily life, biblical patriarchy offers women the opportunity to find fulfillment in what complementarians often refer to as *the highest calling*—namely, motherhood. Though few complementarians categorically forbid women from working outside the home, women are strongly encouraged to pursue marriage and motherhood—and wives and mothers, in turn, are discouraged from pursuing any occupation that might compete with their responsibilities as housekeeper, consort, and primary caregiver. Thus the ideal domestic arrangement, according to complementarians, consists in a nuclear family with a male breadwinner and a female homemaker. Whatever its merits in the 1950s and '60s, prevailing economic conditions since the 1970s have rendered this domestic model increasingly untenable for a majority of American families. In *The Mommy Myth: The Idealization of Motherhood and How It Has Undermined Women*, Susan J. Douglas and Meredith W. Michaels note that "the 'stagflation' of the 1970s . . . propelled millions of mothers into the workforce. In 1970, only 28.5 percent of children under age six had a mother working outside the home. By 1988, the figure had jumped to 51.5 percent."[64] As real wages consistently fail to keep pace with the cost of living, and costs associated with major purchases like housing and postsecondary education have ballooned, this trend continues. A 2019 survey by the US Bureau of Labor Statistics classified two-thirds (66.4 percent) of mothers with children under the age of six as labor force participants. And that percentage surpasses three-quarters (76.8 percent) for mothers whose youngest child is between the ages of six and seventeen.[65]

Men are free to define their identity in relation to life outside the home—a father who does much of the cooking or laundry or who makes a point of remembering his toddler's height and weight at her last checkup is considered extraordinary. By contrast, biblical patriarchy insists that a woman's ultimate calling is to ensure the orderliness of her home and the flourishing of her spouse and children. So, even as the average woman must make a substantial contribution to household income, her *real* work begins when she arrives home from work.

I hasten to add that this dynamic is a product of myriad social and intellectual forces—standing conventions around gender, media depictions of marriage and motherhood, marketing that aims to perpetuate and profit from anxieties engendered by unattainable cultural ideals, and the conservative politics of economic austerity favored by those on the religious right. So complementarianism alone didn't create these conditions. Yet it has baptized this arrangement by legitimizing the notion that a woman's success is defined by her performance in the domestic sphere. This legitimizing narrative forces wives and mothers to bear the burden of resolving the contradiction between conservative family values and conservative fiscal policies that don't, in fact, value families. (More on "family values" below.)

## Conclusion

The introduction provided a heuristic for organizing ideology and propaganda, and this chapter applied that model to a few concrete examples. Here's the picture that emerges. At the center of ideology is some form of social hierarchy—based, for example, on race or gender. Legitimizing narratives serve to justify the hierarchy in question by explaining why it's morally appropriate for some people to have wealth, power, or privileges that others lack. Within the ideology of the religious right, these narratives often flow from prooftexts (such as 1 Tim. 2:11–15 or Gen. 9:22–27), refracted through the hermeneutics of legitimization. These legitimizing narratives are reinforced by propagandistic appeals to the authority of Scripture that obscure what are in fact assertions of ecclesial authority. Rigid gender hierarchy is an important component of authoritarian ideology—especially when combined with racial hierarchy and sexual anxiety around racial purity of the kind discussed in chapter 2. Moreover, propagandistic appeals to biblical authority and so-called common sense serve as a catalyst for anti-intellectualism and unreality—two more key elements in authoritarian ideology. As we'll see in chapters 3 and 4, such appeals are a perennial feature of the rhetoric deployed by ministers of propaganda.

# 2

## *Racial Hierarchy*

The religious right's commitment to racial hierarchy is layered, intellectually and historically, in ways that make it difficult for some evangelicals to recognize white supremacy for what it is. Indeed, many on the religious right—and no doubt an overwhelming majority of white evangelicals—would sincerely disavow any sympathy for racism, especially white supremacy. But when we peel back the layers of ideology and situate them in the context of US history, the most eligible explanation for prevailing evangelical attitudes around race over time—from opposing civil rights reforms to denying the reality of structural racism—is a pathological commitment to white superiority that transcends periodic changes in rhetoric. This commitment is maintained by propagandistic appeals to merit and colorblindness: The notion that wealth in our society is allocated on the basis of individual merit lends credence to the claim that laws and public policies should be colorblind. And colorblindness, in turn, conceals the racism embedded in the claim that wealth in our society is allocated on the basis of merit. Thus propagandistic appeals to merit and colorblindness reinforce one another.

## Meritocracy

In debates about economic justice, those on the religious right typically highlight the importance of personal responsibility and individual merit in determining access to wealth, income, and opportunity. According to the prevailing economic paradigm of the religious right, the United States is a meritocracy—that is, a society in which wealth is distributed on the basis of merit. Insofar as our society fails to allocate wealth on the basis of merit, this failure is due to government redistribution of wealth that prevents the wealthy from keeping as much of their resources as they're entitled to have.

The white evangelical investment in meritocracy is not new. In a 1951 sermon, Billy Graham remarked that government aid to the poor is misguided, since "their greatest need is not more money, food, or even medicine; it is Christ. Give them the Gospel of love and grace first and they will clean themselves up, educate themselves, and better their economic circumstances."[1] A few years later, in 1954, Graham wrote in *Nation's Business* magazine that

> wise men are finding out that the words of the Nazarene: "Seek ye first the kingdom of God and His righteousness, and all these *things* shall be added unto you" were more than the mere rantings of a popular mystic; they embodied a practical, workable philosophy which actually pays off in happiness and peace of mind.... Thousands of businessmen have discovered the satisfaction of having God as a working partner.[2]

Thus, according to longstanding evangelical norms, material poverty is a result of moral and spiritual poverty; and the remedy for material poverty is moral and spiritual reform.

According to this way of thinking, government assistance inhibits free enterprise and places us on the path to communism. In a 1951 "sermon competition" on the theme of "Freedom under God," sponsored by the Committee to Proclaim Liberty, one Kansas minister observed that "socialism in our country has probably progressed farther than most of us fully realize.... Every act or law passed by which the government promises to 'give' us something is a step in the direction of socialism."[3] And in his contest-winning sermon, an Illinois minister proclaimed:

> "Government of the people, by the people, for the people" has become government of the people by pressure groups for the benefit of minorities. "Give me liberty or give me death" has been shortened to just plain "Give me." ... America stands at the cross roads. ... The one road leads to slavery which has always been the lot of those who have chosen collectivism in any of its forms ... communism, socialism, the Welfare State—they are all cut from the same pattern. The other road leads to the only freedom there is.[4]

A quarter century later, in his 1976 sermon "Conditions Corrupting America," the prominent televangelist and political activist Jerry Falwell asserted that

> we are developing a socialistic state in these United States as surely as I am standing here right now. Our give-away programs, our welfarism at home and abroad, is developing a breed of bums and derelicts who wouldn't work in a pie shop eating the holes out of donuts. And they will stand in line at an unemployment office rather than go look for a job.[5]

And in the opening lines of his 2014 book, *Awakening: How America Can Turn from Economic and Moral Destruction Back to Greatness*, Ralph Reed offers an exquisite summary of the civic gospel's basic economic outlook:

> Are we watching our nation commit suicide? The United States of America was founded on the principles of limited government, individual liberty, and personal responsibility based on faith in God. Yet it seems we have abandoned those principles to such an extent that it may be too late for this beacon of faith and freedom to turn around. Is America ... doomed to inevitable decline and demise? This is the central question of our time. While things aren't always as they appear ... , the trends are not encouraging.[6]

As its title predicts, the book goes on to suggest that it isn't too late, provided that we engage in "spiritual searching, revival, and a rediscovery of the principles found in the Bible, the Declaration of Independence, and the U.S. Constitution."[7] So, according to the ideology of the religious right, our political community faces a simple choice. We can continue on the path to communism, driven by government intervention and welfarism, or we can return to God on the wings of individual freedom, industry, and spiritual revival.

As we examine these claims, it's important to observe that those on the religious right often use the terms *communism*, *socialism*, and *Marxism* to describe not only the philosophical legacy of Karl Marx, or a centrally planned economy in the Soviet style, but indeed *any* attempt to upend social hierarchies cherished by political conservatism. It is in this sense that the label *communist* or *Marxist* applies to anyone who seeks to overturn patriarchal gender norms, or rectify racial injustice, or redistribute wealth through progressive taxation and subsidies for public goods that benefit the poor. Moreover, terms like *communism* and *Marxism* are all but synonymous with *atheism* in the vernacular of religious conservatism. All of this culminates in the impression that wealth and power in our society are assigned according to some combination of individual merit and divine favor. Efforts to redistribute wealth or reform established hierarchies constitute an attempt to transfer money and status from the deserving to the undeserving, without regard for God's design.

It's equally important to note that business leaders and ministers conspired to market this economic paradigm to the American public in the middle of the twentieth century. Gerardo Martí observes:

> As corporations grew, their leaders knew their businesses were perceived as avaricious and materialistic. Therefore, they sought to be portrayed in a more favorable light, pushing against the assumptions that their priorities were based only in self-serving greed. Toward that end, Christian businessman J. Howard Pew and Los Angeles minister James Fifield established Spiritual Mobilization. Spiritual Mobilization was an organization that worked to retrain clergy, providing them theological justification for free-

market policies. It innovated and then disseminated religious reasons for the promotion of profit-seeking and entrepreneurship. Indeed, Spiritual Mobilization "took as its mission the invention of theological justification for capitalism." It also sought the removal of government social services, all of which were viewed as unnecessary, wasteful, and dangerously expensive for tax payers. . . . Corporations and businessmen were major donors to the Spiritual Mobilization organization, seeing it as a means to effectively uphold the notion that hard work within the American market economy would be rewarded with profit. Economic ills were traced back to spiritual shortcomings, and liberal policies would only keep spiritually weak people in bondage.[8]

The economic reality, of course, is more complicated than the neoliberal fantasy that was marketed to American evangelicals by organizations like Spiritual Mobilization.

## Choices and Circumstances

Access to resources—wealth, education, opportunity, healthcare, housing, and so forth—is determined by two sets of variables: *choices* and *circumstances*. Generally speaking, we control our choices but we don't control our circumstances.[9] Facts about my personal circumstances that I can't control include, for example, the identity of my parents, their level of education, their social networks, or the amount of wealth that they are willing and able to leverage on my behalf. On a larger scale, we have no control over social conditions like the prevailing economic moment that spans the course of our lives— whether we live through a prolonged period of economic recession, the availability of affordable housing, or the pace of technological innovation and its effect on the labor market. And at the intersection of personal and social circumstances, we have no control over which natural capacities we possess at birth, or the wage that a given set of abilities can command in the place and time in which we're born.

Consider, for example, the ability to propel oneself across a frozen sheet of water on sharpened pieces of metal while hitting a small

rubber disk with a bent wooden stick. In the current economic moment, some who possess this unique combination of talents can earn
a fortune in the National Hockey League (NHL). A mere two centuries ago, this skill set wouldn't have fetched a modest living. Had
Wayne Gretzky been born in 1861 rather than 1961, he'd have been
in his mid-fifties when the NHL was founded (in 1917). Alternatively,
had Gretzky been born in 1960s Patagonia instead of 1960s Canada,
it's possible that he'd never have owned a pair of ice skates, let alone
mastered the game of hockey.

Moreover, Gretzky spent the most lucrative years of his career
playing for the Los Angeles Kings. So he earned much of his fortune
on an ice rink in the middle of Southern California, where the average
temperature hovers around seventy degrees Fahrenheit during the
coldest part of hockey season. Thus the monetary value of Gretzky's
talent was contingent not only on the timing and location of his birth
but also on a background of technical advances that made it possible
to preserve a large block of ice in a subtropical venue—to say nothing
of all the other technology and infrastructure without which a market for professional athletics would be impossible (transportation,
stadium, television, and so on).

It would be an understatement to say that Gretzky is widely regarded as the greatest hockey player of all time. (For perspective:
Gretzky is the only NHL player to surpass two thousand career
points, and he retired with nearly three thousand. He scored his
first one thousand points in 424 games and his second one thousand points in 433 games. Mario Lemieux, the second-fastest player
to reach one thousand points, did it in 533 games.) Yet, as I've just
demonstrated, the economic value of Gretzky's transcendent talent was highly contingent on context: talent generates income only
in cooperation with a favorable economic environment. We might
refer to this convergence between talent and economic moment as
*income-talent*. Income-talent is different from talent, in that talent is
the capacity to do something, while income-talent is the capacity to
do something that commands a paycheck. Thus I have income-talent
only insofar as my abilities are commercially valuable at the time and
place in which I live. Since I choose neither my endowment of natural

abilities nor the timing and location of my birth, income-talent is a feature of my circumstances that I do not control.

Those who emphasize the role of merit in achieving economic success are likely to object that I've overstated the importance of circumstances in general and income-talent in particular: "Sure, athletes like Gretzky possess innate physical gifts that are totally foreign to the average human. But raw, uncultivated potential is worthless. Gretzky didn't just show up at a hockey rink one afternoon and start collecting million-dollar paychecks. Natural ability and environmental factors were necessary to his success but not sufficient. He also devoted countless hours to refining his talents and perfecting his craft. The same goes for successful lawyers, or bankers, or surgeons, or what have you."

These are fair points. I don't intend to ignore the dedication and hard work behind the achievements of many highly successful people, including some who are born into difficult circumstances. Nor do I mean to gloss over the role of indolence in the economic hardship of some capable individuals who are simply averse to the demands of employment. Some people end up in dire circumstances as a result of their own poor choices, despite having been born into perfectly adequate or even ideal conditions. Others fail to overcome their circumstances despite possessing the ability to do so. As individuals, we are all responsible for exploiting the opportunities available to us and cultivating whatever talents we have.

Yet it's easy to overlook the fact that those who overcome difficult circumstances through ambition and industry often enjoy uncommon natural endowments of intellect, attractiveness, creativity, or some other marketable quality—all a function of circumstance, not choice. And it's equally important to observe that we are not responsible for the value that the labor market assigns to our natural abilities once they've been fully refined. Nor do we have a hand in deciding the basic stock of opportunities open to us by virtue of our parents' socioeconomic status or the broader economic trends that span the course of our lives.

Here's an example. Imagine that Frank is born in a midsize industrial town somewhere in Alabama. His parents never finished high school, but they work hard and earn a decent living. Frank is a good kid. He follows all the rules and makes adequate grades in school—he isn't a spectacular student, but he passes all his classes. After graduating from high school, he gets a job in a warehouse down the road from the factory where his father works. Frank fully expects to work hard for the next fifty years, raise a family, and retire with a modest nest egg.

But around age forty, Frank begins to experience crippling back pain. Because he takes pride in his work and he's devoted to his employer, Frank doesn't complain and he doesn't take any time off. Over the next several months, his condition worsens until his back pain becomes totally debilitating—he can barely walk upright. So Frank goes to a back specialist, where he learns that his back is permanently damaged. With physical therapy, he'll regain his ability to walk more or less comfortably. But he will not be able to return to his job at the warehouse. Physically demanding labor of any kind is out of the question: no lifting heavy things, no standing for long periods of time. With great reluctance, Frank quits his job and enters the job market.

Let's take a step back and look objectively at Frank's résumé. His only credential is a high school diploma. And his only employment experience consists of two decades of unskilled manual labor—precisely the kind of work that his injury now prevents him from performing. Relative to any job for which he's qualified, in other words, Frank is effectively disabled.

At this point, those sympathetic to the kind of individualist narrative promoted by the religious right might say that Frank finds himself in this situation because he made a poor choice—namely, deciding to enter the workforce immediately after high school instead of attending college or pursuing some sort of technical training. But I'm skeptical of the notion that Frank *decided* not to attend college. What if, given his family's background and the collective experience of those around him, it just never occurred to Frank to attend college? Perhaps, as a teenager, trade school seemed like a bad investment to Frank, given his family's limited resources and inexperience with postsecondary education. Some people, unlike

Frank, emerge from very humble beginnings to achieve remarkable things, educationally and otherwise. But such people possess exceptional income-talent. What if Frank isn't one of those people? What if, despite his solid work ethic, Frank is just average? Is it appropriate to blame Frank for failing to possess, or failing to cultivate, *exceptional* income-talent?

Some on the religious right might argue that regardless of his circumstances, Frank should have known that continuing his education after high school would enhance his earning potential and protect his finances against the vicissitudes of age and infirmity. So, despite his disadvantages, Frank is at fault for failing to recognize that he should prepare himself for a career path that isn't restricted to unskilled manual labor.

Even if this objection refutes our example, it fails to reach the deeper point. Frank's case is merely a thought experiment, the details of which can be amended until it's just obvious that someone like Frank isn't to blame for his inability to earn an income following his back injury. For example, imagine that instead of working in a factory to provide for his family, Frank's father was a hardened criminal who spent all of Frank's childhood and adolescence in a penitentiary several hours away. Suppose further that Frank's mother was heavily addicted to prescription pain pills. So, when she wasn't at work or out searching for drugs, she was passed out on the couch. And because his mother's apartment was located in a school district with woefully inadequate resources, Frank's overworked and underpaid teachers failed to notice Frank's dyslexia. So he never received appropriate accommodations; and consequently, no matter how hard he worked, his grades were consistently below average. No one, including Frank himself, believed Frank to be a promising student. But in spite of all the obstacles, through sheer force of will, Frank managed to graduate from high school. After graduation, he found a job in a local warehouse, serving as an exemplary employee for over two decades before injuring his back.

Does it now make sense, in this revised scenario, to blame Frank for his inability to earn an income following his back injury? Surely it does not. We blame ourselves for having made poor choices when we reflect on some course of action and admit that we should have acted differently. In some cases, this kind of reflection prompts an effort to reform our character or amend our life goals. By contrast, when we reflect on circumstances over which we never exercised any control, we do not believe that we should have chosen differently. We may regret that our circumstances weren't more conducive to our flourishing in some aspect, and we might grieve the loss of some un-realized ambition foreclosed by circumstances outside our control. But we do not meditate on the date of our birth or the quality of the school district where our childhood home was located and wish that we had chosen differently.[10]

Before moving on, we need to distinguish this question—whether we should blame Frank for his present hardship—from related but very different questions about whether or how our society ought to assist those in Frank's situation. For example: Should anyone in roughly Frank's situation be entitled to public assistance? What about those who come from slightly better circumstances, or who have just a bit more native capacity—are they entitled to public assis-tance as well? Exactly how much assistance should people like Frank receive, and for how long? What form should the assistance take—should Frank receive direct payments, or food subsidies, or some combination of the two? Is Frank entitled to vocational training at the public's expense? Or should Frank be required to undergo vocational training as a condition of receiving public assistance? What if Frank finds employment, but only at a wage that's insufficient to cover his modest needs? What about dependent minors—what level of subsidy should be allocated to the children of those who receive public assis-tance? Who should be responsible for administering all of this; and how will they prevent potential cheaters who are perfectly capable of working from freeriding at the expense of honest taxpayers? Notice that we need not agree on answers to any of these questions in order to agree that Frank isn't to blame for his circumstances.

On the other hand, if we believe that people like Frank *are* to blame for their circumstances, then structural concerns about the allocation of wealth, income, and opportunity recede from view. More generally, if we believe that we're each responsible for whatever financial hardships we face, then the distribution of resources in our society appears legitimate—which is precisely the point of legitimizing narratives that blame poverty on the poor. As Jason Stanley observes, "Without legitimizing myths, hierarchy is merely stratification. With legitimizing myths, hierarchy becomes grounded in superiority and inferiority and formal distinctions become laden with norms."[11] When we blame poverty on the poor, disparities in wealth and income appear justified by the relative superiority of the wealthy. Moreover, if the wealthy deserve their wealth and the poor deserve poverty, then attempts to redistribute resources are by definition unjust—taking from those who deserve what they have in order to give to those who don't deserve anything beyond what they have.

What our analysis of choices and circumstances makes clear is that such appeals to merit are, in fact, propaganda: the notion of meritocracy invokes an ideal of personal responsibility in order to justify withholding resources from those who are not personally responsible for their lack of resources. And insofar as this propaganda engenders public support for policies that withhold resources from those who face financial hardship, it is harmful to the poor.

### Property, Prosperity, and Systemic Racism

Since a majority of those who stand to benefit from public assistance are white, a majority of those harmed by meritocratic propaganda are white people. But because Black Americans are overrepresented among those who stand to benefit from wealth redistribution, meritocratic propaganda is disproportionately harmful to Black Americans. As we will see below, this propaganda is racist insofar as it implies a commitment to white superiority. I'll return to this point in due course, following a brief foray into some relevant US history.

In 1934, the US government created the Federal Housing Administration (FHA) to oversee a mortgage insurance program designed to facilitate homeownership for millions of middle-class Americans. But the FHA only insured mortgages on homes that were located in neighborhoods that systematically excluded people of color. As Richard Rothstein explains,

The FHA insured bank mortgages that covered 80 percent of purchase prices, had terms of twenty years, and were fully amortized. To be eligible for such insurance, the FHA insisted on doing its own appraisal of the property to make certain that the loan had a low risk of default. Because the FHA's appraisal standards included a whites-only requirement, racial segregation now became an official requirement of the federal mortgage insurance program. The FHA judged that properties would probably be too risky for insurance if they were in racially mixed neighborhoods or even in white neighborhoods near black ones that might possibly integrate in the future.[12]

The primary consequence of this FHA policy was, of course, to segregate housing and homeownership along racial lines.[13] Given that school districting is based on residential location, a secondary consequence of the policy was racially segregated public schools across the country. (Hence, in the era of school desegregation, Black students had to ride buses to the other side of town in order to attend schools that had previously been restricted to white students, a practice that became known as *busing*. More on busing in chapter 5.) And a tertiary effect of the FHA policy was to ensure that public schools zoned for white students received better funding than those zoned for Black students: by making it easier for banks to lend to potential buyers in racially exclusionary neighborhoods, the FHA policy increased effective demand for homes in those neighborhoods, driving up property values and thus increasing the property taxes from which public schools derive much of their funding.[14]

Meanwhile, property values in Black neighborhoods were subject to the effects of a broader zoning regime that diverted bars, nightclubs, factories, and toxic waste facilities and other environmental hazards away from white neighborhoods. According to studies conducted in the 1980s by Greenpeace and by the Commission for Racial Justice of the United Churches of Christ, "the percentage of minorities living near incinerators was 89 percent higher than the national median."[15] (All these effects of residential segregation, incidentally, conspired to facilitate a system of racially disparate policing and incarceration.) Notice the social-intellectual feedback loop: FHA policy, based on white supremacy, created market volatility and suppressed real estate values in neighborhoods with Black residents. The resulting uncertainty and suppression of property values in Black neighborhoods then served to legitimize the presumption that lending to Black homebuyers involved more risk—never mind that said volatility was merely a natural by-product of the very FHA policy it was invoked to justify.

The Fair Housing Act of 1968 outlawed *de jure* racial discrimination against renters and homebuyers in the real estate market; and the Housing Financial Discrimination Act of 1977 banned racial discrimination in the mortgage industry. But decades of steadily rising real estate prices in racially exclusionary neighborhoods created yet another obstacle to residential desegregation: affordability. By the end of the 1960s, the process of suburbanization was essentially complete. America's economic hubs were surrounded by single-family homes that had been purchased by white homeowners with the benefit of government-backed mortgages. With a limited supply of real estate and demand buoyed by easy credit, real estate prices soared. From 1973 to 1980, the value of the average American home increased by 43 percent.[16] Increasing real estate prices are good for those who already own homes: if I buy a house for $100,000 and the value increases to $150,000, my family wealth increases by $50,000. That $50,000 in passive income can be handed down as an inheritance or cashed out and used for college tuition or to help make down payments on the homes of one's children.

But for those who don't already own homes, who relinquish more and more of their lifetime income with every month's rent, spiking real estate prices move homeownership further from reach. Rothstein observes that

> by the time the federal government decided finally to allow African Americans into the suburbs, the window of opportunity . . . had mostly closed. In 1948, for example, Levittown [New York] homes sold for about $8,000, or about $75,000 in today's dollars. Now, properties in Levittown without major remodeling (i.e., one-bath houses) sell for $350,000 and up. White working-class

families who bought those homes in 1948 have gained, over three generations, more than $200,000 in wealth.

Most African American families—who were denied the opportunity to buy into Levittown or into the thousands of subdivisions like it across the country—remained renters, often in depressed neighborhoods, and gained no equity.[17]

So, for roughly four decades, white Americans were given an opportunity to accrue equity in real estate with the help of the FHA's mortgage insurance program—a program that was subsidized by *all* American taxpayers, including Black Americans who weren't permitted to benefit from it. In other words, the US government systematically transferred wealth *from* people of color (in the form of taxpayer subsidies for the FHA's mortgage insurance program) *to* white Americans (in the form of home equity, mortgage-interest tax deductions, and so on). And by the time the law was changed—even in places where the change had an immediate effect on local practices--the cost of real estate was prohibitive for all but high-income earners and those whose families already had access to wealth generated by home equity.[18]

The effects of this injustice still resonate in wealth and income disparities that persist to the present day. Home equity is by far the largest source of intergenerational wealth among American families. Even now, young African Americans are eleven times more likely than young white Americans to live in poor neighborhoods (66 percent compared to 6 percent). And less than 10 percent of white families have lived in poor neighborhoods for two or more consecutive generations, compared to nearly half of all Black families (48 percent).[19] As of 2019, according to the Federal Reserve Bank of St. Louis, the median white household in the US has about $184,000 in wealth, whereas the median Black household has about $23,000.[20] We'll return to the racial wealth gap in due course.

## Neutrality and Justice

Imagine a future in which basketball referees have been replaced by artificial intelligence. RoboRef, as it's called, uses hundreds of cameras to surveil every inch of the court, at all times, sending data to a supercomputer that's trained to identify the appropriate call in each case—foul, double dribble, out of bounds, and so on. Unlike human referees, RoboRef can't be distracted by unruly fans, or swayed by the petitions of an angry coach, or biased by personal antipathies toward a particular player or team.[21] In this sense, RoboRef is a neutral official that observes the game and applies the rules with impartiality.

Now imagine that in the course of a regular season matchup between the Blue Team and the Green Team, it becomes apparent that RoboRef is suffering from a small but significant programming glitch. Every time the Blue Team rebounds a missed shot, RoboRef calls a foul on the rebounder—even when there are no Green players in the vicinity. Oddly enough, the glitch only works one way: only Blue players are assessed fouls for rebounding the ball, while Green players are free to rebound with impunity. This has a significant impact on the game. By the end of the first half, the Green Team has amassed a formidable lead—forty points, let's say—and several of the Blue Team's starters have fouled out of the game.

Suppose RoboRef's programmers address the glitch at halftime. Officiating in the second half of the game is flawless: RoboRef applies the rules of the game consistently and without bias, never missing a call. But no matter how good the officiating is in the second half— regardless of how neutral or unbiased—no one would describe this game as a fair contest overall.[22] Yes, the rules were fairly applied after halftime. But because of what transpired before halftime, the Blue Team entered the "fair" portion of the game at a 40-point disadvantage. Unless and until that unfair disadvantage is rectified, the game is fundamentally unjust. Neutral rules and referees will only perpetuate the underlying injustice.

The game is still unjust even if it's technically possible for the Blue Team to overcome the unfair 40-point deficit. Indeed, even in the extremely unlikely event that the Blue Team overcomes the 40-point deficit to win the game, the basic conditions of the game are still fundamentally unjust. Alternatively, even if the Green Team outplays the Blue Team in the second half, the game is still fundamentally unjust. (In some sense, although they're playing the same game, the

Green Team and the Blue Team aren't really playing the same sport. To have any chance of overcoming the deficit, the Blue Team will have to adopt high-risk strategies with little hope of success and zero margin for error. The Green Team, by contrast, can make quite a few mistakes and still be reasonably assured of victory.) Importantly, the game is fundamentally unjust even if no one on the Green Team is to blame for the unfair conditions that obtained in the first half of the game. (For present purposes, culpability is irrelevant: what matters is that the game is unjust. Who is responsible for the injustice is a related but different question—and one that is often highly contentious, which is why we'll place it to one side for the moment.)

Similarly, even if we assume that our current laws and public institutions are perfectly neutral with respect to race—an assumption that is undoubtedly false—neutrality is insufficient to rectify socioeconomic disparities amassed over centuries of racialized oppression. Colorblind policies do nothing to address the significant racial gap in family wealth that persists after many decades during which FHA policies effectively barred people of color from amassing and transferring intergenerational wealth. A neutral system that perpetuates this disparity is fundamentally unjust, even if the rules are such that it's technically possible for people of color to overcome the racial wealth gap and achieve upward mobility. Indeed, even if some people of color do in fact overcome the racial wealth gap, the basic conditions of the system are unjust. Nor should we conclude that the system is just simply because we can't agree on the identity of specific people who are morally culpable for the persistence of racial disparities in wealth.

I'd expect some readers to object that there are important differences between race in the American context and the basketball analogy offered above. This is a fair point. For example, in the basketball analogy, we imagined that half of the game was officiated fairly. But there's no plausible construal of American history in which we've had racially neutral laws or public policies for that long. Suppose we place the beginning of the relevant interval in the year 1619 (with the institution of the Atlantic slave trade), and the end somewhere around the present day—a period of about four hundred years. The Fair Housing Act was passed fifty-five years ago, in 1968, which would be analogous to instituting fair rules with about five minutes left to go in the game. The Supreme Court decided *Brown v. Board of Education* in 1954—less than seven minutes on the clock. The institution of race-based chattel slavery wasn't legally abolished until 1865, which would be about halfway through the third quarter.

Another point of disanalogy is that a basketball game involves two teams, each comprising individuals who identify as a team and attempt to score points collectively in order to achieve a common goal—namely, winning the game. By contrast, our society comprises individuals who each pursue their own interests, and wealth isn't aggregated and shared collectively within racial groups in competition with other racial groups.[23] I concede that these are points of disanalogy, but this fact fails to undermine the point at hand. As a group, Black Americans were placed at a massive economic disadvantage through a system of manifestly unjust laws and social practices. Abandoning those laws and social practices is good. But it's not enough to rectify the injustice, since it does nothing to compensate for the disadvantage that was unjustly conferred. That's the point of the analogy, and that's as far as we need the similarities to go. And while it's certainly true that wealth in our society isn't aggregated and shared collectively within racial groups, it's worth observing that Americans tend to marry people who share their racial identity, and professional networks are heavily inflected by race. So wealth and income flow much more freely within racial groups than across racial lines.

If the foregoing argument is correct, then instituting racially neutral policies is insufficient to rectify centuries of racialized oppression. Thus the white evangelical appropriation of "colorblind" rhetoric is a form of propaganda, insofar as it invokes the ideal of racial equality in service to a social and political agenda that perpetuates racial inequality. Given that our goal is to analyze the ideology of the religious right, it's equally important to understand why white evangelicals fail to recognize their own appropriation of colorblindness as propaganda. And that requires us to grapple with why white evangelicals fail to see that racially neutral policies perpetuate racial inequality. So before turning our attention to the rhetoric of colorblindness, it will be helpful to say something about the white evangelical theology that baptized white supremacy for most of the twentieth century. We'll return to colorblindness below.

## Racial Hierarchy and the Religious Right

In order to understand the illusion of racial justice at the core of colorblindness propaganda, we must examine the pathology of racial superiority at the core of white evangelical theology. We can divide the manifestations of this pathology into those that are *explicit* and those that are *implicit*. Explicit manifestations of white supremacy involve modes of reasoning and social practice predicated on an overt commitment to racial hierarchy, such as racial segregation and the theological narratives used to legitimize it. Implicit manifestations involve modes of reasoning and practice that imply white superiority, like the notion that the racial wealth gap is morally legitimate because resources in our society are allocated on the basis of merit. Although explicit manifestations of white supremacy have been in decline since roughly the 1960s, an implicit commitment to racial hierarchy remains latent in the ideology of the religious right. And evangelical appeals to colorblindness serve primarily to obscure the religious right's implicit commitment to racial hierarchy.

### Explicit White Supremacy

Just as it did for slavery in previous centuries, evangelical theology furnished legitimizing narratives for the racial hierarchy that was legally enforced throughout most of the twentieth century in the United States. Ostensibly these narratives derived from two sources: common-sense observation and biblical prooftexts (via common-sense interpretation). We'll examine each in turn.

In *The Bible Told Them So: How Southern Evangelicals Fought to Preserve White Supremacy*, J. Russell Hawkins reports that

> in one of the most widely circulated defenses of segregation in the 1950s, Reverend G. T. Gillespie insisted that God built racial separation into nature. "The fact that man ... is a gregarious ani-

mal and that human beings everywhere and under all conditions of life tend to segregate themselves into families, tribes, national or racial groups," Gillespie told his audience of white Presbyterians, "only goes to prove that all human relations are regulated by this universal law of nature."[24]

Pastor Carey Daniel claimed that God's fondness for segregating different races of people was confirmed by "Mother Nature, with her huge geographic barriers of oceans, deserts, and gigantic mountain ranges."[25] In a similar line of reasoning that incorporated the white supremacist interpretation of Genesis 9 10, the Reverend A. C. Lawton claimed that "God originally separated his five races by mountains, oceans, continents, language and colors. God does not change and his color scheme should never be obliterated."[26]

As further evidence that God favored segregation, white evangelicals cited America's flourishing under a system of racial hierarchy. According to the Reverend Maylon D. Watkins,

> For over 150 years our nation has prospered under the practice of separation of the white and negro races. With this practice our nation has built the most churches, the best schools, and has become the wealthiest nation with the highest standard of living for all people of any nation of earth.[27]

And in a line of reasoning that combines biblical precedent and notions of manifest destiny with a cultural commentary reminiscent of Douglas Wilson, Georgia minister Montague Cook reasoned that

> as the Jew was the instrument of God's purpose in the development of monotheistic religion, which in turn produced a Messiah, so the white man is God's instrument in the development of modern civilization. . . . As racial segregation was vital in maintaining the racial quality that made the Jew serviceable, so racial segregation is now necessary to maintain in the white race those qualities which can control and advance the civilization which the white race has produced.[28]

As Hawkins points out, Cook's reasoning conflates racial desegregation with racial intermarriage—the latter signifying the degradation
of the superior white race.

White supremacists also claimed no shortage of biblical support
for racial segregation. For example, Marvin Brooks Norfleet found
evidence for segregation in Matthew 25:32, since Jesus will gather
all nations, "and he shall separate them one from another" (KJV).[29]
Hawkins notes that a favorite among segregationists was Acts 17:26,
in which Paul declares that God "hath made of one blood all the nations of men for to dwell on all the face of the earth and hath determined the times before appointed, and the bounds of their habita-
tion" (KJV). When integrationists cited the same verse in support of
their position—that is, given that God created all people from a single
human—segregationists accused them of prooftexting. For instance,
in a remarkable speech defending segregation, replete with an appeal
to common sense, J. Elwood Welsh declared:

> One of the worst things any preacher and any Bible teacher can
> do is take a piece of Scripture out of its context. . . . For many good
> people in our denomination and many in other denominations,
> both clerical and lay, who entertain opposite opinions on [segre-
> gation], I have only the profoundest respect. . . . But having said
> all this, I cannot suppress expressing my surprise at some of the
> conclusions many of these good people come to. . . . I cannot con-
> cur in their conclusions. I am baffled to understand their refusal to
> face many self-evident facts. I am stunned at their urging mixed
> membership in our churches.[30]

Similarly, when integrationists cited Galatians 3:28 in support of their
position—"There is neither Jew nor Greek, neither bond nor free,
neither male nor female: for ye are all one in Christ Jesus" (KJV)—
segregationists insisted that Paul was referring to spiritual unity
rather than physical proximity.

As it was for enslavers in the antebellum South, the so-called
curse of Ham was also a favorite legitimizing narrative among segregationists. According to an interpretation popular among white

supremacists, the "mark" that God places on Cain in Genesis 4:15 (following the murder of Abel) is darkened skin. Though the biblical narrative doesn't indicate that Cain's mark is heritable, this reading assumes that Cain transmitted this mark to his descendants. This informs an interpretation of Genesis 9 according to which Ham's curse is precipitated at least in part by the fact that Ham had married Cain's descendant (whose presence on the ark explains why Cain's progeny survived the flood). In other words, the impetus for the curse of Ham was his "interracial" marriage to a descendant of Cain. Given that racial desegregation was regarded as a slippery slope to interracial marriage, segregationists claimed that their position was justified by this alleged condemnation of Ham's alleged marriage to a descendant of Cain. (We'll revisit this legitimizing narrative in connection with creation science propaganda and the Ark Encounter's portrayal of Ham's wife as a Black woman.)[31]

These theological justifications for segregation fueled the political activism of white evangelicals who embraced them. As J. Russell Hawkins notes,

> The response to the *Brown* decision began a pattern that segregationist Christians repeated over the subsequent decade with the advancement of civil rights. When black Americans procured their constitutional freedoms, white Christians reacted by writing their elected officials to remind them that these changes violated God's plan for humanity. As the South's representatives, these white Christians also insisted that the region's politicians had a Christian duty to fight for segregation. In such respects, segregationist theology proved not to be hollow rhetoric, for it guided the way these Christians saw the world and shaped the expectations they put on their elected representatives.[32]

In a 1959 speech to the South Carolina state legislature, W. A. Criswell—pastor of First Baptist Church of Dallas (whose membership included Billy Graham) and SBC president from 1969 to 1970—offered a characteristic example of white evangelical segregationist rhetoric. In the words of Jesse Curtis, Criswell's speech

effectively combined Southern Baptist identity and white supremacy as a single edifice. Criswell accused integrationists of
attacking everything "we love as good old Southern people and
as good old Southern Baptists." There was no line between Christianity and whiteness; they made each other. Integrationists violated the sanctity of his home and struck at his deepest commitments as a white southerner and a Southern Baptist. . . . But he
insisted he had nothing against black Christians and did not feel
superior to them. He believed human nature dictated that people,
black and white alike, were happier among their own "kind."[33]

Thus evangelical theology provided legitimizing narratives for
racial hierarchy that perpetuated a white supremacist–segregationist
feedback loop well into the second half of the twentieth century. Empirical observations and biblical prooftexts allegedly furnished evidence of white superiority and God's disdain for interracial marriage,
which legitimized segregationist policies like those enacted by the
Federal Housing Administration from 1934 to 1968. Those policies,
in turn, served to reinforce notions of white superiority by denying
Black citizens access to the trappings of economic success.

*Implicit White Supremacy*

Given the many controversies surrounding charges of implicit racism, we should highlight and discard one variety of implicit racism
that is immaterial to my account. So let's divide implicit manifestations of white supremacy into two categories: those pertaining to *human psychology* and those involving *logical implication*. As it pertains
to human psychology, implicit white supremacy involves things like
subconscious biases, stereotypes, and racial prejudices into which
we are enculturated. These features of human psychology raise interesting and important questions, none of which fall within the scope
of my argument.

When I speak of "implicit white supremacy" or "an implicit commitment to white supremacy," I'm referring *not* to a feature of human
psychology but to a matter of logical implication. In order to avoid

any confusion about what I mean by "logical implication," consider the following examples.

- *If* I have two dimes and a nickel in my pocket, *then* I have (at least) twenty-five cents in my pocket.
- *If* I own a red car, *then* I own a car.
- *If* Roger is a bachelor, *then* Roger is an unmarried male.
- *If* Carl is a German shepherd dog, *then* Carl is a mammal.

A common feature of all these statements is that each makes an assertion about the relationship between two discrete claims—namely, that the truth of one proposition *implies* the truth of some other proposition. My having two dimes and a nickel in my pocket *implies* that I have twenty-five cents in my pocket; Roger's being a bachelor *implies* that Roger is an unmarried male, and so on.

Note that if a given logical implication obtains, it does so independently of what we happen to think about it—or whether we've ever thought about it at all. For example, I could believe that "Carl is a German shepherd dog" without believing the implication that "Carl is a member of the phylum Chordata," by virtue of my being unaware that Carl, as a mammal, is a member of the phylum Chordata. (In fact, this is an accurate description of my epistemic situation before I googled "mammal phylum" in the moments prior to composing this paragraph.) So, importantly, we might hold a belief that has any number of logical implications we've never considered or may never consider.

For present purposes, when I speak of an "implicit commitment to white supremacy," this is the kind of implication I have in mind: a belief, or network of beliefs, that *logically implies* white superiority. In this sense, it's possible to sincerely decry white supremacy while at the same time embracing some belief or system of belief that logically implies white superiority.

Here's an example. Above we noted that the median white family has about $184,000 in wealth, while the median Black family has about $23,000 in wealth. Given that fact, the claim that wealth in our society is allocated on the basis of merit *implies* that the median white family deserves $161,000 more wealth than the median Black family. In other words, there's something about the average white family by virtue of which they deserve to have significantly more wealth than the average Black family. It's difficult to imagine why the average white family might *deserve* to have significantly more wealth than the average Black family unless the average white family is in some way superior to the average Black family. Thus, in light of the racial wealth gap, the claim that wealth in our society is allocated on the basis of merit implies white superiority.

As Gerardo Martí observes, when political conservatives reflect on the allocation of wealth, income, and opportunity in our society, including the racial wealth gap,

> instead of acknowledging the historical barriers that have prevented African Americans, Mexicans, Asians, and other ethnic and religious minorities from thriving, conservative neoliberals see a free and fair labor market. They fail to acknowledge that individuals do not start from the same places. At the same time, neoliberal principles are celebrated among the most "successful" of Americans, as the widening wealth gap further accentuates those exceptional persons who interpret their success as solely the result of "hard work."
>
> . . . Those who achieve do so on the basis of pure merit—so it is believed—and collectivism thwarts the laws of nature. Leveling the playing field or helping the less fortunate is immoral. Ending racial discrimination on the basis of manipulating economic realities is equated with socialism and communism and would compromise the "liberty" that is essential to American ways of life. Taking away from the achievements of others to reward the indolence and immoral lives that result in poverty is also decidedly un-Christian. Instead, neoliberals and their conservative Christian allies argue that Americans should eschew group measures by race and only emphasize the achievement of individuals, and everyone should be responsible for themselves and their families.[34]

As we've established, it is an axiom of the religious right that wealth in our society is allocated on the basis of merit—and that insofar as our society fails to allocate wealth according to merit, this failure is due to government intervention that prevents the wealthy from keeping as much of their wealth as they're entitled to have.

The sermons cited at the outset of this chapter attest that white evangelicals have been invoking this meritocratic legitimizing narrative since at least the 1950s. Recall that the FHA's racially exclusionary policies remained in effect until almost 1970 (officially). So at the very moment that explicitly racist evangelical theology was being used to legitimize federal policies that prevented people of color from amassing intergenerational wealth via home equity, white evangelicals were defending the allocation of wealth in our society with implicitly racist appeals to merit.

Note the common denominator. In the 1950s, evangelicals believed that white families had more wealth because white families deserved more wealth—the fact that explicitly racist government policies effectively prevented people of color from accruing wealth was regarded as irrelevant. And today, evangelicals believe that white families have more wealth because white families deserve more wealth—it's irrelevant that the explicitly racist policies of the Federal Housing Administration prevented people of color from accessing the financial instruments with which the US government created the white middle class. Somehow, by virtue of merit, racial oppression is never to blame for racial disparities in wealth: notwithstanding history or present circumstance, white families have more wealth because white families deserve to have more wealth. The ideological constant is an implied commitment to white superiority, veiled in propagandistic appeals to merit.

Survey data confirm that this is precisely what a majority of white evangelicals believe. Even as they vehemently disavow white supremacy, white evangelicals refuse to countenance our nation's history of racial oppression as an explanation for enduring inequities in wealth, income, and opportunity. A 2022 survey by PRRI found that 70 percent of white evangelicals disagree with the statement that "generations of slavery and discrimination have created conditions that make it difficult for blacks to work their way out of the lower class." According to the same survey, 79 percent of white evangelicals "believe that racial minorities use racism as an excuse for economic inequalities more than they should." And in keeping with my claim that meritocratic propaganda is implicitly racist, a majority of white evangelicals (53 percent) agree with the statement that "if Black Americans would only try harder, they could be just as well off as white Americans."[35]

## Colorblindness

The religious right's investment in meritocracy stands in a mutually reinforcing relationship to the rhetoric of "colorblindness." According to the logic of colorblindness, race matters only to racists, and the way to avoid being a racist is to be blind to race, or "colorblind." The core ambition of colorblindness is a society in which people are judged "not by the color of their skin, but by the content of their character," in the oft-appropriated words of Dr. Martin Luther King Jr. According to the politics of colorblindness, racial justice is achieved not by direct efforts to rectify the impact of racial oppression, but through laws and public policies that are racially neutral. And at the level of cognition, colorblindness maintains that we must ignore racial identity—those who insist on the importance of race are the real racists.

As we noted above, unless and until we address the material inequities brought about by racial injustice, neutral policies only serve to perpetuate racial inequality. So colorblindness is propaganda: it appeals to the ideal of racial equality in order to perpetuate racial inequality. This propaganda reinforces, and is reinforced by, appeals to meritocracy: while the myth of meritocracy lends a veneer of plausibility to colorblind rhetoric, colorblindness serves to conceal the white superiority implied by meritocratic legitimizing narratives. Let's elaborate on this point.

Meritocratic legitimizing narratives deny the importance of group membership in determining economic outcomes. On the meritocratic supposition that our society distributes wealth according to individual merit, overcoming social and economic disadvantages—including the disadvantages attached to membership in a historically oppressed group—is simply a matter of hard work and clean living. Historical oppression is irrelevant. If history and group membership are irrelevant, then racially neutral policies offer individuals all the opportunity they need to achieve upward mobility. And if racially neutral policies offer individuals sufficient opportunity for social and economic advancement, then colorblind policies are the appropriate mechanism for achieving racial equality. Thus, at the level of politics, colorblindness is predicated on meritocracy: colorblind policies present an eligible path to racial equality only if we assume that wealth, income, and opportunity in our society are distributed according to individual merit.

Colorblindness, in turn, serves to conceal the white supremacy implied by the mythology of meritocracy. Recall that the average Black family has $161,000 less wealth than the average white family. So the proposition that our society allocates wealth on the basis of merit *implies* that the average white family deserves to have considerably more wealth than the average Black family—which is white supremacy. But this implication remains hidden unless we reflect explicitly on the nature of racial disparities in wealth, which is precisely the sort of reflection that is foreclosed by cognitive colorblindness. If I "don't see color," then I don't see racial disparities in wealth, income, and opportunity—which prevents me from observing that white superiority is implied by the proposition that wealth in our society is allocated on the basis of merit. Thus the feedback loop between meritocracy and colorblindness culminates in an ideology that disavows white supremacy while preserving the racial stratification engendered by generations of white supremacist belief and practice.

At this point, I would expect many white evangelicals to protest that "I'm not racist!" or "I'm not a white supremacist!" These are common refrains among those who express skepticism about the existence or prevalence of structural racism and object to talk of systems that perpetuate white supremacy. My response is twofold.

First, I haven't accused anyone of endorsing white supremacy or holding racist beliefs. Rather, I've argued that in light of the racial wealth gap, white superiority is a *logical implication* of the merito-cratic rhetoric espoused by a majority of white evangelicals. I do not claim that a majority of white evangelicals celebrate or even ac-knowledge this implication of their own economic paradigm. Pre-sumably, those who embrace the myth of meritocracy and disavow white supremacy would claim that there's no such logical entailment between meritocracy and white supremacy. And they're free to think so, in the sense that we are all free to hold beliefs that are false or mu-tually incoherent. All humans are susceptible to lapses in cognitive integrity—especially when confronted with the morally repugnant consequences of some cherished belief (see my discussion of Albert Mohler's 1998 appearance on *Larry King Live* in chapter 1). So, insofar as my argument makes any claim about individual beliefs, that claim is limited to the observation that logical consistency requires those who reject white supremacy to abandon the myth of meritocracy.

Second, to the extent that my argument makes any claim about the persistence of racism or white supremacy, the racism in ques-tion is *systemic*: racial hierarchy is inscribed on social structures and institutions that perpetuate racial disparities in wealth, income, and opportunity. The point isn't that our society suffers from systemic racism by virtue of ongoing racist efforts to produce racial inequal-ity.[36] On the contrary, our society is systemically racist precisely be-cause it produces racial inequality through no human effort at all. So the retort that "I'm not racist!" is perfectly irrelevant.

Here's a simple example. Quite a few universities in the US didn't accept applications from people of color until the 1960s. Many of those same institutions give "legacy points" to applicants whose parents or grandparents attended the university. So white applicants whose parents or grandparents attended the university have an ad-vantage over applicants of color whose parents and grandparents weren't even permitted to apply to the university. This system is ra-cially unjust, since it gives an unjust advantage to white applicants over applicants of color. Crucially, such a system is racially unjust even if there's no racist individual in the admissions office screening out applicants of color. Even in the absence of some racist individual working to exclude applicants on the basis of race, a system of this kind generates unfair advantages on the basis of race: the system, of itself, engenders racial inequality. In other words, the system itself is racist—hence, *systemic racism.*

Meritocracy effectively denies the significance of systemic racism by ignoring the role of history and group identity in determining circumstances and the role of circumstances in determining the range of outcomes that are accessible to any given individual. Colorblindness, in turn, conceals the racist implications of meritocracy. In this way, meritocracy and colorblindness provide those on the religious right with cognitive resources to disavow white supremacy even as they work to preserve social arrangements that perpetuate racial hierarchy.

Those who embrace colorblindness are likely to object that by rejecting colorblindness, I'm endorsing race essentialism, or the idea that race is a biological reality. "Race," they would argue, "is a social construct—a myth, concocted by racists in order to legitimize racial hierarchy. Colorblindness reflects the scientific fact that race isn't a genuine biological reality: there's more genetic variation within a given racial group than across racial groups. Those who reject colorblindness are beholden to the racist, antiscientific supposition that racial identity is real. And that's why those who reject colorblindness, who insist on refracting all social and political ills through the lens of racial identity, are the true racists."

This objection is confused. But since it's remarkably common, we should take a moment to dispel the confusion. Race is *not* a biologically significant category. (The physical features associated with racial identity are governed by biological factors, of course; but race is biologically insignificant in the sense that, for example, we see more genetic diversity within socially constructed racial groups than across socially constructed racial groups.) Yet it is a *social fact* that throughout US history race has been treated as a biological fact that legitimizes white supremacist beliefs and practices. As I've argued throughout this chapter, the repercussions of that social fact are both real and important. Thus we should reject colorblindness *not* because race is biologically significant but because we recognize the significance of the *social fact* that race has been treated as biologically significant throughout our nation's history.

## Conclusion

Legitimizing narratives around racial hierarchy have adapted over time in response to broader cultural trends. In the wake of the civil rights movement, as legally imposed racial hierarchy gave way to racialized socioeconomic stratification, white evangelicals abandoned "biblical" arguments for racial hierarchy and appropriated the rhetoric of colorblindness. In cooperation with meritocratic legitimizing narratives, the rhetoric of colorblindness serves to silence demands for institutional reforms that would mitigate the persisting effects of racist policies and practices once abetted by white evangelical theology. Thus evangelical appeals to colorblindness constitute a form of propaganda, invoking racial equality in order to perpetuate racial inequality. In this way, meritocracy and colorblindness furnish white evangelicals with intellectual resources to decry racism and white supremacy while actively promoting institutional arrangements that perpetuate racial hierarchy. Racial hierarchy, along with related anxieties around sexuality and racial purity—all of which have been legitimized by white evangelical theology for centuries—are core features of authoritarian ideology.

# 3

## Creationism and Theological Propaganda

ccording to the account of ideology I've been developing, the social and intellectual scandals that plague evangelicalism are mutually reinforcing: humans tend to invent narratives that confirm the legitimacy of social norms from which they benefit. This produces a feedback loop in which corrupt social arrangements engender corrupt beliefs—which, in turn, serve to legitimize and reinforce those corrupt practices, and so on. Thus far my analysis has accented the social side of this feedback loop, emphasizing the religious right's embrace of race and gender hierarchy. In this chapter my focus shifts to the intellectual side of the feedback loop.

### Creationisms

In his book *American Creationism, Creation Science, and Intelligent Design in the Evangelical Market*, Benjamin L. Huskinson identifies several distinct versions of what we might call *creationism*, broadly construed:

> *Young-Earth Creationism* (also called *Flood Geology, Creation Science*, and *Scientific Creationism*): The Genesis account describes

six twenty-four-hour days of creation, which took place in the recent past (six thousand to ten thousand years ago).

*Gap Theory* (also called *Ruin and Restoration*): An undetermined period of time (a gap) passed between Genesis 1:1 and Genesis 1:2, allowing for an old earth, while the six twenty-four-hour days of creation describe a restorative, rather than constructive, event.

*Day-Age Theory*: The six days of creation are allegorical and stand for six successive ages of undetermined length during which the universe was constructed, allowing for an old earth.

*Framework Theory* (also called the *Literary Framework View*): The Genesis narrative is a literary device, which constructs parallels between days one through three and four through six, and should be read as allegory rather than history.[1]

Despite their differences, what unites these views under the banner of creationism is that each posits some correlation between the origin of the universe and the creation narratives found in Genesis. This commitment to preserving the Genesis account sets all forms of creationism apart from, for example, the intelligent design movement—which may or may not involve claims specific to Christianity or the book of Genesis.

In keeping with Huskinson's framework, I'll use the term *creation science* to describe the organized effort to vindicate young-earth creationism against modern scientific claims concerning the antiquity of the earth. Note that two commitments set young-earth creationism apart from other forms of creationism. First, young-earth creationism claims that God created the earth and all forms of terrestrial life roughly ten thousand years ago, in a single period of approximately 144 hours (or six twenty-four-hour days).[2] Second, young-earth creationism holds that the creation narrative in the first chapter of Genesis is best understood as a straightforward, historical account of scientific facts about the earth's origins. In an effort to defend these tenets of young-earth creationism against modern scientific claims regarding the antiquity of the earth, creation scientists embrace the notion that the entirety of the earth's geological record reflects events that occurred during or after the flood narrated in Genesis 7, roughly four thousand years ago—a theory called *flood geology*. As we'll see, creation scientists maintain that young-earth creationism and flood geology are motivated by faithfulness to Scripture over and against the modern scientific establishment. I'll use the term *old-earth creationism* to refer collectively to all versions of creationism other than the young-earth view.

The creation science movement's core commitments are neatly captured in the following statement, composed by the founders of the Creation Research Society (CRS) in June 1963, which all members of the CRS were required to sign:

1. The Bible is the written Word of God, and because we believe it to be inspired thruout [*sic*], all of its assertions are historically and scientifically true in all of the original autographs. To the student of nature, this means that the account of origins in Genesis is a factual presentation of simple historical truths.

2. All basic types of living things, including man, were made by direct creative acts of God during Creation Week as described in Genesis. Whatever biological changes have occurred since Creation have accomplished only changes within the originally created kinds.

3. The great Flood described in Genesis, commonly referred to as the Noachian Deluge, was an historical event, worldwide in its extent and effect.[3]

The rise of the creation science movement in the latter half of the twentieth century was predicated on its remarkable success in persuading evangelicals that old-earth creationism is a capitulation to modern science and a rejection of Scripture.[4] As we'll see, the enthusiasm with which evangelicals embraced this notion is inseparable from the social anxieties that galvanized the religious right of the 1960s and '70s. But before turning our attention to the provenance of creation science and its lingering impact on the evangelical mind, we should dwell for a moment on the theological reasons that young-earth creationists offer for rejecting old-earth creationism.

## Objections to Old-Earth Creationism

We can divide theological objections to old-earth creationism into three categories: appeals to the clarity and authority of Genesis; concerns about the effects of old-earth creationism on biblical interpretation in general; and anxieties about the consequences of rejecting Christianity's historical young-earth consensus in favor of modern science.

### Objections 1 and 2: Authority and Interpretation

John MacArthur touches on each of these objections to old-earth creationism in the spring 2002 issue of *The Master's Seminary Journal*. MacArthur, the Southern California pastor introduced in chapter 1, is chancellor emeritus of The Master's Seminary, principal author and namesake of the *MacArthur Study Bible*, and according to *Christianity Today*, among the twenty-five most influential evangelical preachers of the latter half of the twentieth century.[5] On the matter of biblical authority, MacArthur reasons that

> many in the church are too intimidated or too embarrassed to affirm the literal truth of the biblical account of creation. They are confused by a chorus of authoritative-sounding voices who insist that it *is* possible—and even pragmatically necessary—to reconcile Scripture with the latest theories of the naturalists. . . . The simple, rather obvious, fact is that no one would ever think the timeframe for creation was anything other than a normal week of seven days from reading the Bible and allowing it to interpret itself. . . . The basic presupposition behind [old-earth creationism] is the notion that science speaks with more authority about origins and the age of the earth than Scripture does. Those who embrace such a view have in effect made science an authority *over* Scripture.[6]

In a talk given at the 2010 Ligonier Ministries National Conference, themed around "Tough Questions Christians Face," Southern Baptist Theological Seminary president and young-earther Albert Mohler wrestles with the question of why the universe appears to be more than ten thousand years old. Echoing MacArthur's appeal to the clarity and authority of Genesis, Mohler asserts that

> what we have here in Genesis 1:1–2:3 is a sequential pattern of creation, a straightforward plan. A direct reading of the text would indicate to us seven 24-hour days, six 24-hour days of creative activity and a final day of divine rest. . . .
>
> We need to recognize that disaster ensues when [science] or general revelation is used in some way to trump scripture and special revelation. And that is the very origin of this discussion.[7]

A century before MacArthur and Mohler, Ellen G. White, a cofounder of the Seventh-day Adventist Church, expressed similar concerns about theological efforts to accommodate "infidel geologists" by interpreting the first chapter of Genesis in ways that render "indefinite and obscure that which God has made very plain."[8] (In view of upcoming concerns, it's interesting to note that White's accounts of trancelike visions and messages from God inspired George Mc-Cready Price to develop the pseudoscience of flood geology on which creation science is based. I'll return to White and Price below, in tracing the genealogy of the creation science movement.)

A related objection to old-earth creationism holds that rejecting young-earth creationism establishes a dangerous precedent for biblical interpretation more generally. MacArthur alleges that

> what "old-earth creationists" (including, to a large degree, even the evangelical ones) are doing with Genesis 1–3 is precisely what religious liberals have always done with *all* of Scripture—spiritualizing and reinterpreting the text allegorically to make it mean what they want it to mean. It is a dangerous way to handle Scripture. And it involves a perilous and unnecessary capitulation to the . . . presuppositions of [scientific] naturalism—not to mention

a serious dishonor to God. Evangelicals who accept an old-earth interpretation of Genesis have embraced a hermeneutic that is hostile to a high view of Scripture. They are bringing to the opening chapters of Scripture a method of biblical interpretation that has built-in anti-evangelical presuppositions. Those who adopt this approach have already embarked on a process that invariably overthrows faith.[9]

Mohler concurs that "when it comes to the exegetical issues I will tell you that . . . the exegetical cost—the cost of the integrity in interpretation of scripture—to rendering the text [of Genesis] in any other way [than young-earth creationism] is just too high."[10] As I understand their concern, MacArthur and Mohler are anxious that embracing old-earth creationism will engender a proliferation of nonliteral modes of biblical interpretation: they reason that if we can justify a nonliteral reading of Genesis 1, then we can justify a nonliteral reading of anything else in the Bible.[11]

The cure for this anxiety is mild scrutiny. We might begin by observing that no theologically literate Christian interprets every word of Scripture according to its plainest, most literal sense. (No serious person reads the prophecies in Revelation 16 and understands them to mean that on some future occasion, seven angels will literally pour God's actual wrath out of bowls. Wrath is a sentiment. How does one place sentiment in a bowl, let alone pour it out?) And yet, despite reading some parts of Scripture nonliterally, plenty of evangelicals manage to read most of the Bible according to its plainest sense (as they understand it). So, how do we separate nonliteral interpretations that threaten to unravel the rest of Scripture from those that don't?

The most reliable interpreter of Scripture is Scripture itself. So we must allow that nonliteral interpretations of Scripture are appropriate when Scripture itself indicates that a nonliteral interpretation is in order. I'll refer to this position as *principled literalism*—the belief that we should understand Scripture according to the plain, literal sense of the text, except when Scripture itself indicates that we should do otherwise. Note that principled literalism makes two claims about how we should approach biblical interpretation. The first is that our default mode of interpretation should be anchored in the plain, literal sense of the text. (Naturally, in establishing what constitutes the "plain, literal sense of the text," we must be sensitive to cultural assumptions and other background beliefs that we impose on the text—see my critique of common sensism in chapter 1.) Second, principled literalism provides the caveat that we should abandon this default mode of interpretation at the direction of Scripture itself.[12]

In keeping with principled literalism, the following is a sensible line of reasoning that an old-earth creationist might offer for rejecting the young-earth interpretation of Genesis. Importantly, this line of reasoning poses no threat to biblical interpretation overall. Beginning in verse 13, the first chapter of Genesis tells us that

> evening came and then morning: the third day. Then God said, "Let there be lights in the expanse of the sky to separate the day from the night. They will serve as signs for seasons and for days and years. They will be lights in the expanse of the sky to provide light on the earth." And it was so. God made the two great lights—the greater light to rule over the day and the lesser light to rule over the night—as well as the stars. God placed them in the expanse of the sky to provide light on the earth, to rule the day and the night, and to separate light from darkness. And God saw that it was good. Evening came and then morning: the fourth day. (Gen. 1:13–19)

So according to the origin narrative in Genesis 1, three days elapsed—three mornings and three evenings—before God created the sun and other lights "to separate the day from the night."

I'm aware of young-earth creationists who claim the ability to envision the progress of three days, from dawn to dusk, in the absence of a sun. I confess that my own powers of imagination are not equal to the task: I can't conceive of what a day would be, if not a complete rotation of the earth *relative to the sun*. Echoing MacArthur and Mohler, Ken Ham—founder and CEO of the creation science organization Answers in Genesis—insists that "it is important for us to let the language of God's Word speak to us. . . . If we let the language speak to us, all six days are ordinary earth days."[13] Ham is, of course, entitled to his common-sense intuitions. But as we've observed, an "ordinary earth day" involves a complete rotation of the earth relative to the sun. So, when I let the text speak to me, what I hear it saying is that the "days" that elapsed prior to the creation of the sun were, by definition, *anything but* "ordinary earth days."

Perhaps Ham only means to say that the "days" before the sun were "ordinary" in the sense that they were twenty-four hours in length. But that won't do: twenty-four hours is merely the average interval of time it takes the earth to complete a full rotation relative to the sun. Some days are longer, due to the eccentricity of the earth's orbit. And some days are *much* longer—or so we are told in the tenth chapter of Joshua:

> On the day the LORD gave the Amorites over to the Israelites,
> Joshua spoke to the LORD in the presence of Israel:
>> "Sun, stand still over Gibeon,
>> and moon, over the Valley of Aijalon."
>> And the sun stood still
>> and the moon stopped
>> until the nation took vengeance on its enemies.
> Isn't this written in the Book of Jashar?
>> So the sun stopped
>> in the middle of the sky
>> and delayed its setting
>> almost a full day.
> There has been no day like it before or since, when the LORD listened to a man, because the LORD fought for Israel. (Josh. 10:12–14)

The use of the word *day* in verses 12 and 14 constitutes a biblical precedent for defining a day as a full rotation of the earth relative to the sun, notwithstanding the span of time required to complete said rotation. Thus a twenty-four-hour interval of time isn't what constitutes a day: it just happens to be the case that a day, defined as a complete rotation of the earth relative to the sun, typically lasts around twenty-four hours.

Ham alleges that "the sun is not needed for day and night. What is needed is light and a rotating earth. On the first day of creation, God made light (Gen. 1:3). The phrase 'evening and morning' certainly implies a rotating earth. Thus, if we have light from one direction, and a spinning earth, there can be day and night."[14]

I'm not sure how seriously to take this proposal, given that it fails to acknowledge the intricate cooperation of gravitational forces that sustain the earth's rotation in its orbit around the actual sun. Naturally, I don't deny that God would be capable of illuminating the earth and causing it to rotate even in the absence of a solar system. Yet I fail to see how the supposition that God created (and then presumably annihilated) a proxy sun that's nowhere in the text is somehow more faithful to Scripture than old-earth creationism.

Indeed, Ham's reasoning is intelligible only if his guiding assumption is that the most faithful rendering of Genesis *must* involve the earth being created in six twenty-four-hour days, regardless of the violence this assumption inflicts on the text. But in that case we're no longer contemplating how best to understand the book of Genesis; the subject has changed to whether young-earth assumptions can be coherently imposed on the creation narrative. This, as we'll see, is the same tactic that creation scientists employ in conversation with conventional science: instead of contemplating how best to understand the book of nature, creation science changes the subject to whether young-earth assumptions can be coherently imposed on creation itself. In both cases, the priority is vindicating young-earth assumptions rather than seeking to understand what God reveals through his authorship of Scripture and creation.

Before moving on, a couple of clarifying remarks are in order. Note first that my purpose here is *not* to demonstrate that a faithful rendering of Genesis might lead us to conclude that the earth is millions or billions of years old. Rather, my point is that there is a sensible reading of the text according to which the text itself indicates that it's not primarily concerned with relating factual details about intervals of time. So according to the interpretation I'm proposing, Genesis doesn't say that the earth was created in a span of 144 hours roughly six thousand years ago—*not* because the text says the earth was created at some other moment over some other span of time, but because the text just isn't meant to address those sorts of questions.

Second, in light of much young-earth and creation science rhetoric, I should emphasize that this gloss on the text is occasioned not by a lack of faith but by close attention to the text of Genesis. I'm not skeptical of the young-earth interpretation because I doubt that God would be capable of creating everything that exists in six ordinary days roughly six thousand years ago, in a manner that would lead modern scientists to be quite badly mistaken about the age of the earth. Had it pleased him to do so, God might have created the universe in six hours, or six months, or six seconds, or a fraction of one second. (This was the sticking point for many of the church fathers who rejected the young-earth interpretation: Why think it would've taken God *so long* to create the universe? Surely he would have brought the universe into existence instantaneously, the moment he willed it into being.) My skepticism of the young-earth interpretation has nothing at all to do with reservations about God's capacity or doubts about the infallibility or inerrancy of Genesis. Based entirely on the details of the text, I just don't think the first chapter of Genesis presents itself as a historical account of the timeline involved in God's creation of the universe.

This reading is supported by the distinct creation narrative found in the second chapter of Genesis, which stands in some apparent tension with the narrative of Genesis 1. (Technically, the creation narrative in Genesis 1 carries over into the second chapter of Genesis, stopping at the end of Genesis 2:3. A second creation narrative begins at verse 4 and runs through verse 25 at the end of Genesis 2.) There are a number of subtle differences between the two accounts. But the principal difficulty in reconciling the two narratives is a rather unsubtle divergence in the order of events described in Genesis 1 versus the order presented in Genesis 2.

In the first chapter of Genesis we find the earth's surface covered in water, which God separates in order to reveal dry land. God then creates plants, followed by animals, and finally humans (plural):

> Then God said, "Let us make man [i.e., human beings] in our image, according to our likeness. They will rule the fish of the sea, the birds of the sky, the livestock, the whole earth, and the creatures that crawl on the earth."

> So God created man [i.e., humankind]
> in his own image;
> he created him in the image of God;
> he created them male and female.
>
> God blessed them, and God said to them, "Be fruitful, multiply, fill the earth, and subdue it. Rule the fish of the sea, the birds of the sky, and every creature that crawls on the earth." God also said, "Look, I have given you every seed-bearing plant on the surface of the entire earth and every tree whose fruit contains seed. This will be food for you, for all the wildlife of the earth, for every bird of the sky, and for every creature that crawls on the earth—everything having the breath of life in it—I have given every green plant for food." And it was so. God saw all that he had made, and it was very good indeed. Evening came and then morning: the sixth day. (Gen. 1:26–31)

By contrast, Genesis 2 begins with land, followed by water, and then the creation of a single human male (later identified as Adam). After creating Adam, God creates plants and animals, followed by a single human female (Eve).

At this point some commentators note the discrepancies between these respective accounts of creation and declare the young-earth interpretation of Genesis to be bankrupt. They reason that the author of Genesis 1–2 placed these clearly inconsistent narratives side by side, in full awareness of their incompatibility. And that obvious contradiction, they reason, is the author of Genesis indicating that the text isn't meant to be read as an account of six "ordinary earth days" in which God called the universe and all its contents into being.

What makes this assessment of the text attractive is that it foregrounds authorial awareness of, and evident indifference to, the apparent tensions between Genesis 1 and Genesis 2: it's not an error. This underscores the fact that the book of Genesis doesn't present itself to the reader as a collection of ancient newspaper clippings that report scientific facts about the origins of the universe. That said, notwithstanding the objectives or genre of the text, perhaps we should expect the word of God to exhibit greater continuity than a poorly curated anthology of fan fiction. So, for reasons as much aesthetic as theological, I'm unsatisfied with the notion that the Bible's first two chapters offer two competing accounts of creation that are obviously contradictory.

Instead, we might integrate the disparate creation accounts by reading Genesis 2 as a detailed rendering of specific, localized events that unfold during or after day six in Genesis 1. (Based on conventions found throughout the book of Genesis, the introduction to the second creation narrative in Genesis 2:4 supports this reading.) In this view, the narrative in Genesis 1:1–2:3 describes the creation of the universe, the earth as a whole, land, plants, animals, and humans, followed by a day of rest. In Genesis 2, the text circles back to day six and narrows its gaze to a particular location, the garden of Eden, in order to document God's interactions with a specific human.

The picture that emerges is this. According to the first chapter of Genesis (1:27), God creates both male and female humans on the sixth day. In the second chapter of Genesis, God creates Adam alone (Gen. 2:7), and Eve isn't created until the end of the narrative (Gen. 2:22). In the interval between the creation of Adam in Genesis 2:7 and the creation of Eve in Genesis 2:22, the text informs us that (at a minimum):

- God relocates Adam to the garden of Eden (Gen. 2:9), whereupon:
- God makes trees grow out of the ground—including, in the center of the garden, the *tree of life* and the *tree of the knowledge of good and evil* (Gen. 2:8–9);
- Adam is assigned responsibility for tending the garden (Gen. 2:15);
- God gives Adam The Talk about the tree of the knowledge of good and evil (Gen. 2:16);
- God brings "every wild animal and every bird of the sky" to Adam to see what he will name them (Gen. 2:19);
- Adam gives names to "all the livestock, to the birds of the sky, and to every wild animal" (Gen. 2:20);
- Adam uses language for the first time (implied by conjoining Gen. 2:7 and 2:20);
- Adam realizes he's lonely (Gen. 2:20);

- Adam takes a nap—not a couch nap or an on-the-bed-but-over-the-covers nap, but a divinely induced "deep sleep" (Gen. 2:21), during which:
- Adam undergoes major surgery to remove one of his ribs (Gen. 2:21).

Finally, in Genesis 2:22, God creates Eve out of Adam's excised flesh. Adam wakes up and declares his fondness for Eve, and the creation narrative comes to a close.

Provided we reject the young-earth interpretation of Genesis 1–2, we seem to have reconciled the two creation accounts in a fairly straightforward way. God creates the universe and all its contents in Genesis 1. In Genesis 1:27, during the interval referred to as day six, God creates an unspecified number of male and female humans (perhaps a whole group or groups, as in the case of the other creatures described throughout the narrative). Genesis 2 gives us a detailed account of one of the humans God created in Genesis 1:27—namely, Adam. Thereafter, Adam learns about horticulture, God explains the tree of the knowledge of good and evil, God introduces Adam to all the animals, Adam names all the animals, and Adam realizes he's lonely. Judging that it's not good for Adam to be alone, God creates Eve.

For young-earthers, however, this integrated narrative raises further questions. A major theological selling point of young-earth creationism, according to young-earth creationists, is that their view makes Adam and Eve the mutual ancestors of all humankind. (Allegedly, imputing original sin to every human being is fair only if we're all biologically descended from the original sinners.) In the young-earth view, therefore, the male and female humans referenced in Genesis 1:27 are none other than Adam and Eve—literally: Adam, Eve, and no one else. This means that young-earthers are committed to the view that Adam and Eve were created in the same twenty-four-hour day. And if Adam and Eve were created in the same twenty-four-hour day, then the events recounted between Genesis 2:7 and Genesis 2:22 comprise the itinerary for *Adam's first day on earth*.

As of 2023, there are some ten thousand species of birds and well over five thousand species of mammals on our planet. (For simplicity, we'll ignore species of mammals and birds that passed into extinction in recent millennia, along with all species of amphibians and reptiles.) So, very conservatively, young-earthers are committed to the proposition that Adam named no less than fifteen thousand animals within the same twenty-four hours that he: began to exist, met God, moved to the garden of Eden, used language for the first time, learned gardening, learned about the tree of the knowledge of good and evil (about which, presumably, there were follow-up questions), had a formidable nap, underwent orthopedic surgery, and met his companion, Eve. Perhaps most remarkably, in the midst of this whirlwind, and despite having existed for less than twenty-four hours—much of which he spent in the company of God—Adam somehow experiences loneliness.

I find it difficult to imagine a member of our species, even with the capacities of a prelapsarian Adam, accomplishing so much so quickly after arriving on our planet. It's noteworthy that the narrative goes out of its way to mention in Genesis 2:19 that God was curious to see what Adam would name each of the animals. So it seems we must resist the temptation to explain Adam's incredible efficiency by supposing that he was merely acting as a sort of conduit for God's agency. This is a question not of God's capacity but of Adam's.

In a 1999 sermon, John MacArthur confirms that he reads the narrative in Genesis 2 as a detailed account of the sixth day of creation. Yet he doesn't share my skepticism about Adam's capacity to name all the animals in a single day, along with everything else on the itinerary. On the contrary, MacArthur reasons that

> God collected all the animals and He brought them before Adam. And Adam, who is more intelligent than you can ever imagine because his mind had never been corrupted by sin—in his unfallen condition six thousand or so years ago, Adam was far more intelligent than anything we could imagine six thousand years later the victims of constant degeneration. And Adam had the capacity in his mind to look at all these creatures and to determine some characteristic about them and give them a name. Now, at this particular point we don't know what language he spoke; but

in whatever language he spoke, he gave them a name. . . . Now, if Adam—and he certainly could have done this, it's not unreasonable—if he could name ten of them a minute as they passed by, he could do three thousand of them in five hours; and that just gives you a little idea. That would be covering some significant ground in naming the animals and the birds that God brought before him.[15]

Apart from noting the absence of sin and its effects, MacArthur doesn't specify any reasons for supposing that Adam's cognitive capacities would enable him to effortlessly complete tasks that modern humans assign to supercomputers. No reason whatsoever. He also makes his case appear stronger by grossly underestimating the number of species Adam would have had to name. (MacArthur is adamant that evolution is impossible, and equally convinced that God created no new species after the week of creation. There are over fifteen thousand species of birds and mammals today. So there must have been at least that many for Adam to name—again, ignoring extinct species, amphibians, and reptiles.) Even at the breakneck pace of ten per minute, it would've taken Adam twenty-five hours to name all fifteen thousand species of birds and mammals included in our conservative estimate. Assuming that the first half of the itinerary in Genesis 2 required about a minute to complete, at a pace of ten animals per minute, the shot clock on day six would expire with three thousand animals left to name and roughly half the itinerary to go—including the creation of Eve. Incidentally, in order to name fifteen thousand birds and mammals in five hours, Adam would need to proceed at a pace five times faster than MacArthur estimates, or roughly fifty animals per minute. That's one animal every 1.2 seconds—which is rather more like a stampede than the petting zoo on parade that MacArthur seems to imagine.

While I'm happy to acknowledge that Adam would have enjoyed some intellectual advantages over postlapsarian humans, I fear that MacArthur's vision of Adam more closely resembles the protagonist in a Marvel comic than an actual member of our own species. I don't know what reasons MacArthur has, or could possibly have, for believing that Adam competently named ten (let alone fifty) animals per minute for hours on end. I do, however, understand the reasons for my own difficulty in accepting that proposal—namely, my experience of being a human and knowing other humans.

Aside from my reservations about the abilities MacArthur ascribes to Adam, I can't imagine why God would be in such a rush to have Adam name all the animals in creation. That strikes me as out of character for a God who doesn't generally seem to be in a hurry anywhere else in Scripture—at least not in his interactions with humans. It makes sense only if our guiding assumption is that the most faithful rendering of Genesis *must* involve the earth being created in six twenty-four-hour days, regardless of the violence this assumption inflicts on the text. As best I can discern from the public comments of Ken Ham, Albert Mohler, and John MacArthur, their stated reasons for embracing that guiding assumption are a matter of intuition, or perhaps a mood that overtakes them when they survey the first two chapters of Genesis. I suppose I just don't share their intuitions about the biblical faithfulness of claiming that God created and annihilated a proxy solar system (or something with relevantly similar properties) to govern time before creating the actual sun. And "naming fifty animals a minute for five hours is a good plan or even a live option" isn't the mood that strikes me when I read Genesis 2, or contemplate Adam's humanity, or reflect on the nature of God. I'm open to the proposition that God created the universe in six twenty-four-hour days less than ten thousand years ago. But I won't abuse the text of Genesis in order to preserve that proposition.

I understand that any number of young-earthers will find the foregoing analysis of Genesis unsatisfying. (Some of them are theologians whose employment depends on finding objections to young-earth creationism unsatisfying—at least publicly.) So it bears emphasizing that my purpose here is *not* to persuade young-earthers that they should abandon their view in favor of an old-earth interpretation of Genesis. Rather, my aim is merely to demonstrate that there are perfectly respectable reasons for doubting the young-earth interpretation of Genesis, based on a plain reading of the text itself—reasons that pose no conceivable threat to biblical interpretation in general.

In keeping with that modest objective, I should also acknowledge that an adequate picture of the Genesis creation narratives would attend to the literary, cultural, and historical world of the text, which my analysis simply ignores. (Not to mention *language*: several pages in, we've yet to consider the Hebrew word for *day* and the multitudes it contains.) None of those details would improve the case for a young-earth interpretation of Genesis, and I'm content with the strength of my position as it stands. I am, however, prepared to make one concession regarding the "exegetical cost" of principled literalism: if applied consistently, it may require us to abandon the kind of motivated literalism involved in the hermeneutics of legitimization (see Introduction). But in my judgment, that's a cost we should be delighted to pay.

As we'll see, the theological heritage of the old-earth position has been obscured in recent decades by creation science propaganda. So before proceeding, I'll offer the reader a gentle reminder that the following stars in the firmament of modern Christianity either defended or expressed sympathy for an old-earth interpretation of Genesis 1–2:

- Charles Hodge—nineteenth-century Princeton theologian known for his resistance to theological liberalism
- Charles Haddon Spurgeon—nineteenth-century Particular Baptist minister, renowned for his preaching and commitment to theological conservatism
- C. I. Scofield—principal engineer of the Scofield Reference Bible
- B. B. Warfield—nineteenth- and twentieth-century Princeton theologian known for defending the Bible's divine inspiration
- William Jennings Bryan—famous creationist and infamous prosecutor in the *Scopes* trial of 1925 (not a theologian, but noteworthy given his public profile and antievolution advocacy)
- William Bell Riley—founder of the World's Christian Fundamentals Association and the Anti-Evolution League of America
- C. S. Lewis—Christian author of some note
- Billy Graham—Christian evangelist of some note
- James Montgomery Boice—prominent theologian, pastor in the

Presbyterian Church in America, and the only chairman of the International Council on Biblical Inerrancy, which produced the Chicago Statement on Biblical Inerrancy (widely regarded as the evangelical gold standard for biblical inerrancy)[16]

It bears highlighting that *this* is the theological caliber of those whom Albert Mohler, Ken Ham, Ligon Duncan, and John MacArthur presume to indict on charges of theological liberalism, inadequate regard for biblical authority, undue deference to science, hermeneutical barbarism, and forsaking basic common sense.

This brings us to the first theological objection to old-earth creationism: namely, that rejecting the young-earth interpretation of Genesis is an affront to the clarity and authority of Scripture. We've established that the young-earth interpretation of Genesis is contested. So, for reasons examined at length in chapter 1, this objection to old-earth creationism is nothing more than propaganda. For the sake of illustration and proof of concept, we should take a moment to draw out the application to present concerns.

Consider the claim that we should reject old-earth creationism because Genesis *clearly* teaches that creation took place in the course of 144 hours roughly six thousand years ago. The notion that old-earth creationism is at odds with the clear teaching of Genesis simply presupposes that the young-earth interpretation of Genesis is correct (indeed, clearly correct). But that's precisely the point at issue in the debate. Young-earthers say that the Genesis account supports the claims of young-earth creationism, and old-earth creationists say that it doesn't. So this line of argument is hopelessly question-begging: unless I've already accepted the conclusion that Genesis supports the claims of young-earth creationism, I have no reason to accept the premise that old-earth creationism is at odds with the clear teaching of Genesis. But as we observed in chapter 1, this isn't how arguing works. An argument doesn't demand that we accept its conclusion in order to find its reasons persuasive—it invites us to accept its conclusion with persuasive reasoning.

What makes this assertion of biblical clarity interesting, for our purposes, is that it fits the pattern of common-sense propaganda that we identified in chapter 1. Specifically, it invokes a basic human capacity to perceive the clear meaning of the biblical text, only to claim that those who disagree lack the capacity in question. So this appeal to biblical clarity is propaganda, in that it invokes universal common sense in service to an argument that's predicated on denying that common sense is, in fact, universal.

Likewise, the claim that "rejecting the young-earth interpretation of Genesis implies a lack of regard for the Bible's authority" fits the pattern of illegitimate appeals to biblical authority identified in chapter 1. (Whenever the authority of Scripture comes up in a debate about how to interpret Scripture, that's a massive red flag. The Bible's meaning is the point at issue—not the Bible's authority.) Recall that chapter 1 distinguishes between *at-issue content* (which refers to the parts of a statement that are up for discussion) and *not-at-issue content* (or the parts of a statement that furnish the factual backdrop that must be assumed in order to engage in further discussion).

The claim that "rejecting the young-earth interpretation of Genesis implies a lack of regard for the Bible's authority" contains both at-issue content and not-at-issue content. The at-issue content asserts that rejecting the young-earth interpretation of Genesis implies inadequate regard for biblical authority. This presupposes that the young-earth interpretation of Genesis is not only correct but obviously correct—so that those who question it are guilty not merely of misreading the text but of willfully disregarding the clear message of the text.

Thus, embedded within the claim that "rejecting the young-earth interpretation of Genesis implies a lack of regard for the Bible's authority," there's a not-at-issue assertion to the effect that the young-earth reading of Genesis is obviously correct. And as we've established, that assertion is nothing more than common-sense propaganda. So this appeal to biblical authority rests on the notion that men like Ken Ham, Albert Mohler, and John MacArthur possess the competence and authority to decide what the Bible means on behalf of you, me, C. S. Lewis, James Montgomery Boice, and everyone else. That notion is utterly antithetic to the Protestant ideal of *sola scriptura*, which is the very theological principle invoked by appeals to the Bible's authority.

As we observed in chapter 1, the Reformation ideal of *sola scriptura* is meant to attenuate ecclesial power. Yet the opposite is achieved when men with power dictate the meaning of Scripture and then assert the sovereign authority of their own decrees. Such appeals to "biblical" authority only serve to amplify the power of influential pastors and seminary administrators who use the language of biblical authority to cement the orthodoxy of their own intuitions.

This propaganda carries over into the creation science industry's ubiquitous use of the modifier *biblical* to describe its young-earth presuppositions: if the Bible's authority is sovereign and the young-earth position is the "biblical view," it strictly follows that anyone who rejects the young-earth position rejects the biblical view. We'll return to this point in chapter 4.

*Objection 3: Undue Deference to Modern Science*

A final theological objection to old-earth creationism is that the young-earth understanding of Genesis represents the Christian consensus for most of church history. Young-earthers maintain that old-earth creationism's departure from this consensus is a capitulation to modern science that perpetuates a dangerous trend: the growing tendency to trade faith in God's word for confidence in the modern scientific establishment. Ligon Duncan alleges that

> historically the church has always viewed these days to be literal days, speaking of the same kind of days that you and I know about. But within the last 150 years, even within evangelical circles, there has been considerable difference and discussion about the nature of these days. In church history, prior to 150 years ago, you can name on one hand the folks who viewed these days other than literal days, other than six natural twenty-four hour days.[17]

Similarly, Mohler claims that the young-earth interpretation of Genesis

> was the untroubled consensus of the Christian church until early in the 19th century. It was not absolutely unanimous. It was not always without controversy. But it was the overwhelming, untroubled consensus of the church until the dawn of the 19th century.

... We would not be having this [old- versus young-earth] discussion today—this would not be one of those tough questions Christians ask—if these questions were not being posed to us by those who assume that general revelation and [science] is presenting to us ... compelling evidence that is so forceful and credible that we're going to have to reconstruct and re-envision our understanding of the biblical text.[18]

Expanding on the picture painted by Duncan and Mohler, John MacArthur worries that old-earth creationists

are willing to reinterpret Genesis to accommodate evolutionary theory. . . . The result is that over the past couple of decades [ca. 1980s–'90s], large numbers of evangelicals have shown a surprising willingness to take a completely non-evangelical approach to interpreting the early chapters of Genesis. More and more are embracing the view known as "old-earth creationism," which blends some of the principles of biblical creationism with naturalistic and evolutionary theories, seeking to reconcile two opposing worldviews. And in order to accomplish this, old-earth creationists end up explaining away rather than honestly exegeting the biblical creation account.[19]

Observe that this objection depends on three distinct claims. The first is a claim about what Christians believed in the distant past: young-earth creationism was the consensus among Christians until about two centuries ago. The second is a claim about what Christians have come to believe in the more recent past: the historical consensus around young-earth creationism has deteriorated over the last two centuries—especially in recent decades (at least according to MacArthur). And the third is a causal claim about the reason why this young-earth consensus began to deteriorate in or around the nineteenth century: Christians have come to place their faith in the deliverances of science over and against God's clear and authoritative word.

I confess that I find each of these claims more puzzling than the last. Consider the fanciful notion that we can count "on one hand"

the number of Christians who rejected the young-earth interpretation of Genesis prior to the mid-1800s. Within the patristic era alone,
we find: Justin Martyr (ca. 100–ca. 165), Irenaeus (ca. 130–ca. 202),
Origen of Alexandria (ca. 185–ca. 253), Athanasius of Alexandria
(ca. 296–373), Jerome (ca. 342–420), and (as Duncan acknowledges)
Augustine (354–430).[20] That's six prior to the middle of the fifth century. So we've exceeded the enumerating capacity of the average human hand with fourteen centuries to spare—which is more centuries
than we can count on two hands.

   Moreover, this list is restricted to the names of men regarded as
church fathers: ancient Christians who aren't merely orthodox or
influential but whose influence shaped the contours of Christian orthodoxy as we know it. So conspicuous is the absence of a patristic
consensus in favor of young-earth creationism that Martin Luther
felt it necessary to qualify his defense of the young-earth position
as follows:

> We must understand that these days were actual days, contrary
> to the opinion of the Holy Fathers. Whenever we observe that
> the opinions of the Fathers disagree with Scripture, we rever-
> ently bear with them and acknowledge them to be our elders.
> Nevertheless, we do not depart from the authority of Scripture
> for their sake.[21]

Indeed, Luther's remarks suggest that there was something like a
consensus *against* the young-earth reading of Genesis among the
church fathers. So, at least among the Christian theologians and
philosophers whose views on the matter are known to us, we can
state definitively that there is nothing resembling an "untrou-
bled consensus" in favor of young-earth creationism prior to the
nineteenth century.[22]

   More bewildering is John MacArthur's suggestion that "large
numbers of evangelicals" abandoned young-earth creationism in
the closing decades of the twentieth century. Since MacArthur's
essay offers no support for this claim, it's difficult to assess his rationale. But available evidence suggests that in fact the popularity

of young-earth creationism grew in the latter half of the twentieth century and remained more or less stable from the beginning of the 1980s to the end of the 2010s, perhaps peaking around 1999. According to Ronald Numbers, the premier historian of modern creationist movements,

> Until the last few decades [of the twentieth century] most creationists would have regarded [young-earth creationism] as unnecessarily extreme. By the late nineteenth century even the most conservative Christian apologists readily conceded that the Bible allowed for an ancient earth and pre-Edenic life. With few exceptions, they accommodated the findings of historical geology either by interpreting the days of Genesis 1 to represent vast ages in the history of the earth (the so-called day-age theory) or by separating a creation "in the beginning" from a much later Edenic creation in six literal days (the gap theory). Either way, they could defend the accuracy of the Bible while simultaneously embracing the latest geological and paleontological discoveries.[23]

A Gallup poll in January 1982 found that 44 percent of Americans affirmed the proposition that "God created human beings pretty much in their present form at one time within the last 10,000 years or so." In the summer of 1999, Gallup found that the proportion of Americans who affirmed that statement had grown to 47 percent. And in 2008 that figure was back down to 44 percent.[24]

Given that the proposition in question is consistent with versions of old-earth creationism, these poll results don't demonstrate conclusively that young-earth creationism has enjoyed steady popularity among evangelicals for the last four decades. (Indeed, more refined polling suggests that many of those who affirm the recent, special creation of humankind are old-earth creationists.)[25] But there's no evidence that evangelical support for the young-earth view has substantially declined at any point in the past fifty years. (MacArthur certainly doesn't provide any.) Furthermore, as we'll see in the next chapter, young-earth creationism is far more popular among evangelicals now than at any point prior to about 1960.

We've now established that two of the three claims at issue have
no basis in fact. At least among the theologians and philosophers
whose views on Genesis are known to us, the notion of a historical
consensus in favor of young-earth creationism is a fantasy. Likewise,
we have no reason to think that evangelicals' fondness for young-
earth creationism has substantially declined in recent decades—
quite the opposite, in fact.

## The Assumption

This brings us to the matter of why, according to MacArthur, Duncan, and Mohler, the historical Christian consensus on young-earth
creationism is in disrepair: misplaced faith in science over the word
of God. Having established that no such consensus ever existed,
it seems unfair to blame its demise on the popularity of science.
From beginning to end, the alarmist narrative that scores of evangelicals have abandoned young-earth creationism because they've
traded Scripture for science is pure fiction. Nonetheless, it's worth
addressing the baseless assumption that Christians who reject the
young-earth view must be motivated by undue deference to modern
science. This assumption is so integral to the way the creation science industry operates that I'll refer to it simply as *The Assumption*.
The Assumption is that the only reason a Christian would reject the
young-earth interpretation of Genesis is that they trust modern science more than Scripture. (Observe that other evangelical defenses
of purportedly "biblical" views employ variations on The Assumption that trade on the cultural antagonisms of conservative evangelicals—e.g., the complementarian notion that opposition to "biblical"
patriarchy must involve a capitulation to feminism or secular culture.
More on these parallels below.)

For clarity, The Assumption doesn't claim merely that *some* Christians reject the young-earth view because they trust modern science
more than Scripture. (That claim may well be true.) Rather, it claims
that *all* Christians who reject the young-earth position do so because
they trust modern science more than Scripture. But that claim isn't

merely unsupported by evidence; it's demonstrably false. Modern methods of science didn't factor into the thinking of the church fathers listed above, who rejected the young-earth reading of Genesis long before the inception of modern geology, paleontology, glaciology, archaeology, and so forth.

Moreover, although some modern theologians and philosophers who embrace old-earth creationism attest that science has influenced their thinking on the matter, it is by no means obvious that in so doing they have allowed science to supplant the authority of Scripture. (In his commentary on the book of Genesis, for example, James Montgomery Boice cites modern science among his reasons for rejecting the young-earth interpretation of Genesis.[26] And I can't comprehend how anyone might entertain serious doubts about Boice's commitment to the inerrancy or authority of Scripture.) For reasons noted above, it's not at all clear that Genesis presents itself as a scientific or historical account of the earth's origins. So this isn't a straightforward case in which Scripture asserts that "X" and science asserts that "not-X," such that deferring to one means rejecting the other.

Rather, the creation narratives in Genesis present us with a situation in which Scripture is open to interpretation, and science offers us compelling reasons to prefer some interpretations over others. We must distinguish the practice of deferring to science when Scripture is silent or unclear from the very different practice of deferring to science when Scripture says the opposite. One implies a failure to recognize the sovereignty of Scripture. The other merely recognizes that God, in his sovereignty, has provided us with the light of reason to supplement the light of Scripture. The Assumption fails to appreciate that distinction.

For our purposes, what makes The Assumption interesting is its function in framing the discourse around the opening chapters of Genesis. If the only reason for rejecting the young-earth interpretation of Genesis is deference to modern science, then there cannot be a reason for rejecting the young-earth interpretation of Genesis based on the biblical text itself. This implies that the only defensible treatment of Genesis—the only reading of the text that actually takes the Bible seriously—is the young-earth interpretation. Thus The Assumption transforms the creation science movement from a pseudo-scientific defense of a parochial interpretation of Genesis into a holy crusade to defend the Bible's integrity against the arrayed forces of secularism, science, and theological liberalism.[27]

# 4

## *Creation Science and the Culture War Machine*

I concluded the previous chapter by highlighting The Assumption: the only reason why a Christian would reject the young-earth interpretation of Genesis is that they trust modern science more than Scripture. For our purposes, The Assumption is important because it gives young-earthers license to describe their suppositions about the age of the earth as the "biblical view" without acknowledging that what constitutes the biblical view of creation is a contested question. This purportedly "biblical view" of creation is the operative feature of the "biblical worldview" that creation scientists cite as the source of their many intractable disagreements with "secular" science.

By means of this fiction, the creation science industry has come to inhabit a kind of intellectual no-man's-land in which creation scientists advance ostensibly biblical and scientific claims while avoiding substantive engagement with either biblical scholarship or legitimate science. Over time, this intellectual no-man's-land has proven to be a hospitable base of operation for enterprising theologians and ambitious ministers who exercise social control by framing their opposition to "secular" expertise as the definitive "biblical view"—of gender, race, parenting, politics, public school curricula, Walt Disney, progressive income tax, financial capitalism, international relations, and so on and so forth.

## The Methods of Creation Science

Answers in Genesis (AiG), the creation science organization that oversees the Creation Museum and the Ark Encounter, has perfected the procedure. We find an exquisite example in a 2016 exchange between Bill Nye ("the Science Guy") and Ken Ham (founder and CEO of AiG, and the author of more than a dozen books on subjects that range from creation science to parenting and race). Ham invited Nye to tour the Ark Encounter, and AiG recorded their conversation for posterity. Early in the tour, Nye spots an "Ice Age" exhibit. Showing himself in, he asks, "So, what goes on here in the Ice Age?"

Just inside the entrance, a large sign depicts two alternative timelines: one consistent with the findings of conventional science, the other based on flood geology (the foundation of modern creation science). The composition of this sign is remarkable—a fitting backdrop for the conversation that unfolds in the foreground. Its title asks, "ONE ICE AGE OR MANY?" Beneath it, the subtitle advises us that "different worldviews lead to different conclusions." Above the flood geology timeline, a subheading advertises its contents as the "BIBLICAL VIEW," with a note assuring museumgoers that "our *biblical model* maintains that there was only one ice age, and it came about as a result of the global flood" (emphasis in original—note the repeated use of the modifier *biblical*). The timeline based on conventional science is labeled "SECULAR VIEW." Nye pauses to take in the "biblical view," and the following dialogue ensues.

> NYE.  I'm sorry, so your claim is that there was an ice age four thousand years ago?
>
> HAM.  The Ice Age was back towards the flood, yeah.
>
> NYE.  What do you base that on?
>
> HAM.  What do we base that on? Well . . . as you know . . .
>
> NYE.  Here—we have evidence for this [*pointing to the "secular view"*]. But what's the evidence for that [*pointing to the "biblical view"*]?
>
> HAM.  No, we don't have evidence for that [secular view]. That's an interpretation. You can't find ice that has labels on it.
>
> NYE.  Yes, you can.

HAM.  Labels?

NYE.  Absolutely.

HAM.  That say, "I'm three hundred thousand years old"?

NYE.  Yes. Sir, you're a science educator.

HAM.  I've never seen one of those. Where do you see one of those?

NYE.  You count neutrons and oxygen atoms. That's how it's done. It's as though it has a label on it, very much.

HAM.  But it doesn't say, "I'm three hundred thousand years old."

NYE.  Not in English, no.

HAM.  You have to interpret it on the basis of certain assumptions, right?

NYE.  Well, certain discoveries.

HAM.  No, assumptions.

NYE.  Let's go with *discoveries*. Go ahead. Go ahead, how do you get an ice age four thousand years ago?

HAM.  Let's go with *assumptions* because whenever you're interpreting the past, you have to have certain basic assumptions about elements that were there, and rates of change, and all that sort of thing.[1]

For the next several minutes, Nye and Ham engage in an extended sidebar concerning Ham's eccentric views on the philosophy of science. Ham alleges that there is an important difference between what he calls *observational science* and *historical science*. Observational science involves conducting experiments and making observations in order to reach conclusions about the world around us—conclusions on which, all else being equal, creation science and conventional science would agree. But Ham insists that observational science is very different from what he calls *historical science*, which deals with questions about the distant past. What makes historical science different, according to Ham, is that we can't observe the distant past or subject it to experiments. So, he reasons, scientific conclusions about the distant past depend on assumptions embedded in our worldview. These assumptions determine how we interpret the scant evidence concerning the distant past that is available to us in the present.

Once Ham finishes explaining how he conceives of the distinction between observational and historical science, Nye repeats his original question for the third time.

> NYE.  So let's talk about this again [*pointing to the timeline under the "biblical view"*]. What makes you think this was four thousand years ago?
>
> HAM.  What makes us think that that was four thousand years ago? Well first of all, we take the chronology in the Bible. And the chronology in the Bible is that Noah's flood was about 4,300 years ago. And so that gives us a date at the end of the flood. Then we look at the evidence we have today of the fact that we know that there was ice in the past, we know there were glaciers in the past that advanced, because we see the evidence in the present.

By established standards of conventional scholarship, the pattern of reasoning that Ham narrates is highly irregular. What he offers isn't evidence of an ice age having occurred four thousand years ago, but rather an acknowledgment that the earth has undergone an ice age, followed by assurances that flood geology can accommodate this fact in a way that's consistent with the assumptions of young-earth creationism. Indeed, according to Ham, this is exactly how the "historical science" game is played: we make assumptions about the distant past based on our worldview, and those assumptions determine how we interpret the available evidence. Thus, as far as it concerns the distant past, the task of the scientist is to furnish an interpretation of the evidence that confirms the assumptions embedded in his worldview.

This procedure for evaluating evidence bears a striking resemblance to the phenomenon of *confirmation bias*: the human tendency to interpret information or evidence in a way that confirms the beliefs we already hold. Mainstream scientists (and academics more generally) regard confirmation bias as undesirable. Like all humans, researchers have biases. But professional researchers and research institutions invest a great deal of effort in identifying and mitigating the biases that may adversely impact the results of their research. So, while it would be harsh to say that what Ham describes as "historical science" is the *exact opposite* of actual science, it must be observed that actual scientists take great care to avoid precisely the style of reasoning that Ham calls historical science.

From a marketing perspective, Ham's emphasis on "historical" science appears to be a technique for selling conservative evangelicals on the importance of creation science education. It evokes images of the professional scientist toting his lunch pail to work, day after day, determined to vindicate his assumption that God doesn't exist, or prove that the timeline in Genesis is factually inaccurate. This narrative leverages popular misconceptions about the alleged antipathies between "secular" science and religious faith—misconceptions that are no doubt amplified by the extracurricular efforts of celebrity scientists like Richard Dawkins, who goes well out of his way to antagonize people of faith and ridicule religious belief. Nonetheless, as attested by the quality of his philosophical arguments on the subject, when Dawkins reflects on the question of God's existence, he does so not in his professional capacity as an Oxford biologist but as a hobbyist.

In professional contexts, when a scientist sits down to examine a cross-section of ice core[2] from Antarctica, they're probably not interested in proving that the earth is billions of years old. Do they believe that the earth is billions of years old? Almost certainly. But it's highly unlikely that this belief is directly relevant to their research[3] (largely because the longest ice cores—i.e., those with the deepest and therefore oldest samples of ice—typically date back only hundreds of thousands of years).[4] The scientist's interest in analyzing glacial ice is probably restricted to the details of volcanic activity or the state of the earth's atmosphere at some moment in the past. The point is that they go about their work on ancient cylinders of ice with their beliefs about the earth's antiquity in the background, and in the process of conducting their research, they never encounter any evidence that contradicts those background beliefs. This experience is repeated countless times, in dozens of scientific subdisciplines, by thousands of scientists—the vast majority of whom aren't immediately concerned with the age of the earth. This collective body of work, stretching across centuries and continents, culminates in a mass of evidence that is uniformly consistent with the earth's antiquity. And virtually none of it involves efforts on the part of scientists to confirm their background beliefs regarding the age of the earth, the existence of God, or the merits of Scripture.

Ham's description of "historical science" does, however, resemble the creation science industry's approach to "science." And he demonstrates the procedure to perfection in explaining how he arrives at the conclusion that the earth underwent an ice age four thousand years ago. Creation science begins by accepting the "biblical view" of the earth's origins, according to which God created the earth roughly six thousand years ago. If we assume that the earth's geological record was produced by physical processes that unfolded in a uniform way, all available evidence seems to indicate that the earth is easily hundreds of millions of years old. So creation science must provide an alternative "interpretation" of the evidence, according to which the geological record was *not* produced by uniform physical processes. And flood geology does exactly that.

According to flood geology, a global catastrophic flood covered the entire earth in water for an entire year, reorganizing every feature of the earth's geological record in the process—fossils, sediment, manmade structures, etc. So anything we find in the geological record must be a product of either the flood or events that transpired thereafter.[5] According to the "biblical view," the Genesis flood occurred roughly 4,300 years ago. So any evidence of an ice age found in the geological record *must* correspond to events that occurred within the last 4,300 years. There is evidence of an ice age in the geological record. Thus, he reasons, the earth underwent an ice age within the last four thousand years or so.

Creation scientists follow the same procedure for discounting the apparent age of ice cores recovered from the depths of apparently ancient glaciers. An ice core is a column of solid ice that's been drilled out of a glacier, typically in Antarctica or Greenland. Ice cores vary widely in length, ranging from less than a few feet to more than two miles. Longer ice cores resemble a large telephone pole made of neatly stacked, translucent discs. (Imagine a mile-high stack of oversize hockey pucks that are semi-transparent and fused together by thinner layers of solid ice.) The ice discs toward the top of the column are the youngest in age; discs at the bottom are the oldest. Thus, as we proceed down the column, we proceed back in time.

Testing reveals that the chemical composition of each disc is unique. Some discs have relatively high concentrations of lead, for example, while others have higher concentrations of radioactive particles, or copper, or volcanic ash, or what have you. And it turns out that when we count the number of discs between the very top disc and the lowest (i.e., oldest) disc containing relatively high concentrations of radionuclides, the sum is identical to the number of years between the date the core was drilled and the year we commenced atmospheric testing of thermonuclear bombs. Similarly, the number of discs between the top disc and discs with relatively high concentrations of lead is identical to the number of years between the date the core was drilled and the peak consumption of leaded gasoline—and when we count back up the cylinder, chemical testing reveals a gradual reduction in lead concentration brought about by the introduction of unleaded fuel.[6] The number of discs between the top and the oldest discs that have high concentrations of industrial pollutants is identical to the number of years between the date the core was drilled and the onset of the industrial revolution. The number of discs between the top and a disc with high concentrations of volcanic ash is identical to the number of years between the date the core was drilled and the eruption of Mount Vesuvius in 79 CE, and so on.[7] Without making any assumptions about the age of the earth, it's reasonable to suppose that each layer in an ice core represents a single year in the earth's history.

Apparently these annual layers are produced by seasonal variations in temperature that trap colder snow between thin layers of relatively warmer snow. These annual layers are then compressed into solid ice under the weight of subsequent snow accumulation. Longer ice cores contain hundreds of thousands of these annual layers. So, based strictly on the evidence found in glacial ice, the earth appears to be much older than young-earthers would have it.[8]

In sharp contrast to the process I've just described, creation scientists begin with the assumption that earth can't possibly be more than about six thousand years old, because that would be inconsistent with the "biblical view" of the earth's age. So, they reason, it must be possible for many layers of snow-ice to form within a single year. I could go on, but we've established that creation science isn't actually a form of science (unless "historical science" counts as science, which it does not). Rather, creation science is an organized framework for casting doubt on scientific conclusions that pose a threat to the allegedly "biblical" view of creation. Thus creation science is propaganda: in marketing itself as a scientific enterprise, the creation science movement invokes the intellectual ideals associated with scientific rigor—but it does so only in order to further an agenda that denies the reliability of research conducted according to those very ideals, while promoting research that violates them.

Since the 1960s, creation science propaganda has enjoyed enormous success in the evangelical marketplace of ideas. I turn now to the origins of the modern creation science movement in the 1920s. We'll then ask why this movement gained traction among white evangelicals beginning in the 1960s, and examine the impact of creation science on the evangelical mind even today.

### The History of Creation Science

Henry Morris (1918–2006), the hydraulic engineer and coauthor of the bestselling 1961 book *Genesis Flood*, is widely regarded as the father of modern creation science. That would make the architect of flood geology, George McCready Price (1870–1963), the grandfather of the creation science movement. So we might say that the great-grandmother of creation science is Ellen G. White (1827–1915).

*Smithsonian Magazine* lists Ellen G. White among the "100 most significant Americans of all time."[9] She was a prolific author, influential advocate of vegetarianism, and cofounder of the Seventh-day Adventist Church. Regarded as a prophet in the Adventist tradition, White recounted hundreds of visions in which she witnessed events in the past or future under the direction of Jesus or angels. In a document titled "The Inspiration and Authority of the Ellen G. White Writings," the Biblical Research Institute of the General Conference of Seventh-day Adventists states, "One of the gifts of the Holy Spirit is prophecy. This gift is an identifying mark of the remnant church and was manifested in the ministry of Ellen G. White. As the Lord's messenger, her writings are a continuing and authoritative source of truth which provide for the church comfort, guidance, instruction, and correction."[10]

In his definitive history of modern creationist movements, *The Creationists: From Scientific Creationism to Intelligent Design*, Ronald Numbers documents three of White's claims that are salient to the genealogy of modern creation science. First, White recounted one vision in which she was "carried back to the creation and was shown that the first week, in which God performed the work of creation in six days and rested on the seventh day, was just like every other week."[11] Second, unlike most of her Christian contemporaries, White held that the flood narrated in Genesis 7–9 covered the surface of the entire earth. Thus, according to White, the earth's geological record was produced by the flood, *not* by uniform physical processes unfolding over many millions of years. Similarly, fossils were the remains of animals that were buried following the global flood, when God caused "a powerful wind to pass over the earth . . . in some instances carrying away the tops of mountains like mighty avalanches, forming huge hills and high mountains where there were none to be seen before, and burying the dead bodies with trees, stones, and earth."[12] And third, according to White,

> Every species of animal which God had created were preserved in the ark. The confused species which God did not create, which were the result of amalgamation, were destroyed by the flood. Since the flood there has been amalgamation of man and beast, as may be seen in the almost endless varieties of species of animals, and in certain races of men.[13]

White's visions turned out to be a decisive factor in the thinking of a young science teacher named George McCready Price.

*George McCready Price and Flood Geology*

As a young man, Price agonized over how to reconcile Scripture with
evidence of the earth's antiquity. Virtually none of the creationists of
his time believed in a young earth. In the 1920s, in fact, young-earth
creationism was considered so ridiculous that fundamentalists like
William Jennings Bryan, who defended creationism in the infamous
*Scopes* trial of 1925, accused evolutionists of ascribing the young-
earth view to creationists in order to unfairly discredit them. (In
other words, creationists considered it a "straw man" tactic.)[14] Price,
a committed Seventh-day Adventist, finally became convinced of
the young-earth view by reflecting on accounts of White's visions—
which contained, in Price's words, "revealing word pictures of the
Edenic beginning of the world, of the fall and the world apostasy,
and of the flood."[15] It was White's account of the flood in particular
that led Price to the key insight that spawned the creation science
movement: that the evidence for evolution "all turned on its view of
geology, and that if its geology were true, the rest would seem more
or less reasonable."[16] Thus Price set out to remake the field of geology in the image of White's visions, in the process showing "how the
actual facts of the rocks and fossils, stripped of mere theories, splen-
didly refute this evolutionary theory of the invariable order of the
fossils, which is the very backbone of the evolution doctrine."[17]

   Despite his misgivings about Darwinian evolution, Price took a
capacious view of species' potential to change over relatively brief
spans of time. This isn't unusual among young-earth creationists
who allow for the possibility of evolution (based, let's say, on evidence found in the fossil record). Given that they have only a few
thousand years to work with, young-earth creationists who concede
the possibility of evolution often allege that evolution happens much
more rapidly than most evolutionary biologists would claim. In fact,
this is how some young-earth creationists, such as Price, account
for the incredible diversity of land-dwelling species we see around
us given the limited space available on Noah's ark. In Price's words,
evolution enabled him to explain "how the great diversity of our
modern world may have come about after the world disaster of the

Deluge, from a comparatively few kinds which were salvaged from the great cataclysm."[18]

According to Price's idiosyncratic view of evolution, species evolve as a result of changes to their environment and what he calls genetic "mixing" or "hybridizing." (For the record, conventional evolutionary theory holds that species evolve as a result of natural selection, which is governed by random genetic mutation and reproductive fitness. Environmental changes are relevant, but only insofar as changes in environment might impact what constitutes fitness for survival and reproduction.)[19] Numbers explains that most Adventists of Price's era interpreted Ellen G. White's remarks concerning "amalgamation of man and beast" as a reference to "interbreeding *between* man and beast."[20] Price, however, took White's comments to mean "the mixing of races of mankind and the crossing or hybridizing of races of animals which God never meant to mix or cross." In Price's view, Satan was "the real instigator of all the mixing and crossing of the races of mankind, and also the mixer of thousands of kinds of plants and animals which God designed should remain separate."[21]

Thus, according to Price, the phenomenon known as *evolution* is in fact a process of degradation and regression, producing lower forms of plants, animals, and even humans. In *The Phantom of Evolution*, Price maintains that the mixing of different races of people, contrary to God's design, brought about a precipitous decline in the human species following the tower of Babel, resulting in different races of humans and possibly apes, which Price speculated might be "degenerate or hybridized men." This regression, according to Price, accounts for the fossils that paleontologists mistakenly believe to be those of humankind's ancestors.[22] This sense of creation's steady, inevitable decline is a durable aspect of creation science that would feature prominently in the culture war rhetoric of creation science for years to come.

In 1923, Price published *The New Geology*, in which he proposes a theory called the *new catastrophism* to contest the "uniformitarian" assumptions of conventional geology. According to uniformitarianism, the earth's geological record is the product of uniform physical processes unfolding over vast amounts of time. According to Price's new catastrophism, the geological record presents evidence of a global catastrophic flood that reshaped the surface of the earth a few thousand years ago. The details surrounding how the flood occurred and the specifics of how it allegedly shaped the geological record came to be known as *flood geology*. Since Price viewed conventional geology as prerequisite to evolutionary biology, he believed that his flood geology refuted Darwinian evolutionary theory. He thus wasted little energy arguing over biological details, which he regarded as an afterthought.

While Price's work enjoyed popularity among prominent American fundamentalists in and around the 1920s, it seems not one of those prominent fundamentalists had a tolerable grasp of Price's central thesis.[23] Apparently they were given to citing Price's refutation of evolutionary biology, only to endorse prevailing day-age or gap interpretations of Genesis in the next breath. By all appearances, they failed to understand that Price's account of flood geology undermines evolutionary biology only if, and only insofar as, it defeats the account of geology presupposed by Darwinian evolution—which happens to be the very same account of geology that motivates old-earth creationism. According to Price's letters, this misunderstanding of his work was a perennial source of irritation.[24] He was particularly cross with William Jennings Bryan, who commended Price's research at the 1925 *Scopes* trial, only to concede "the entire geological argument to the evolutionists, with the pitiful results now known to all the world."[25]

### Henry Morris and The Genesis Flood

Undoubtedly the most prolific of Price's disciples were the coauthors of *The Genesis Flood*—John C. Whitcomb, a professor of theology, and Henry M. Morris, a professor of hydraulic engineering who is widely considered the father of modern creation science. Published in 1961, two years before the death of George McCready Price, *The Genesis Flood* is credited with generating a renaissance of young-earth sentiment among American evangelicals. It had sold over two hundred thousand copies by the mid-1980s; as of 2010, it had undergone forty-eight printings across five languages, producing over three hundred thousand copies.[26]

Regarded as highly derivative of Price's *The New Geology* by contemporary commentators and historians—and indeed by the authors themselves, according to letters they exchanged—the geological argument of *The Genesis Flood* was a repackaging of Price's flood geology.[27] Nor was the book's theological framework especially provocative or original. In a passage that might just as easily have been written by George McCready Price, Ellen G. White, Albert Mohler, Ken Ham, Ligon Duncan, or John MacArthur, the introduction to *The Genesis Flood* notes that "modern scholarship will be impatient with [our] approach. Our conclusions must unavoidably be colored by our Biblical presuppositions, and this we plainly acknowledge."[28]

In addition to hermeneutics and geology, Morris shared Price's commitment to theological racism. In *The Beginning of the World*, Morris furnishes a white supremacist legitimizing narrative according to which

> the descendants of Ham were marked especially for secular service to mankind. Indeed they were to be "servants of servants," that is "servants *extraordinary!*" Although only Canaan is mentioned specifically (possibly because the branch of Ham's family through Canaan would later come into most direct contact with Israel), the whole family of Ham is in view. The prophecy is worldwide in scope and, since Shem and Japheth are covered, all Ham's descendants must be also. These include all nations which are neither Semitic nor Japhetic. Thus, all of the earth's "colored" races, yellow, red, brown, and black—essentially the Afro-Asian group of peoples, including the American Indians—are possibly Hamitic in origin and included within the scope of the Canaanitic prophecy.
>
> Somehow they have only gone so far and no farther. The Japhethites and Semites have, sooner or later, taken over their territories, and their inventions, and then developed them and utilized them for their own enlargement. Often the Hamites,

especially the Negroes, have become actual personal servants or even slaves to the others. Possessed of a genetic character concerned mainly with mundane matters, they have eventually been displaced by the intellectual and philosophical acumen of the Japhethites and the religious zeal of the Semites.[29]

These words were published in 1991, during Morris's twenty-five-year tenure as president of one of the largest creation science research organizations in the world—namely, the Institute for Creation Research (ICR), which Morris cofounded in 1970. We'll come back to Morris in just a moment, following a quick sidebar.

AiG is also among the largest creation science organizations in the world, and arguably the most visible. It operates two creation science museums—the Creation Museum and the Ark Encounter. According to AiG, these museums welcomed their ten millionth visitor in 2022.[30] One of the Ark Encounter's exhibits features wax figures of Noah, his wife, their three sons (Shem, Japheth, and Ham), and the wives of their three sons—eight people in all. One of those eight figures has a noticeably darker complexion than the other seven. And which member of Noah's family do you suppose has a noticeably darker complexion than the others? If you suspect the museum's curators of harboring sympathy for the racist legitimizing narrative that Black bodies inherited the mark of Cain—whose progeny survived the flood because a descendant of Cain married Noah's youngest son, Ham—then you would guess that the member of Noah's family depicted with noticeably darker skin would be Ham's wife. And your guess would be correct.[31] (For context, see discussion of Genesis 9 and theological legitimizing narratives around racial segregation in chapter 2.) Now back to Morris.

By 1961, the year that *The Genesis Flood* went to press, Morris's work on creation science was attracting attention from his colleagues at Virginia Tech—and not in a good way. Morris, who served as head of the civil engineering department, was invited to deliver a lecture on the geological significance of Noah's flood. Many of Morris's colleagues in the departments of biology and geology attended the lecture. His talk featured an overview of the argument presented in

*The Genesis Flood*—which is to say, the argument presented in Price's *The New Geology*. It was not well received. Particularly strong was the resistance of Morris's colleagues to the notion that scientific disciplines such as biology and geology rested on assumptions no more scientific than those of young-earth creationism.[32] (Note that we find the same tension in the dialogue between Bill Nye and Ken Ham concerning "assumptions" in what Ham calls *historical science*. Interestingly, Ham worked with Morris at the ICR before leaving to found AiG in the mid-1990s.)

A few months later, Morris was summoned to the office of the dean of engineering to discuss Morris's public profile—in particular, the matter of the *New York Times* quoting Morris as "estimating the age of the earth at ten thousand to fifteen thousand years." According to Ronald Numbers, "the dean called Morris into his office to warn him about collegial concerns that his 'peculiar and unscientific beliefs' were embarrassing the [Virginia Tech] community" in Blacksburg, Virginia.[33] By 1968, Morris informed Whitcomb that "my relations with the administration are more tenuous than ever and the eventual outcome will probably be that either I or the Dean will have to leave."[34] The following year, Morris resigned his position at Virginia Tech in exchange for a year's severance pay. And at the invitation of Tim LaHaye, Morris moved to San Diego in 1970 to found the ICR as a division of Heritage College (now San Diego Christian College).

Decades before coauthoring the wildly successful *Left Behind* series, LaHaye's guides to marital intimacy established his reputation as something of an evangelical sex guru in the late 1960s. LaHaye, at any rate, regarded his reputation as sufficiently established by May of 1968 that he thought it worthwhile to send a note to the president of Wheaton College expressing his disapproval of Wheaton's having hosted a memorial service honoring Dr. Martin Luther King Jr. in the wake of his assassination that April. In the note, which appears under the official letterhead of the San Diego church where he pastored, LaHaye attests to his own disbelief that "a Christian college could participate in honoring an out-right theological liberal heretic whose 'non-violent' demonstrations have resulted in the deaths of seventeen people."

LaHaye goes on to report that "as a pastor, I am asked every year by parents and prospective students to express my sentiments of Wheaton College." The note closes with an invitation to correct the record if LaHaye is mistaken about the memorial service—which correction, LaHaye indicates, he would be "quite delighted" to have.[35]

Before joining LaHaye at the ICR in San Diego, Morris converted another prominent culture warrior in neighboring Lynchburg, Virginia, to the cause of young-earth creationism: Jerry Falwell. In an obituary authored by neuroscientist David A. DeWitt, AiG notes that Falwell

> had not always been a young earth creationist. In fact, for a while after becoming a Christian, he believed in the gap theory. . . . However, it was Dr. Henry Morris (a professor at nearby Virginia Tech at the time) who helped Dr. Falwell come to a better understanding of Genesis and the importance of a young earth creation perspective. Dr. Morris spoke several times at Thomas Road Baptist Church. Dr. Falwell once told me that when he invited Dr. Morris to the church, almost no one else seemed to be promoting biblical creation at the time.[36]

Thus, in the wake of the civil rights movement, at the very moment that cultural currents had forced them to relinquish explicit arguments for school segregation and other forms of legalized racial oppression, the architects of the modern religious right were taking an intense interest in creation science—which, as we've established, was engineered by documented theological racists.

I should pause here to emphasize what I'm *not* going to allege in the pages that follow (or anywhere else, for that matter). I'm not about to argue that creation science is inherently racist, or that anyone who embraces young-earth creationism harbors racist beliefs. I'm certainly not going to argue that creation science is part of a vast conspiracy to perpetuate white patriarchal hegemony. Such conclusions would, in fact, run counter to the arguments of this book.

Ideology is importantly different from conspiracy. Some features of a given ideology may be more explicit than others—for example, many evangelicals proudly endorse gender hierarchy while disavowing any affinity for racial hierarchy. What interests me is ideology's capacity to shape the beliefs and practices of those under its spell without their knowledge, and perhaps even in opposition to their own stated desires. Conspiracies are explicit and intentional, a result of concerted reflection and effort on the part of the conspirator(s). Ideology is more subtle, doing its work through systems of coded language, propaganda, and manifold signals that operate beneath the plane of conscious reflection. What makes ideology interesting is that it prompts us to take whatever information happens to be at hand and fold it into narratives that legitimize the social hierarchies we prefer—often unconsciously, and often to our own detriment. Such is the role of creation science within the ideology of the religious right.

**Creation Science as a Weapon of Culture War**

For a couple of reasons, if we ignore the social and political context of the 1960s, the rise of young-earth creationism and creation science in the United States is mysterious. The first is historical: prior to the 1960s, outside the Seventh-day Adventist Church and some Lutheran circles, young-earth creationism was regarded as a fringe view even by fundamentalists. The arguments for young-earth creationism that we see in the 1960s and '70s are neither new nor compelling. So what prompted large numbers of American evangelicals to decide that young-earth creationism was theologically defensible? Second, there's never been much enthusiasm for young-earth creationism outside the United States. And in places outside the US where young-earth creationism enjoys any popularity at all, the phenomenon is almost entirely a cultural export of the creation science industry in the United States.[37] What has made American evangelicals over the last fifty years uniquely susceptible to creation science propaganda?

When we attend to the way that young-earth creationism functions culturally, the social conditions that gave rise to the creation science movement in the 1960s come into sharp focus.

In *Building God's Kingdom*, Julie Ingersoll recounts her experience of attending a creation science conference at First Baptist Church in Jacksonville, Florida—one of thirty-seven "Demand the Evidence" conferences produced by the ICR in fall 2009. Ingersoll finds that these conferences are about much more than the factual truth of young-earth creationism or the best way to interpret the book of Genesis.

> One might think that the purpose of the conference was the presentation of evidence in favor of young earth creationism over against evolution. But one would be wrong. There were no skeptics there weighing evidence. The conference goers were already convinced of the "truth" of creationism and that young earth creationism is the only biblically legitimate interpretation of the Genesis account of creation. Instead, the conference served as an exercise in social formation; the building of a community through myth and ritual. The "myth" at issue is more than the creation narrative itself. In retelling the Genesis story, describing the fight to defend it, identifying the enemies of God, and ridiculing them as sinister and ungodly, the storytellers mark the boundaries of who is inside the group and who is not. The "myth" in question is the story of an embattled but faithful remnant, holding fast to God's truth in the face of persecution. The ritual is the public enactment of the identity through storytelling.[38]

At the core of this identity is opposition to the enemies of God: atheists, secularists, humanists, secular humanists, Marxists, cultural Marxists, feminists, nihilists, and so on. The front line in this battle is the struggle between young-earth creationism and evolution—the latter being the gateway to all the social ills that have plagued American culture for the last fifty years or more. In keeping with The Assumption, the old-earth interpretation of Genesis is a dangerous concession to the enemy—a slippery slope that leads inexorably to compromising what young-earthers regard as the "biblical worldview."

Given that the "enemy" in this narrative is the scientific establishment as a whole, the creation science movement has a complicated relationship with expertise. The industry depicts "secular" scientists and their credentials as illegitimate—and indeed intellectually inferior to the informed common sense of ordinary Christians. Yet creation scientists go well out of their way to represent themselves as highly credentialed scientists, often bending the truth in the process. Ingersoll notes that, consistent with a well-established pattern in the creation science industry, one speaker at the "Demand the Evidence" conference "is a rather impressive MD, but he's still not a research scientist working on issues related to evolutionary biology or genetics, despite the fact that he cultivates that misperception." Two other conference speakers hold doctoral degrees in ministry from seminaries,

> though they make it difficult to know that they hold doctorates in ministry rather than in scientific fields. They go to great lengths to cultivate the impression that they are scientists by using the title and saying that they have degrees from particular schools, without being clear about what those degrees are and which ones come from which schools.[39]

Ingersoll documents an extreme example of this phenomenon—even by creation science industry standards—in one Jerry Bergman, a prolific author and speaker in the world of creation science.

One of Bergman's books, *Slaughter of the Dissidents: The Shocking Truth about Killing the Careers of Darwin Doubters*, describes a conspiracy on the part of the scientific establishment to deprive young-earth creationists of jobs, funding, and influence. Ingersoll recounts a lecture of Bergman's titled "Killing Careers of Creationists," in which he alleges that

> atheists push evolution because it's the key to atheism. So you can see when you send your kids to college or grad school what worldview they're going to get. The goal seems to be to get students to drop Christianity and become atheists. Both evolutionism and creationism are theories of creation. Truth will come out. Darwinists will prove themselves wrong. [But for now] we're locked out of science; [we] can get degrees [but] can't get jobs, can't get grants.[40]

Bergman cultivates the impression that he is a highly credentialed research scientist—which is to say, one who has been "locked out of science" and "can't get jobs" or "grants" despite having been able to "get degrees." The official website of Creation Ministries International (which split from AiG in 2005) reports that

> Jerry Bergman has taught biology, genetics, chemistry, biochemistry, anthropology, geology, and microbiology at Northwest State College in Archbold OH for over 25 years. He has 9 degrees, including 7 graduate degrees. Dr. Bergman is a graduate of Medical College of Ohio, Wayne State University in Detroit, The University of Toledo, and Bowling Green State University. He has over 800 publications in 12 languages and 20 books and monographs.[41]

Bergman's biography lists two doctorates. One is a PhD in "measurement and evaluation" from Wayne State University. According to Wayne State University, this is a doctorate in the field of education that deals with *educational* evaluation and research.[42] The other is a PhD in "human biology" from Columbia Pacific University, a distance-learning institution formerly based in California. According to the State of California, Columbia Pacific University wasn't a legitimate postsecondary institution, and it was ordered to close its (virtual) doors in 1997.[43] As Ingersoll observes, "In a highly competitive academic job market, it is just as likely that [Bergman's] lack of formal science credentials and his academic training in other areas at marginal or questionable institutions are better explanations for his career path than systemic discrimination because of his religious views."[44]

The picture of creation science that emerges from Ingersoll's analysis is not that of a movement that revolves around legitimate scientific inquiry or serious theological reflection. Rather, it is that of an industry engaged in the production of conspiracy theories and narratives that legitimize the social objectives of political conservatism as "biblical" and delegitimize competing sources of authority as "secular." Among white evangelicals in the latter half of the twentieth century, this product was in high demand. Historian Adam Laats notes that

> over the course of the twentieth century, some radical creation-
> ists have come to the conclusion that their vision of good and evil
> is not shared by the mainstream scientific establishment. It's not
> science itself that radical creationists are mad at. Rather, it is the
> notion that some prominent members of that scientific establish-
> ment—along with other elites in fields such as education, jour-
> nalism, and academia—have abandoned the traditional moral
> code that bound together American society. Even worse, some
> creationists feel, is that some of those elites haven't only aban-
> doned America's moral code, they have also actively attacked it.[45]

As educational anthropologist David Long observes, in the minds of creationists, evolution is merely a "placeholder for a larger and much deeper conflict of ideologies or worldviews."[46]

Laats notes that in 1964, Bob Jones Jr., president of Bob Jones University, "warned that evolutionary theory must be understood as more than just a scientific idea." According to Jones, evolution was an "attack upon the citadel of faith" that Jones considered as "equally satanic and equally dangerous" as the threats he perceived from Catholicism and communism.[47] In 1980, Jerry Falwell—the Liberty University chancellor who converted to young-earth creationism under the tutelage of Henry Morris—alleged that those who embrace evolutionary biology are bound to abandon "basic values such as morality, individualism, respect for our nation's heritage, and the benefits of the free-enterprise system."[48] (See chapter 2 for more on the intersection of racism, meritocracy, neoliberal economics, and "anticommunism.")

Culture war rhetoric around evolution has been remarkably durable over time. Mohler's 2010 remarks on evolution echo the sentiments of Jones and Falwell:

> Darwinist evolution is the great destroyer of meaning. Not only
> the meaning of the book of Genesis, but of almost every dimen-

sion of life. The background of this is also panic among the cultural and intellectual elites. In the United States and increasingly
in Great Britain and in Europe and beyond, the intellectual elites
are absolutely frantic. They're scratching their heads in incre-
dulity. How is it that after the Darwinist revolution, after the
hegemony of evolutionary theory in the sciences, a majority of
Americans still reject the theory of evolution? It is driving them
to distraction.[49]

A few sentences later, Mohler goes well out of his way to mention
that a prominent advocate of old-earth creationism, Francis Collins, served in the Obama administration. (Collins is a born-again
Christian who published a book on apologetics in 2006. Christopher
Hitchens described Collins as "one of the most devout believers I've
ever met.")[50] Mohler doesn't elaborate on the relevance of Collins's
service as director of the National Institutes of Health under President Obama to the subject at hand—namely, the question of how we
should understand the opening chapters of Genesis.

Even for seasoned creation science professionals like Henry Morris and Ken Ham, creation science is about more than just science
and Scripture. Morris blames the popularity of evolutionary theory
for everything from the proliferation of "premarital sex, adultery,
divorce, and homosexuality" to "unrestrained pornography . . . pros-
titution, both male and female," and "the modern drug crisis (rock
music, peer pressure, organized crime, etc.)."[51] And according to
Ham, evolution is to blame for the war on Christmas.[52] Thus, at least
in the eyes of creation scientists, the fight against evolution is a proxy
battle in the war over who gets to define America and its values. The
choice is stark and the stakes are almost too high to be believed.

In the 1960s and '70s, public education was perhaps the most
active theater in this proxy culture war. As Laats observes, "Creationism was only one dramatic part of a profound conservative religious
dissent against the new directions of modern public education."[53] In
particular, conservatives objected to a pattern of Supreme Court rul-
ings in the 1960s that curtailed official prayer and official Bible reading in public schools, followed by the introduction of sex education

and social studies curricula emphasizing social science. Laats notes that "throughout the 1950s, 1960s, and 1970s, folks who wanted to keep public schools the way they always had been felt as if they were losing ground, inch by inch, battle by battle. The Bible was out. Prayer was out. Schools were teaching sex; schools were teaching bad morals; and schools were no longer racially segregated; and thus no longer under parents' control."[54] According to Tim LaHaye, these innovations in public education constituted an "ingeniously evil technique" of "atheistic humanist educators" aimed at corrupting America's youth.[55]

## The Nomadic Culture War Machine

Within the sizable cross-section of evangelicalism that is receptive to creation science, fully three generations of conservative evangelicals have been enculturated to associate mainstream science with misinformation.[56] No doubt some who are sympathetic to creation science would allege that there are bad (perhaps even "ingeniously evil") actors involved in this conspiracy to establish the cultural hegemony of evolutionary biology (or, as it were, "atheistic humanism"). But we mustn't overstate the point: creation science propaganda leaves room for the possibility that most mainstream scientists are sincerely misguided—by mass delusion, elite hubris, groupthink, as a consequence of spiritual warfare, or what have you. Be that as it may, conservative evangelicals have been conditioned to believe that "secular" scientists, in cooperation with "cultural and intellectual elites" in mainstream media and education, habitually misrepresent the nature of reality.

The anti-intellectual impulse within American evangelicalism predates the creation science movement.[57] But the creation science industry organized this impulse and channeled it into institutions that actively perpetuate the intellectual ghettoization of conservative evangelicals. I hasten to add that white evangelicals are not hapless victims of creation science propaganda. As we've established, the surge of evangelical enthusiasm for creation science in the 1960s and '70s is inseparable from the social anxieties that forged the politics of the modern religious right: women's liberation, civil rights, and the desegregation of public schools. Thus it is no accident that the creation science industry trades in the very habits of mind that enable evangelicals to reject the consensus of experts whenever that consensus is in tension with the social, economic, or political objectives of the religious right.

Evangelicals who have been thusly conditioned do not distrust *all* science. They visit the doctor and take their cholesterol medication. They use GPS navigation and ride on airplanes. They *ask Siri.* They trust science when it's convenient. Yet when expert consensus threatens the interests of the religious right, evangelical theology furnishes an endless supply of "biblical" narratives that justify skepticism of "secular" expertise.

Thus, under the guise of subjecting human reason to biblical scrutiny, American evangelicals have transformed Christian theology into a nomadic culture war machine: seminary officials, celebrity preachers, and parachurch influencers roam from place to place, offering "biblical" pronouncements on a range of technical subjects—without regard for disciplinary boundaries, scholarly convention, or indeed their own intellectual heritage—toppling centuries of accumulated knowledge in their haste to legitimize the social, political, and economic impulses of American conservatism.

The creation science industry is an exquisite example of this machinery at work. It begins with the pretense of deferring to the sovereignty of God's word—which, in this context, is indistinguishable from deference to certain idiosyncratic human intuitions about God's word. The pretense of biblical authority requires serious Christians to believe that seminary presidents and celebrity preachers possess a deeper, more accurate grasp of the earth's physical history than the collective wisdom of professional scientists now working in the fields of geology, physics, paleontology, anthropology, stratigraphy, glaciology, and archaeology. Not to mention botany: there are pine trees in the United States that are nearly five thousand years old (which, according to flood geology, there shouldn't be). Indeed, there are spruce trees in Sweden that are nearly ten thousand years old.[58] (According to the version of young-earth creationism we've been tracing, the earth itself is less than seven thousand years old.) Mohler makes the striking suggestion that perhaps the earth looks old for its age *because of sin*—though he doesn't specify a causal mechanism or process by which some evergreens might come to look older than the flood.[59]

Experience has taught me that at this point I'll be accused of committing a genetic fallacy. (A *genetic fallacy* rejects a claim on the basis of its source, ignoring the merits of the claim itself. Perhaps the best-known form of genetic fallacy is the ad hominem argument, which attacks one's opponent personally rather than engaging with their ideas.) "Just because someone is a minister," the objection goes, "doesn't mean he's incapable of making valid observations about geology or anthropology, or anything else. We should evaluate arguments based on their merits, not based on the occupation or credentials of the one presenting the argument."

I completely agree with this objection in principle. But I fail to see what it has to do with my own argument. I don't allege that theologians or preachers, as such, are incapable of making cogent observations about geology—or any other subject, for that matter. And naturally I agree that arguments should be evaluated on their merits rather than the credentials or alleged authority of the one(s) making the argument. Indeed, this is essentially my point: geologists offer arguments and empirical evidence to support their conclusions about geology—that's what makes them geologists. The same goes for physicists, paleontologists, and so on. By contrast, the young-earth theologians and creation scientists we've examined offer no argument for their claims about the earth's history, apart from *how things seem to them*: because the Bible is authoritative and they feel very strongly that the opening chapters of Genesis are consistent with the claims of young-earth creationism, they think they know something about the age of the earth that geologists don't. For reasons we've noted, that's not an argument: it's common-sense propaganda, shrouded in a propagandistic assertion of authority.

Those of us who embrace the sovereignty of Scripture, by definition, reject the sovereignty of human intuitions.[60] I'm happy to grant that John MacArthur's intuitions about Genesis 1 constitute a reason for *John MacArthur* to believe that young-earth creationism is true.

But John MacArthur's intuitions don't give *anyone other than John MacArthur* a reason to believe that young-earth creationism is true. So I reject the notion that my analysis rests on a genetic fallacy, for the simple reason that it's impossible to acknowledge the merits of an argument that doesn't exist. MacArthur, Mohler, Ham, and Duncan provide no argument for young-earth creationism: they merely describe the intuitions that occur to them when they survey the opening chapters of Genesis, proclaim the sovereign authority of how things seem to them, and proceed to denigrate the faith of those who disagree.

The fact that such rhetoric is greeted with complete seriousness by evangelical audiences is symptomatic of deeper social and intellectual infirmities.

The evangelical marketplace of ideas is resplendent with the uncultivated intuitions of theological entrepreneurs promoting "biblical" perspectives on geology, political theory, developmental psychology, economics, critical race theory, psychopharmacology, gender and sexuality, media and entertainment, public health, and on and on. Particularly noteworthy is the proliferation of factual claims that do not even pretend to rely on factual support. For example, in the course of researching their recent book, *The Great Sex Rescue: The Lies You've Been Taught and How to Recover What God Intended*, authors Sheila Wray Gregoire, Rebecca Gregoire Lindenbach, and Joanna Sawatsky investigated the history of a bizarre factual claim that is ubiquitous in popular evangelical literature on marriage and sexuality. According to this piece of conventional wisdom, a flourishing human male requires sexual release at least once every seventy-two hours. Countless evangelical marriage guides encourage wives to observe this "seventy-two-hour rule" whether they want to or not, lest their husbands stray as a consequence of physical neglect. (One best-selling evangelical marriage guide advises us that male biological needs must be borne in mind during the postpartum period, noting that the weeks immediately following childbirth are difficult for many husbands.[61] And no, dear reader, you didn't misread the preceding sentence.) When Gregoire, Lindenbach, and Sawatsky looked into the provenance of the seventy-two-hour rule, they didn't find a single study supporting it, or any discussion of it in peer-reviewed literature. Instead, they discovered that James Dobson just made it up in the 1970s, for reasons that aren't entirely clear. And evangelical marriage gurus have been repeating it ever since.[62]

Over roughly three generations, this nomadic culture war machine has conditioned evangelicals to trust the untutored common sense of enterprising ministers over the carefully reasoned, peer-reviewed arguments of "secular" experts. Whether the subject is the antiquity of the earth, the reality of climate change, epidemiology, the existence and prevalence of systemic racism, the violence of financial capitalism, the history of American imperialism, mass incarceration, civil rights, women's liberation, or any number of other subjects, the moment that evangelicals sense a threat to the established order or their status therein, they turn to ambitious ministers who furnish "biblical" reasons to embrace unreality. The predictable result is a system of belief rooted not in wisdom or truth but in a patchwork of myths alleging the moral and intellectual legitimacy of evangelical norms despite overwhelming evidence to the contrary.

The religious right's allergy to "secular" expertise is thus a product of the tension between these fictional legitimizing narratives and facts that call those narratives into question. Similarly, the religious right's increasingly open hostility to liberal democracy reflects white evangelical efforts to preserve their status within the established order amid a popular reckoning with the racist and misogynistic axioms on which that order rests. The fondness for unreality and authoritarian politics that has come to define the religious right is the culmination of a decades-long feedback loop between evangelical social preferences and the legitimizing narratives that flow from the pulpits and power centers of the evangelical culture war machine.

# 5

## *Race, Reagan, and the Twilight of Democracy*

In democratic societies, conservative politicians perform a delicate balancing act. Political scientist Daniel Ziblatt calls this the *conservative dilemma*: how to recruit enough popular support to win elections while preserving the interests of relatively few voters at the top of the existing social order.[1] The source of the dilemma lies in the fact that conservatives ostensibly seek to *conserve* the established order. So their most natural constituents are those who stand to benefit from that order—in particular, those who currently enjoy wealth and power. So, on one hand, conservatives must pursue a policy agenda that preserves the wealth and power of a small (and, as we'll see, shrinking) fraction of the population. On the other hand, in order to remain in power, they must win elections—which means persuading a significant (and growing) percentage of the electorate to vote against their own economic interests. Importantly, the problem can't be solved by modest economic concessions to middle- and working-class voters; conservatives simply cannot, without aggrieving their core constituency, match the kind of economic redistribution on offer from their progressive rivals. So conservatives can't hope to attract popular support with policies that transfer wealth and power to the unwashed masses, because voters who find such policies attractive will inevitably be more attracted to progressive candidates.

Conservatives in the United States rely on two main strategies for negotiating this dilemma. One is voter suppression: making it inconvenient, ineffectual, or impossible for progressives to vote. Fewer progressive votes means fewer middle- and working-class voters conservatives must recruit in order to win elections. In 1980, one of the principal engineers of the modern religious right, Paul Weyrich, commended this strategy to an audience of evangelical political activists that included Tim LaHaye, W. A. Criswell, Pat Robertson, and Republican presidential candidate Ronald Reagan:

> Many of our Christians have what I call the goo-goo syndrome: good government. They want everybody to vote. I don't want everybody to vote. Elections are not won by a majority of people. They never have been from the beginning of our country, and they are not now. . . . As a matter of fact, our leverage in the elections quite candidly goes up as the voting populace goes down.[2]

This sentiment has become a durable feature of the religious right's approach to elections. Phyllis Schlafly—the antifeminist who led the conservative religious insurgency that defeated the Equal Rights Amendment in the 1970s—was in the audience for Weyrich's 1980 remarks. In 2013, Schlafly observed that "the reduction in the number of days allowed for early voting is particularly important because early voting plays a major role in Obama's ground game. The Democrats carried most states that allow many days of early voting."[3] Early voting, of course, enables those who can't take time away from work to vote on Election Day to participate in our democracy. A disproportionate percentage of voters in this situation are people of color, who tend to favor progressive candidates. Hence, limiting the availability of early voting gives conservative candidates a competitive advantage by suppressing progressive votes (a disproportionate percentage of which are the votes of people of color). In 2015, as a candidate in the Republican presidential primary, Mike Huckabee—the Baptist minister and former governor of Arkansas—explained his own nuanced views on voter turnout in the following terms: "I know that most politicians say we want everyone to vote. I'm gonna be honest with you: I don't want everyone to vote. . . . If they're gonna vote for me, they need to vote; if they're not gonna vote for me, they need to stay home."[4] I'll return to various voter suppression efforts in the next chapter, where our focus will be the religious right's growing fondness for antidemocratic, authoritarian political tactics.

The other conservative strategy for winning elections is to recruit middle- and working-class allies who are willing to tolerate social and economic inequality as long as their own status within the established order is preserved (or restored, as the case may be). Ideally, from the conservative perspective, these allies are already organized into groups with recognized leaders who are willing to act as campaign surrogates on behalf of conservative politicians. Ideally, these groups are embedded in an established network of institutions, replete with mailing lists and a system for distributing campaign literature. And ideally, these allies have well-documented cultural grievances that have been nurtured over decades, allowing conservative politicians to tailor their message to the specific social anxieties of their constituents. In the political realignment that developed out of the civil rights movement, such an alliance was forged between political conservatism and white evangelicalism, converging on the Republican Party in the Reagan era.

Thus the Republican Party has come to rely on evangelical votes as it negotiates the conservative dilemma. And negotiate it they have. Emboldened by the unwavering support of our nation's single largest voting bloc and underwritten by the evangelical culture war machine, Republican policies since the Reagan administration have engendered levels of economic inequality that would make a robber baron blush.

## Economic Austerity

At least since the Reconstruction era (1865–1877), when conservatives exploit cultural resentment, they almost always choose to highlight racial division in particular. And they leverage racial division by persuading poor and working-class white people that their interests are aligned with *other people who are white* rather than *other people who suffer economic hardship* within the established order. Before turning to the way that the New Right has exploited this historical pattern with the blessing of white evangelicals, it will be instructive to demonstrate that this practice does indeed constitute a historical pattern.

### Reconstruction

Vanessa Williamson, a senior fellow in governance studies at the Brookings Institution, observes that during the Reconstruction era, with the help of a progressive Congress and federal troops enforcing voting rights throughout the South,

> black legislators in coalition with white allies from the North and from the South's poorer regions set to work rebuilding their states' infrastructure and constructing a public school system. Reconstruction-era economic policies were relatively moderate, eschewing land reform, but included new forays in social spending in support of the poor and sick, as well as efforts to increase taxes paid by landowners.[5]

In South Carolina—where newly enfranchised Black voters outnumbered whites, and the state legislature was majority-Black—the aristocracy developed a strategy to undermine the alliance between freedmen and poor whites:

> they focused their critique of Reconstruction on rising government debt and excessive spending, painting government by black people and poor whites as intrinsically corrupt. Adopting a new identity as concerned taxpayers helped the rich bridge the divide with small white farmers, for whom new land taxes were heavy, while avoiding explicit opposition to black male suffrage, which might smack of treason to Northerners.[6]

Indeed, this group of concerned taxpayers—which included a number of former Confederate generals, one of whom (Martin W. Gary)

had declined to surrender at Appomattox—insisted that their anxieties about South Carolina's state government were based not on
race but on the fact that those imposing the taxes were not property owners. The taxpayers were entirely colorblind, according to
the taxpayers.

Available evidence suggests that the taxpayers' colorblindness
was a recent development. A few years prior, in 1868, "a number
of Tax-Payers had signed a petition to the U.S. Congress, entitled a
'Respectful Remonstrance on Behalf of the White People of South
Carolina,' that opposed black male suffrage because 'the superior
race is to be made subservient to the inferior.'" By the early 1870s,
the same taxpayers no longer claimed to speak on behalf of the white
race, but only in defense of "over-burthened tax-payers," complain-
ing that "they who lay the taxes do not pay them, and that they who
pay them have no voice in the laying of them."[7] Williamson notes
that Southern aristocrats in the Reconstruction era were

> astonished to find that straightforward appeals to racism had not
> produced consistently favorable electoral outcomes. A troubling
> number of whites in the hilly, poorer "upcountry" were willing
> to vote with the freedmen. . . . Taxes offered a different electoral
> entry point for the aristocracy of the Old South. Reconstruction
> governments desperately needed revenue for infrastructure and
> schools, and the resulting tax increases hit small farmers hard. By
> focusing on their identity as "taxpayers," [southern aristocrats]
> could elide the vast economic gulf between themselves and sub-
> sistence farmers in Appalachia.[8]

The taxpayers' logic is echoed in the sentiments of the white supremacist theologian and unreconstructed Confederate R. L. Dabney. In
reflecting on Reconstruction efforts to build a robust system of public
education, Dabney bemoans

> the *unrighteousness* of expending vast sums, wrung by a grinding
> taxation from our oppressed people, upon a pretended education
> of freed slaves; when the State can neither pay its debts, nor at-

tend to its own legitimate interests. Law and common honesty both endorse the maxim: "A man must be just before he is generous." The action of the State, in wasting this money thus, which is due to her creditors, is as inexcusable as it is fantastical. I do know that not a few of our white brethren, before the war, independent and intelligent, are now prevented from educating their own children, because they are compelled to keep them in the cornfield, laboring from year's end to year's end, to raise these taxes to give a pretended education to the brats of the black paupers, who are loafing around their plantations, stealing a part of the scanty crops and stock their poor, struggling boys are able to raise. Not seldom has this pitiful sight made my blood boil with indignation, and then made my heart bleed with the thought: "How mournfully complete is that subjugation, which has made men, who were once Virginians, submit tamely to this burning wrong?" "The offense is rank, and smells to Heaven." Thank God, that I have only to pay, and have nothing to do with the imposition, collection and disbursement of this shameful exaction.[9]

Incidentally, John MacArthur regularly cites the work of R. L. Dabney in his sermons and books. One such citation is worthy of a brief aside.

In a February 2009 sermon, MacArthur opines that "one of the wonderful old past-generation American preachers was a man named R. L. Dabney—R. L. Dabney. And reading him is always refreshing. He's like a Puritan out of his time and out of his place." MacArthur continues,

He said, "The power of the great revolution that we know as the Reformation was the restoration of scriptural preaching. It came with the authority of God. It came with the power of the Holy Spirit. It came under the clear leadership of Christ, and people submitted to the Word of God in the pulpit, and people followed and submitted to the Word of God in the pew." And Dabney then goes on to draw a little . . . a kind of paradigm that helps us to understand this. He said, "The golden age of preaching is Scripture truth in Scripture dress," that's the words he used. Scripture truth in Scripture dress, that's the golden age.[10]

After invoking the Reformation, Dabney appears to conflate the authority of Scripture with the authority of "scriptural preaching," praising those who "submitted to the Word of God in the pulpit . . . and in the pew." This is essentially a blueprint for propagandistic appeals to the authority of Scripture: when theologians ascribe "the authority of God" to their own "scriptural preaching," the Reformation ideal of *sola scriptura* serves to amplify rather than attenuate the authority of men like Dabney. This procedure is precisely what enabled white supremacists like Dabney to weaponize the hermeneutics of legitimization in defense of race-based chattel slavery.

## Jim Crow

When Reconstruction ended in 1877, the South quickly reverted to a social order featuring racial hierarchy ensconced in law (evangelical sympathy for which is documented in chapter 2). In the Jim Crow era, whites exercised social control through the racial terrorism of organizations like the Ku Klux Klan and the practice of lynching. Jim Crow also utilized the formal apparatus of law enforcement, imposing segregation by law and instituting the convict-lease system. Historian Jemar Tisby describes convict leasing as

> a "legal" way for corporations to gain cheap labor and for state and county governments to get money. The process of convict-leasing began by entrapping black people, usually men but occasionally women, for minor offenses . . . and then saddling them with jail time and court fees. If the person could not pay the fee, as was often the case, they could have their sentence increased. A company, or even an independent employer, would then contract with a prison for inmate labor, putting them to work in mines, factories, or fields. . . . The workers themselves, as prison inmates, were never paid for their labor. They worked in appalling conditions that bred disease and violence. Many died and were dumped into unmarked graves.

The convict-lease system made black inmates "slaves in all but name."[11]

Nor was the Jim Crow system restricted to the South. In chapter 2 we observed the role of federal policy in imposing racially segregated housing across the United States. And as Jemar Tisby describes, regions outside the South were home to

> "sundown towns"—communities where black people had to be out before sundown or face violent repercussions. . . . Towns such as Appleton, Wisconsin; Levittown on Long Island; and the Chicago suburb of Cicero, among hundreds of others, kept their communities intentionally all-white. Larger cities, including New York and Tulsa, . . . conducted periodic "purges" of black neighborhoods to intimidate residents into moving out or staying confined to certain parts of the city. Other Jim Crow laws and customs mandated that black and white baseball teams could not play on the same field, black and white people had to be buried in separate cemeteries, white students could not have textbooks that originally had been assigned to black students, and prison inmates had to be divided by race.[12]

As Reconstruction gave way to Jim Crow, the politics of austerity receded. Arguments for economic austerity had little purchase among an American electorate that witnessed the soaring inequalities of the Gilded Age, followed by pervasive poverty and unemployment during the Great Depression. Hence the overwhelming popularity of Roosevelt's New Deal—which, notably, reserved the benefits of steeply progressive taxation and expansive social programs almost exclusively for whites.

## The New Right

As the civil rights movement gained traction in the 1950s and '60s—with the promise to distribute public subsidies for housing, education, and other social programs across racial lines—the rhetoric of economic austerity returned to the foreground of American politics.

And as we observed in chapter 2, having been cultivated throughout the 1940s and '50s by right-wing organizations like Spiritual Mobilization, white evangelical ministers helped promote the midcentury turn to austerity politics via their sermonizing on behalf of "Christian libertarianism." These two developments—the expansion of social welfare programs and the evangelical embrace of neoliberal economics—informed the "Southern Strategy" that would enable the modern right to split the horns of the conservative dilemma and win elections while dramatically increasing economic inequality.

*George Wallace*

In his infamous 1963 inaugural speech as governor of Alabama, George Wallace stood before the state capitol and swore his allegiance to the institution of racial segregation. Roughly a century after the end of the Civil War, Wallace declared,

> Today I have stood where once Jefferson Davis stood, and took an oath to my people. It is very appropriate that from this cradle of the Confederacy, this very heart of the Great Anglo-Saxon Southland, that today we sound the drum for freedom. . . . Let us rise to the call of freedom-loving blood that is in us, and send our answer to the tyranny that clanks its chains upon the South, in the name of the greatest people that have ever trod this earth. I draw the line in the dust, and toss the gauntlet before the feet of tyranny, and I say: *Segregation now. Segregation tomorrow. And segregation forever.*[13]

Far less infamous is Wallace's record on issues of race prior to his 1962 campaign for governor. Ian Haney López observes that

> Wallace had not been a rabid segregationist; indeed, by Southern standards, Wallace had been a racial moderate. He had sat on the board of trustees of a prominent black educational enterprise, the Tuskegee Institute. He had refused to join the walkout of Southern delegates from the 1948 Democratic convention when they

protested the adoption of a civil rights platform. As a trial court judge, he earned a reputation for treating blacks civilly—a breach of racial etiquette so notable that decades later J. L. Chestnut, one of the very few black lawyers in Alabama at the time, would marvel that in 1958 "George Wallace was the first judge to call me 'Mr.' in a courtroom." The custom had been instead to condescendingly refer to all blacks by their first name, whatever their age or station. When Wallace initially ran for governor in 1958, the NAACP endorsed him; his opponent had the blessing of the Ku Klux Klan.[14]

The 1958 gubernatorial campaign was the first following the Supreme Court's 1954 decision in *Brown v. Board of Education*, over which much of the Alabama electorate was still seething. It seems that white Alabama voters weren't interested in a governor with "moderate" views on race—let alone a Tuskegee Institute trustee endorsed by the NAACP.

For present purposes, what's interesting about Wallace is his political journey from racial moderate in 1958 to rabid segregationist in 1963. In the judgment of Wallace biographer Dan T. Carter, "Wallace was a politician first who embraced racism second."[15] According to Carter, the candidate who defeated Wallace in the 1958 gubernatorial campaign, John Patterson, later remarked that the "primary reason I beat [Wallace] was because he was considered soft on the race question at the time. That's the primary reason."[16] It seems Wallace agreed with his rival's assessment. As López recounts,

> On the night he lost the 1958 election, Wallace sat in a car with his cronies, smoking a cigar, rehashing the loss, and putting off his concession speech. Finally steeling himself, Wallace eased open the car door to go inside and break the news to his glum supporters. He wasn't just going to accept defeat, though, he was going to learn from it. As he snuffed out his cigar and stepped into the evening, he turned back: "Well boys," he vowed, "no other son-of-a-bitch will ever out-nigger me again."[17]

In his successful 1962 campaign, Wallace vowed to prevent Black students from entering segregated schools, promising to block the doorway himself if necessary. And in the summer of 1963, Wallace had an opportunity to keep that promise.

Federal courts ordered the University of Alabama to integrate. Sensing that the State of Alabama might require further direction, the Department of Justice dispatched a deputy attorney general, in the person of Nicholas Katzenbach, to encourage compliance with the court order. According to López,

> More than 200 national reporters and all three of the major broadcast networks were on hand for the promised confronta-tion. From behind a podium, Wallace . . . read a seven-minute per-oration that avoided the red-meat language of racial supremacy and instead emphasized "the illegal usurpation of power by the Central Government." . . . The nation watched as Wallace hec-tored Katzenbach, culminating with Wallace declaiming, "I do hereby denounce and forbid this illegal and unwarranted action by the Central Government."[18]

Nonetheless, the University of Alabama's first two Black students were on campus within two hours of Wallace's speech. The whole confrontation was a performance, staged for the benefit of Wallace's white supremacist base.[19]

In the week that followed, Wallace received over one hundred thousand telegrams and letters regarding his speech, 95 percent of which expressed support, and over half of which originated outside the southern region. This occasioned two insights that would reshape Wallace's political career and, in turn, American political discourse for the next half century or more.[20]

The first was that resentment over federal efforts to enforce civil rights was not limited to the South. Wallace concluded that at least in this respect, "they're all Southern. The whole United States is South-ern." Wallace's second insight was that dog whistles succeed where overt white supremacy fails. As López observes,

> The key lay in seemingly non-racial language. . . . Talking not about stopping integration but about states' rights and arrogant

federal authority—and visually aided by footage showing him facing down a powerful Department of Justice official rather than vulnerable black students attired in their Sunday best—Wallace was a countrywide hero. "States' rights" was a paper-thin abstraction from the days before the Civil War when it meant the right of Southern states to continue slavery.... Yet this was enough of a fig leaf to allow persons queasy about black equality to oppose integration without having to admit, to others and perhaps even to themselves, their racial attitudes.[21]

Wallace took his dog whistle show on the road in 1968, running for president as an independent candidate against Democrat Hubert Humphrey (sitting vice president to Lyndon B. Johnson) and Republican Richard Nixon.

A month before the election, in October 1968, polls showed that Wallace had more support in the South than Nixon or Humphrey. Wallace also commanded attention outside the South, drawing crowds of twenty thousand and seventy thousand to rallies at Madison Square Garden and in the Boston Common, respectively. Republican strategists determined that an overwhelming majority of Wallace's supporters in the South, and a near majority in the North, preferred Nixon to Humphrey. Thus, with a month to go in the 1968 presidential campaign, Nixon leaned into the rhetoric of racial division.[22]

### Richard Nixon

As a means of securing his endorsement in the 1968 Republican primary, Nixon had secretly promised Strom Thurmond that as president, he would curtail the federal government's role in overseeing the integration of southern schools. Thurmond, a rabid segregationist, represented South Carolina in the US Senate from 1954 to 2003. It was Thurmond, then governor of South Carolina, who led the 1948 walkout at the Democratic National Convention to protest the civil rights plank in the party's platform—the very protest that George Wallace, at the time a "racial moderate," declined to join.

Ahead of the 1964 election, rather than support President Johnson's Great Society plan to eradicate poverty and racial injustice, Thurmond changed his affiliation to the Republican Party and endorsed Republican presidential candidate Barry Goldwater. In the decades that followed, as debates over civil rights exposed racialized fissures in the New Deal coalition, other conservative Democrats (generally from the South) followed Thurmond to the Republican Party, pushing socially progressive Republicans (generally associated with Eastern "elites") to the Democratic Party. The result of this party realignment was an increasingly polarized political landscape: in the middle of the twentieth century, both major parties claimed conservative and progressive factions, and both parties contributed to civil rights reforms. By the 1980s, the Democratic Party was known for progressivism and racial diversity, while the Republican Party was socially conservative, fiscally libertarian, and mostly white.

Thurmond's choice for president in 1964, Barry Goldwater, was a US senator from Arizona and heir to a department store fortune, given to lecturing the public on the virtues of rugged individualism and private enterprise.[23] Though he was no George Wallace, the arc of Goldwater's racial politics took a similar shape. As a senator, Goldwater voted for civil rights legislation in 1957 and 1960. But by 1961, Goldwater had joined the growing number of Republicans who felt that the survival of their party depended on cultivating votes in the South, which meant tacking hard to the right on policies around race and federal enforcement of civil rights. In Goldwater's words, "We're not going to get the Negro vote as a bloc in 1964 and 1968, so we ought to go hunting where the ducks are."[24] Evidently Goldwater judged that the ducks were to be found among the racists. In addition to standard "states' rights" rhetoric, Goldwater's 1964 campaign featured appeals to "freedom of association," which was well-established code for permitting businesses the "freedom" to deny service to people of color.

Goldwater's campaign faced two obstacles that proved insurmountable. First, Goldwater was a Republican, and the ducks he was hunting were committed Democrats. Strom Thurmond's defection to the Republican Party was a harbinger of a political realignment that would not reach maturity until the 1980s. In the mid-1960s, many white southerners wouldn't even contemplate voting for a candidate from the party of Abraham Lincoln.

Second, Goldwater waged his campaign in the shadow of the New Deal, and the electorate was not yet attuned to the racial undertones of austerity politics. While conservative southerners resented federal enforcement of civil rights, southern voters had little appetite for cuts to federal spending on social programs that aimed to benefit poor and working-class whites and were therefore perceived as legitimate. Biographer Rick Perlstein recounts a poignant episode from a West Virginia campaign rally in which Goldwater "called the War on Poverty 'plainly and simply a war on your pocketbooks,' a fraud because only 'the vast resources of private business' could produce the wealth to truly slay penury." Perlstein notes that "in the land of the tar-paper shack, the gap-toothed smile, and the open sewer—where the 'vast resources of private business' were represented in the person of the coal barons who gave men black lung, then sent them off to die without pensions—the message just sounded perverse. As he left, lines of workmen jeered him."[25]

Johnson won in a landslide. The overwhelming unpopularity of Goldwater's economic agenda demonstrated that the political right had yet to arrive at a sustainable answer to the conservative dilemma. Exploiting racial division could win them some votes. But in order to win elections, they needed an economic platform that aligned with the interests of middle and working-class voters, even if it meant alienating their wealthier constituents.

By all appearances, Nixon's 1968 campaign learned from Goldwater's failure. In a book reflecting on the 1968 campaign and casting a vision for the future of the party, Nixon strategist Kevin Phillips observes that Republicans needed to assuage voters' "fears that a Republican administration would undermine Social Security, Medicare, collective bargaining and aid to education."[26] Thus Nixon's 1968 economic platform featured a strong social safety net, federal support for labor unions, and wealth redistribution through progressive taxation. In the words of political scientists Jacob Hacker and Paul Pierson,

Nixon was a big spender who signed on to a huge expansion of Social Security and nationalized the Food Stamps program; a social policy innovator who supported a guaranteed family income and national health plan; a Keynesian pump-primer who imposed wage and price controls; and a command-and-control regulator who established a string of agencies protecting workers, consumers, and the environment—from the Environmental Protection Agency, to the Occupational Safety and Health Administration, to the Consumer Product Safety Commission. On racial and cultural issues, Nixon was the harbinger of a new kind of Republicanism in the White House. On economic policy, he was the last social democrat of the twentieth century.[27]

Nixon also learned from Goldwater's electoral successes, meager as they were. Thus, in addition to economic policies that favored middle- and working-class voters, Nixon developed what came to be known as the "Southern Strategy" for exploiting racial resentments in the wake of the civil rights movement. As Corey Robin explains,

Pioneers of the Southern Strategy in the Nixon administration ... understood that after the rights revolutions of the sixties they could no longer make simple appeals to white racism. From now on, they would have to speak in code, preferably one palatable to the new dispensation of color blindness. As White House chief of staff H. R. Haldeman noted in his diary, Nixon "emphasized that you have to face the fact that the whole problem is really the blacks. The key is to devise a system that recognized this while not appearing to."[28]

A month before the 1968 election, with Wallace outpolling both major-party candidates in the South, Nixon took a hard right turn on race.

On October 7, Nixon announced his opposition to "forced busing"—an established euphemism for opposition to school integration—essentially publicizing what had previously been a private accord with Strom Thurmond. The only conceivable advantage to be gained from this announcement was garnering the support of white voters who were hostile to integration. Nixon's campaign ran television ads that were heaving with racist dog whistles. One such ad featured a montage of riots, civil rights protests, and police, with a voiceover instructing its audience to "recognize that the first right of every American is to be free from domestic violence. So I pledge to you, we shall have order in the United States." Upon reviewing one of his own television ads, Nixon remarked: "Yep, this hits it right on the nose.... It's all about law and order and the damn Negro–Puerto Rican groups out there."[29] Nixon's special counsel, John Ehrlichman, confirmed that "subliminal appeal to the anti-black voter was always present in Nixon's statements and speeches."[30]

Nixon defeated Humphrey by a margin of less than 1 percent of the popular vote; Wallace received nearly 14 percent of the vote. In the months that followed, Nixon and his political advisers arrived at the conclusion that the future of the Republican Party lay in exploiting cultural divisions, and racial resentment in particular. According to Phillips, "Ethnic and cultural division has so often shaped American politics that, given the immense midcentury impact of Negro enfranchisement and integration, reaction to this change almost inevitably had to result in political realignment."[31] Arthur Finkelstein, a perennial Republican political consultant who worked with Jesse Helms, Strom Thurmond, Ronald Reagan, and others, wrote a memo in 1970 advising Nixon that he should "try to polarize the election around that issue which cuts best in your direction, i.e., drugs, crime, race."[32]

In view of these assessments, Nixon's 1972 campaign featured a much heavier emphasis on racist dog whistles, particularly "law and order." It's worth observing that in the US context, appeals to "law and order" are generally a form of propaganda, gesturing toward the ideal of justice in order to deprive people of justice. Specifically, the phrase *law and order* signals the intent to deploy the coercive power of law enforcement for the sole purpose of safeguarding the established social order, over and against the protests of those who claim that the established order is unjust. In other words, "law and order" isn't about justice at all. Rather, it's about power—specifically, legitimizing the use of power to perpetuate an unjust social order. Reflecting on his presidency in a 1977 interview with David Frost, Nixon captured the essence of his law and order paradigm with the shocking (though not altogether surprising) admission that, in his view, "when the president does it, that means that it is not illegal."[33]

This blend of dog whistle politics and progressive economics won Nixon a second term in 1972. His victory over George McGovern marked the last time that a candidate for US president has received more than 60 percent of the popular vote. Nixon's Southern Strategy, refined over the course of his first term, garnered the support of 67 percent of white voters. (Eight years prior, by contrast, Goldwater's agenda featuring "states' rights" and economic austerity attracted only 36 percent of white voters.) The Watergate scandal brought Nixon's administration to an early conclusion, and disillusionment with the Republican Party helped to usher Democratic candidate Jimmy Carter into office in 1976. But in 1980, thanks in large part to a struggling economy at home and Carter's perceived failures abroad (notably the Iran hostage crisis), the stage was set for a Republican candidate who would consummate the post–New Deal political realignment that began with Strom Thurmond in 1964.

## The Reagan Revolution

The Republican who finally presented his party with a durable solution to the conservative dilemma was Ronald Reagan, patron saint of the religious right. It was Reagan who harnessed the alchemy that would enable conservatives to consistently win elections by advancing the interests of economic elites. Reagan's revolutionary innovation was to couch economic austerity in terms of racial resentment, rendering the two inextricable. Goldwater failed because he couldn't persuade enough middle- and working-class white voters to choose racial resentment over their own economic interests. Nixon succeeded because he presented middle- and working-class white voters with a policy platform that indulged their racial resentment ("forced busing," "law and order") while furthering their financial interests at the same time (robust social welfare, support for organized labor). And Reagan surpassed Nixon by using racial resentment to convince those very same voters that their financial interests would be served by massive cuts to social spending.

He accomplished this by persuading middle- and working-class voters that the biggest threat to their financial prosperity was located not in economic exploitation by corporate interests and wealthy elites but in bloated government bureaucracies that enabled lazy (Black) welfare recipients to steal from hardworking (white) taxpayers. Regarded by many as a gifted storyteller, Reagan used narratives to breathe life into racist tropes. One such narrative featured a Cadillac-driving "welfare queen" from Chicago, who had "eighty names, thirty addresses, [and] twelve social security cards, collecting veteran's benefits on four non-existing deceased husbands. She's got Medicaid, getting food stamps, and she is collecting welfare under each of her names. Her tax-free cash income is $150,000."[34] (For context: the median household income in 1980 was just over $21,000; adjusted for inflation, $150,000 in 1980 dollars would amount to well over $500,000 in 2023 dollars.)

Another of Reagan's favorite punchlines involved the fanciful notion that food stamps might enable "some young fellow [to cut in line] ahead of you to buy a T-bone steak" while "you were waiting in line to buy hamburger."[35] When Reagan first introduced the line about the T-bone steak, the food stamp recipient cutting in line was "some strapping young buck." (As López points out, *buck* is an epithet that connotes "the threatening image of a physically powerful black man, often one who defies white authority and who lusts for white women.") After some focus-grouping, the Reagan campaign decided that this was too on the nose, and the phrasing was revised.[36] But the message was clear enough: the gravest economic threat to honest, hardworking (white) Americans came not from above but from below. Thus Reagan vowed to safeguard the hard-earned incomes of middle- and working-class Americans—not from corporations seeking to profit at all costs, or financial speculators, or tax-dodging one-percenters, but from (Black) welfare cheats. As López notes,

Conservative dog whistling made minorities, not concentrated wealth, the pressing enemy of the white middle class. It didn't seem to matter that the actual monetary transfers to nonwhites were trivial. If all of the anti-poverty and social welfare dollars paid to blacks during the Kennedy and Johnson administrations had instead been given to low- and middle-income whites, it would have added less than three-eighths of 1 percent to their actual disposable income. What mattered was the sense that blacks were getting more than they deserved, at the expense of white taxpayers. The middle class no longer saw itself in opposition to concentrated wealth, but now instead it saw itself as beset by grasping minorities.... Racial attacks on liberalism shifted the enemy of the middle class from big money to lazy minorities, and transmuted [New Deal] economic programs that helped to build the nation into welfare for undeserving groups.[37]

Moreover, by embedding his case for economic austerity within coded appeals to racial resentment, Reagan effectively resolved the conservative dilemma. No longer did conservative politicians need to weigh winning elections against serving the interests of economic elites. The moment Reagan convinced middle- and working-class white voters that their economic interests were served by slashing government programs, the path to winning elections merged with the path to advancing the interests of economic elites. The two had become one. The fusion of racial resentment and economic austerity was the real Reagan Revolution, and radical economic inequality is its enduring legacy.

Importantly, conservatives' unwavering commitment to color-blindness furnished Reagan and his supporters with a degree of deniability against charges of racism. Because Reagan's message was delivered in coded language, however vulgar and transparent it may have been, those who objected to Reagan's race-baiting faced bitter accusations of "making everything about race" and other such nonsense.[38] So it's instructive, if unpleasant, to note the hateful language of Lee Atwater, an ascendant Republican operative and political strategist in the Reagan administration. In a recorded interview in 1981, Atwater gave an infamous, epithet-laced assessment of his own party's rhetoric:

> You start out in 1954 by saying, "Nigger, nigger, nigger." By 1968 you can't say "nigger"—that hurts you. Backfires. So you say stuff like forced busing, states' rights, and all that stuff. You're getting so abstract now [in 1981] you're talking about cutting taxes, and all these things you're talking about are totally economic things and a byproduct of them is blacks get hurt worse than whites.[39]

Atwater went on to serve as the political director of Reagan's 1984 campaign, the manager of George Bush's 1988 campaign, and chair of the Republican National Convention.

On November 7, 1984, Reagan won reelection in a landslide, receiving just under 60 percent of the popular vote and carrying forty-nine states in the Electoral College. On November 8, Atwater accepted a senior partnership at the DC lobbying firm of Black, Manafort, Stone, and Kelly. Three decades later, two named partners in that firm—Paul Manafort and Roger Stone—would be convicted by federal juries of crimes including financial fraud, conspiracy to defraud the United States, and making false statements to Congress.[40]

### A Tale of Two Bushes

George Bush, Reagan's vice president, retained Lee Atwater to manage his 1988 campaign for president. In keeping with Bush's patrician image, he personally avoided Reagan-style race-baiting in the '88 campaign. But when he found himself trailing Democratic opponent Michael Dukakis by seventeen points in the polls, he authorized Atwater to run perhaps the most notoriously racist advertising campaign known to modern American politics.

Willie Horton was a convicted murderer serving a life sentence in the state of Massachusetts. As governor of Massachusetts, Dukakis vetoed a bill that would have rendered convicted murderers, including Horton, ineligible to participate in a program that permit-

ted prisoners to leave the prison grounds for occasional weekend fur-
loughs. While on furlough one weekend, Horton invaded the home
of a young couple, stabbing a man and raping his fiancée.

For Atwater's purposes, what mattered most was the fact that
Horton was Black and his victims were white. As one Bush aide said
at the time, "Willie Horton has star quality. Willie's going to be politically furloughed to terrorize again. It's a wonderful mix of liberalism
and a big black rapist."[41] López recounts that

> in true dog whistle style, the most effective Willie Horton ad never
> mentioned race at all. Instead it showed a grainy mugshot of Hor-
> ton, clearly black, staring blankly into the camera. Over this image,
> a disembodied voice declared, "Dukakis not only opposed the
> death penalty, he allowed first-degree murderers to have week-
> end passes from prison. One was Willie Horton. . . . Despite a life
> sentence, Horton received 10 weekend passes from prison. Horton
> fled, kidnapped a young couple, stabbing the man and repeatedly
> raping his girlfriend." . . . The production values were deliberately
> terrible, making the ad "the political equivalent of a supermarket
> tabloid, emphasizing the personal and the sensational."[42]

In the month following the Horton ad campaign, 12 percent of vot-
ers abandoned Dukakis in favor of Bush—a twenty-four-point swing.
According to Dan T. Carter, "No campaign ever turns on one issue,
but no one—*no one*—who followed the campaign believes George
Bush had any more devastating ally than the homicidal black rapist
Willie Horton."[43]

A decade later, Bush's son, George W., would likewise turn to
race-baiting in an effort to salvage his own bid for the presidency. On
February 1, 2000, George W. suffered a devastating nineteen-point
loss to underdog John McCain in the New Hampshire Republican primary. Senator McCain's platform called for campaign finance reform
and a tax plan that challenged the Reaganite economic paradigm
that had engendered spiraling inequality since the 1980s—policies
favored by an overwhelming majority of Americans.[44] Hacker and
Pierson explain that

McCain's tax plan in particular was fundamentally at odds with the Bush-Cheney program: it would have set aside a sizable chunk of then-anticipated budget surpluses to shore up Social Security. It also would have closed a variety of corporate tax loopholes to fund a tax cut for the middle class. Bush's tax plan promised to deliver nearly 40 percent of its benefits to the top 1 percent. Independent estimates suggested that the McCain plan would deliver less than 2 percent of its benefits to the top 1 percent. In introducing his plan, McCain declared, "Let the warning go out to the army of lobbyists who so stoutly resist our campaign. Every tax dollar now wasted on special breaks for oil companies, ethanol giants, insurance companies and the multitude of other powerful special interests with their army of lobbyists are now at risk."[45]

While McCain's campaign relied on small-dollar contributions from many donors, George W.'s campaign drew its support from more conventional Republican donors—that is, the very special interests whose economic and political power McCain declared "at risk."

It's crucial to note that in order to become the favorite of the Republican establishment in 2000, George W. had to repudiate the moderate economic policies espoused by his father. For his part, the elder Bush was consistently skeptical of Reagan's economic fever dreams, which he referred to as "voodoo economics" in the 1980 Republican primary. When the elder Bush entered the White House eight years later, he worked with congressional Democrats to pass tax increases that were "laser-targeted on the superrich: an increase in the top marginal tax rate, a strengthened alternative minimum tax on affluent taxpayers, new excise taxes on luxury items like furs, yachts, and private planes."[46] Despite the overwhelming popularity of these reforms, congressional Republicans were having none of it: the economic elites who funded their campaigns had tasted the sweet succor of Reaganomics, and they had no intention of abandoning the promise of the Reagan Revolution—which is to say, they had no intention of allowing McCain to win the nomination. At stake was nothing less than the Republican Party's commitment to populist plutocracy.

On February 2, 2000, the day after McCain's landslide victory over George W. in the New Hampshire primary, the campaigns headed to Lee Atwater's home state of South Carolina.

Before rising to national prominence with the Reagan campaign in 1980, Atwater had established himself as a legend in South Carolina politics. In 1978, while managing Strom Thurmond's Senate campaign, Atwater served as an informal adviser to congressional candidate Carroll Campbell, a state senator best known for leading an anti-"busing" protest. Campbell's Democratic opponent was the popular two-term mayor of Greenville, Max Heller, a native of Austria who narrowly escaped the Holocaust by immigrating to Greenville as a teenager.[47] According to Mark Shields, who helped manage Heller's campaign, Heller "had been enormously popular, enormously successful as mayor, but beyond that he had just been the ultimate employer. When he sold his factory, he spent all his time making sure that all his employees were placed."[48]

Richard Gooding reports that early in the campaign, likely at the direction of Atwater, Campbell carried out a secret poll—specifically, a "push poll," designed to push ostensibly unflattering information about one's opponent under the guise of collecting data. (This tactic has major advantages over more conventional smear campaigns. It's essentially impossible to trace back to the campaign's principals. It's also inexpensive—since "pollsters" aren't actually compiling any data, they're essentially telemarketers rehearsing a script. In fact, it's not uncommon to outsource the whole operation to a telemarketing firm.) Campbell enlisted "pollsters" to call subjects and ask if they were more or less likely to vote for "a South Carolina native" or "a Jewish immigrant." They then asked which characteristics best describe each candidate:

1. Honest
2. Christian man
3. Concern for the people
4. A hard worker
5. Experienced in Government
6. Jewish[49]

With a week to go before Election Day, Heller led in the (actual) polls by fourteen points. Then an independent candidate, "Don Sprouse, new to the race, announced that religion was the 'hush-hush' issue in the campaign. Heller wasn't qualified, he said, because 'he doesn't believe in Jesus Christ.'"[50] Heller lost the election by six points. Coincidentally, that same year, Strom Thurmond's bid for reelection to the US Senate also benefitted from the late addition of a third-party candidate who seemed primarily interested in attacking Thurmond's opponent.

Having died of brain cancer in 1991, Atwater didn't participate in the 2000 South Carolina primary. But his spirit presided over the proceedings. George W.'s campaign was stacked with Atwater loyalists who knew his tactics well, including: George W. himself, who befriended Atwater when the two worked closely together on the elder Bush's 1988 campaign; Strom Thurmond, then in his fourth decade as a US senator from South Carolina; Carroll Campbell, who went on to serve two terms as governor of South Carolina (1987–1995) following his Atwater-engineered congressional victory over Heller in 1978; Pat Robertson, the Christian media mogul, televangelist, and founder of the Christian Coalition; and lobbyist Ralph Reed, the former executive director of the Christian Coalition (1989–1997), whose guiding professional ambition was, in his words, "to be a Christian Lee Atwater."[51]

Reed famously described his role as executive director of the Christian Coalition in the following terms: "I paint my face and travel at night. You don't know it's over until you're in a body bag. You don't know until election night."[52] Reed garnered notoriety for his part in a lobbying scheme undertaken with his longtime friend and colleague Jack Abramov in the late 1990s and early 2000s.[53] A bipartisan Senate investigation found that Reed accepted payments in excess of $5.3 million from a consortium of casino interests. In return, Reed agreed to lobby for stricter casino regulations *on behalf of the casino industry*. Specifically, Reed leveraged his Christian Coalition connections to unleash scores of evangelical activists who demanded tougher gambling regulations. And yet, apparently, Reed neglected to inform his evangelical friends that their lobbying efforts aligned with the interests of his clients in the casino industry, in that the regulations they sought to implement would effectively prevent new competitors from entering the casino market.[54]

In 2000, Reed promised the Bush campaign that he and his friends on the religious right could deliver South Carolina. A key part of Reed's strategy called for pandering to evangelical voters. In keeping with that objective, on February 2, George W. made his first campaign stop in the state of South Carolina at Bob Jones University—a fundamentalist college in Greenville that, at the time of the 2000 South Carolina primary, maintained an official ban on interracial dating. As it happens, the president of Bob Jones University, Bob Jones III, officially lifted the school's ban on interracial dating a month later amid public scrutiny that reflected poorly on the university and, by extension, presidential candidate George W. Bush. In an interview with Larry King on March 3, 2000, Jones complained that "we're being defined as a racist school. That's all the media is talking about." He assured King and his viewers that when the rule was implemented in the 1950s, it was as part of a perfectly sensible effort "to enforce something, a principle, that is much greater than this. We stand against the one world government, against the coming world of the antichrist."[55]

It was a member of the Bob Jones faculty who spearheaded one of the most incendiary narratives of the South Carolina primary. Richard Hand, a professor of biblical studies, sent out a mass email falsely alleging that "McCain chose to sire children without marriage." At the same time, Ralph Reed's lobbying firm blanketed "400,000 self-described Christian conservatives in the state with negative phone calls and mailings about McCain."[56] Among the negative phone calls was a push poll—reminiscent of Campbell's 1978 congressional campaign—in which "pollsters" asked, "Would you be more or less likely to vote for John McCain for president if you knew he had fathered an illegitimate black child?"[57] Flyers began to appear on car windshields all over South Carolina. One Democratic consultant described the flyers as "a kind of cheesy Kinko's pamphlet" featuring a picture of the McCain family. "It was just so obvious. . . . It was one of the few shots you've ever seen of the McCains that so prominently featured that particular girl."

The young lady at the center of the phone calls, flyers, and email was the McCains' nine-year-old daughter. Richard Gooding reports that "in 1991, when Cindy McCain [John's wife] was on a relief mission to Bangladesh, she was asked by one of Mother Teresa's nuns to help a young orphan with a cleft palate. Flying her to the U.S. for surgery, Cindy realized she couldn't give her up. At the Phoenix airport, she broke it to her husband, and they eventually adopted the child."[58] The George W. campaign and its allies in the Christian Coalition knew this, of course. But by the time South Carolina voters figured it out, the primary race was over.

Meanwhile, Pat Robertson warned that "a large portion of the Republican base would walk away" if McCain won the nomination.[59] The Christian Coalition sent out a mailer advising recipients of "10 Disturbing Facts About John McCain"—claiming, among other things, that McCain was too permissive on abortion and favored casino gambling. The latter accusation was particularly rich given Reed's involvement in the smear campaign, in light of Reed's lobbying efforts: email records filed with the US Senate Committee on Indian Affairs reveal that while he was campaigning on behalf of George W. in the 2000 South Carolina Republican primary, Reed was actively conspiring with Jack Abramov to launder Reed's lobbying fees through third-party entities in order to disguise the fact that Reed was being paid by casino interests.[60] Lois Eargle, head of the Horry County Christian Coalition, resigned in protest following the primary, citing concerns about the organization's distortions of McCain's views.

## Reagan's Legacy

The Reagan Revolution has set the stage for the rise of a religious authoritarian movement, the specter of which I'll consider in the chapter to follow. This outcome is the culmination of three trends that have conspired to fundamentally transform our nation's political landscape: radical economic inequality, racial resentment, and growing enthusiasm for ethno-religious nationalism among white evangelicals. None of these factors is new to American politics. But the unique combination of these dynamics that has emerged over the last few decades is particularly volatile.

*Economic Inequality*

While the white middle class in the US has spent several decades clutching its collective pocketbook and eyeing people of color with suspicion, economic elites have been robbing them blind. Over the course of eight years in the White House, Reagan managed to cut the top marginal tax rate by more than half, from 70 percent to 28 percent. According to Hedrick Smith, "The windfall from [Reagan's] tax cuts for America's wealthiest 1 percent was massive—roughly $1 trillion in the 1980s and another $1 trillion each decade after that. The Forbes 400 Richest Americans, enriched by the Reagan tax cuts, tripled their net worth from 1978 to 1990."[61] The other 99 percent of Americans were assured that these profits would "trickle down," creating new jobs and expanding the tax base. That prediction turned out to be false.

Between 1980 and 2016, the share of national income flowing to the richest 1 percent of households has roughly doubled—from 11 percent in 1980 to 20 percent in 2016. ("Richest 1 percent" is potentially misleading: most of that 20 percent share in fact goes to the top 0.1 percent.) During that same span, the share of national income flowing to the bottom half of households has been cut in half—from about 20 percent in 1980 to 10 percent in 2016. So in 1980, the wealthiest 1 percent of American households had *half* the income of the bottom 50 percent; by 2016, the wealthiest 1 percent had *double* the income of the bottom 50 percent.[62] Hacker and Pierson point out that

> over the four decades between 1979 and 2016, the share of the national wealth held by the richest 0.1 percent of Americans increased from 7 percent to roughly 20 percent. To put this staggering figure in perspective, the top 0.1 percent (fewer than 200,000 families) now holds almost as much wealth as the bottom 90 percent of Americans combined (about 110 million households). . . . These are levels of wealth inequality much higher than seen in

the United States since the late 1920s, or than seen in other affluent nations: the wealthiest households in the United Kingdom
(one of our main competitors for the title of most unequal democracy) own only around half as large a share of national wealth as
the wealthiest households in the United States do. We should not
be surprised these extraordinary trends have coincided with widening opportunities for the very rich to shape politics and policy,
nor that these widening opportunities have resulted in political
and policy trends that make the wealth gap even larger.[63]

Thus the enduring economic legacy of the Reagan Revolution is a cy-
cle of spiraling inequality that has eviscerated the middle class and,
for reasons explored in the next chapter, has precipitated the decline
of American democracy.

The most recent episode in the ongoing conservative effort to divest working- and middle-class Americans of as much wealth as possible gives the lie to conservatives' alleged commitment to "family
values." The US Census Bureau found that the temporary expansion
of the child tax credit reduced child poverty by 46 percent.[64] According to a report from Brookings, it lifted 3.7 million children out of
poverty. (This undoubtedly understates the benefits of the program,
since some families in the most desperate financial circumstances—
those that benefitted most—might be much better off as a result of
the credit while remaining below the poverty line.) The study found
that 70 percent of families receiving the credit reported using it to
pay for routine expenses such as housing and utilities. Over half
said they used it to buy more and healthier food for their family, and
42 percent used it to pay off debt. Accordingly, eligible households
saw significant declines in credit card debt and reliance on high-cost
financial services like payday loans. Nearly a third of parents used
some of the money to purchase tutoring for their children.[65]

In December 2021, every single Senate Republican voted to end
the expanded child tax credit. According to the Columbia University
Center on Poverty and Social Policy, the rate of child poverty grew
5 percent the following month (from 12.1 percent in December 2021
to 17 percent in January 2022).[66]

*Racial Resentment*

In a healthy democracy, the conservative dilemma requires conservative politicians to make some concessions to popular interests, even as they seek to exploit cultural grievances in an effort to recruit voters. Thus Goldwater lost because he asked voters to set aside their economic interests and indulge their racial resentments; Nixon won because in addition to racial resentment, he offered policies that served the economic interests of middle- and working-class voters. Reagan transcended the dilemma by convincing white middle-class voters that the source of their economic woe and the source of their racial resentment were one and the same: bloated government spending on programs that transferred wealth from hardworking Americans to Black Americans.

The persistence of the racial resentment stoked by Reagan's demagoguery is neatly captured in some public remarks made by Rick Santorum, former US senator from Pennsylvania, a quarter century after Reagan left office. While campaigning in the Republican presidential primary for the state of Iowa—which he went on to win—Santorum's dog whistle slipped into a fully audible register:

> I was in Indianola [Iowa] a few months ago, and I was talking to someone that works in the Department of Public Welfare here, and she told me that the state of Iowa is going to get fined if they don't sign up more people under the Medicaid program. They're just pushing harder and harder to get more and more of you dependent upon them so they can get your vote. That's what the bottom line is. I don't want to make Black people's lives better by giving them somebody else's money. I want to give them the opportunity to go out and earn the money and provide for themselves and their families, and the best way to do that is to get the manufacturing sector of the economy rolling again.[67]

Scott Pelley of *CBS Evening News* later asked Santorum to clarify: "You said that you don't want to make Black people's lives better by giving them somebody else's money. Why did you say that?" As if he'd been asked to comment on something that someone else said, Santorum responded, "I've seen that quote; I haven't seen the context." Santorum then wondered aloud if perhaps he was referring to a film when he made the comment in question. (He was not.) Days later, in an interview with CNN, Santorum denied that he'd said the word *Black* at all—suggesting that, in effect, he got his words mixed up and mumbled a nonword that sounded vaguely like the word *Black*.[68] Pelley went on to report that, according to the research department at *CBS Evening News*, 9 percent of food stamp recipients in Iowa at the time were Black; 84 percent were white.[69]

The inescapable truth, of course, is that Santorum accidentally stated in plain English what he very much intended to imply: that white middle- and working-class Iowans should vote for Santorum because he's going to look out for their economic interests—he's the candidate who's going to cut government programs that "make Black people's lives better by giving them other [non-Black] people's money." Such rhetoric hopes to divert the attention of white middle- and working-class voters away from the fact that Republican economic policies since the Reagan administration have devoured the middle class in order to further enrich the wealthiest 1 percent of Americans.

### White Evangelical Complicity

More than any other voting bloc in the United States, white evangelicals have enabled this outcome. Beginning in the middle of the twentieth century, organizations like Spiritual Mobilization cultivated support among evangelical leaders for the economic austerity of so-called Christian libertarianism. And in every single election since 1980, an overwhelming majority of white evangelicals have supported the Republican candidate for president. This means that in every presidential election for the last forty years, an overwhelming majority of white evangelicals have rewarded the race-baiting rhetoric of Republican campaigns—which is particularly unsavory when we recognize that prior to the 1980s, white evangelicals openly defended racial hierarchy (see chapter 2). So white evangelicals transitioned more or less seamlessly from explicit defenses of racial hierarchy to unwavering support for political candidates known for exploiting thinly veiled appeals to racial resentment. In the process, white evangelicals have supported economic policies that engender ever-increasing levels of material inequality and threaten the stability of our nation's democratic institutions. And the evangelical culture war machine has been the vanguard of evangelical complicity in bringing these conditions about—a point we'll explore in the next chapter.

# 6

## *Christo-Authoritarianism*

We noted in chapter 5 that in democratic societies, conservative politicians face what political scientists call the conservative dilemma: namely, how to recruit enough popular support to win elections while preserving the interests of only a small fraction of the electorate. There are two complementary strategies for negotiating this dilemma. One, which we explored in the preceding chapter, involves persuading much of the electorate to vote against their own economic interests. This is typically accomplished by persuading voters to prioritize cultural grievances (around race, ethnicity, religion, and so forth) over their own economic interests. Reagan's innovation was to couch the argument for economic austerity in terms of cultural grievance, convincing swaths of white middle- and working-class voters to embrace the counterintuitive proposition that it was in their own interest to cut taxes on the wealthy and slash government spending. He did this by persuading a large percentage of the white middle and working class that the gravest threat to their own economic security came not from wealthy elites and corporate interests but from government programs that transferred wealth to undeserving (Black) welfare recipients.

The other strategy for negotiating the conservative dilemma is to manipulate the electoral system in ways that allow conservatives to retain power without winning the support of a majority of the electorate, effectively instituting a system of minority rule. This involves a range of tactics, all of which conservatives currently employ. In its mildest form, this strategy involves discouraging progressive voter turnout by, for example, restricting the availability of mail-in voting, or reducing the number of polling places available in those areas with high concentrations of likely progressive voters, resulting in hours-long lines to vote. Gerrymandering is a stronger tactic that involves "cracking" and "packing" congressional districts in ways that enable the governing party to achieve representation that is disproportionate to the electoral support they actually enjoy. (Republicans and Democrats both do this, but in the vast majority of cases—for reasons to do with the confluence in 2010 of developments in computing technology, the census and apportionment schedule, and predictable midterm backlash following the election of a new president—it heavily favors the Republican Party.)[1] "Cracking" splits up voters from the disfavored party into separate districts in order to dilute their impact. "Packing" concentrates disfavored voters in a single district so that the disfavored party wins that district by a wide margin but has no base of support in surrounding districts—effectively sacrificing a single district in order to gain a major advantage in several others.

On the ragged, antidemocratic edge of conservative attempts to achieve minority rule, we find the fringe doctrine of the "independent state legislature," which received a hearing before the Supreme Court in 2022 (*Moore v. Harper*). Advocates of this theory make two claims that pose a serious threat to our democracy. The first is that the elections clause provides state legislatures the authority to make election laws that are not subject to judicial review. This would allow state legislatures to draw districting maps however they please, on whatever basis they please, and state courts have no authority to stop them. The other is that the presidential electors clause gives state legislatures the authority to effectively nullify the popular vote in their state and appoint a slate of electors to the Electoral College that would vote for a candidate who actually lost their state. According to the distinguished conservative jurist J. Michael Luttig, a George H. W. Bush appointee who served for fifteen years on the US

Court of Appeals for the Fourth Circuit, the independent state legislature doctrine is an important feature of "the Republican blueprint to steal the 2024 election."[2]

## Founders and Victims

In her book *Saving History: How White Evangelicals Tour the Nation's Capital and Redeem a Christian America*, Lauren R. Kerby observes that white evangelicals take on different identities depending on the rhetorical demands of the moment. She notes that

> when they speak as founders, white evangelicals argue that their Christian values are normative in American society and should be reflected in American laws. As victims, in contrast, they deplore their mistreatment by those in power and demand equal protection. White evangelicals move fluidly among these roles, as each offers a different position from which to claim moral authority.[3]

Both of these identities—*founder* and *victim*—are key to Christo-authoritarian ideology. The founder identity invokes a mythic past that imbues white evangelicals with a sense of ownership over the United States: as the ideological descendants of the nation's founders, the nation is rightfully theirs. Victimhood, in turn, serves as a catalyst for political mobilization: cultural elites (and others) have stolen our nation and we (white evangelicals) need to take it back. Thus the founder-victim identity activates a politics of grievance that pits *us* (white evangelicals) against *them* (progressives, secularists, cultural elites, and so forth), creating a strong sense of in-group identity over and against the out-group that must be overcome.

The movement from founder to victim to political action is neatly captured in the "Freedom Sunday" message delivered by Robert Jeffress in June 2018 at First Baptist Church of Dallas. Jeffress grew up attending First Baptist Dallas in the days of W. A. Criswell, his parents having joined the church upon learning that Billy Graham was a member.[4] Jeffress's predecessor in the pastorate at First Baptist Dallas was Mac Brunson, who departed for First Baptist Church of Jacksonville in 2006. A vocal supporter of the Institute for Creation Research, Brunson was pastor of First Baptist Jacksonville during ICR's "Demand the Evidence" conference in 2009 (see chapter 4).

Jeffress's 2018 "Freedom Sunday" message begins by decrying a "secular" vision of America's founding:

> Listen long enough to organizations like the American Civil Liberties Union or the Freedom from Religion Foundation or any other left-wing group and you will come to believe this history of America: that America was founded by men of a wide diversity of religious beliefs, some deists, some atheists, and a few Christians. But they were all united by one dream: they wanted to build a completely secular nation that was devoid of any religious, especially Christian, influence. Their goal was to build an unscalable wall around this country that would protect this country from any religious influence seeping into public life.[5]

Jeffress maintains that the purpose of the "secular" founding narrative is political rather than historical. (The irony, of course, is that Jeffress goes on to narrate a version of America's founding that is, in the judgment of professional historians across the ideological spectrum, fictional. And Jeffress's purpose in presenting this fictional narrative is transparently political.) According to Jeffress, the reality is that

> America was founded predominantly—not exclusively, but predominantly—by Christians who wanted to build a Christian nation on the foundation of God's will [*interrupted by applause*]. And furthermore, these men believed that the future success of our country depended on our fidelity to the Christian beliefs. And that's why we can say, though it's politically incorrect to do so, we say without hesitation or apology that America was founded as a *Christian* nation [*pounds pulpit*], and our future success depends on our country being faithful to those eternal truths of God's word [*thunderous applause*].[6]

Jeffress concludes his message with an account of conservative evangelical victimhood that motivates a call to political action:

Now here's the question: What has changed? In these hundred and fifty years, has the Constitution changed and nobody told us? Is that what happened? Of course not. What has happened is we've allowed the secularists, the humanists, the atheists, the infidels to pervert our Constitution into something our founding fathers never intended. And it is time for Americans to stand up and say, "Enough! We're not going to allow this in our Christian country anymore!" It is time to put an end to this.[7]

The effort to "put an end to this," as it were, is becoming increasingly fraught in contemporary American politics. The cultural grievances that endeared evangelicals to Reagan command the allegiance of a pronounced but shrinking minority of America's electorate. And as cultural grievances lose purchase, the religious right and its political allies are poised to embrace antidemocratic measures in order to achieve minority rule.

## (Inter)national Conservatism

A more intellectually ambitious rendering of the founder-victim narrative is found in a manifesto produced by the Edmund Burke Foundation (EBF) titled "National Conservatism: A Statement of Principles." The statement appeared in the *American Conservative* in June 2022, a month ahead of the EBF-sponsored National Conservatism Conference in Miami.[8] That conference's keynote speakers included:

- Ron DeSantis—current governor of Florida and likely contender for the 2024 Republican presidential nomination, known for reaching the Little League World Series quarterfinals in 1991 and, more recently, defrauding Venezuelan refugees by luring them onto a chartered flight to Massachusetts with false promises of food, shelter, and employment;
- Josh Hawley—US senator from Missouri and enthusiastic Christian nationalist, featured in countless memes commemorating his sprint away from rioters as they breached the US Capitol on

January 6, 2021, just hours after he stood before the Capitol with his fist raised in solidarity with said rioters;

- Albert Mohler—president of the Southern Baptist Theological Seminary, young-earth creationist, and complementarian, who declared in a June 2022 conversation with EBF chairman Yoram Hazony that "we have the left routinely speaking of me and of others as Christian nationalists as if we're supposed to be running from that. I'm not about to run from that. I'm not about to join their one world order";[9]
- Rick Scott—former governor of Florida and current US senator from Florida, who recently proposed legislation that would enable Congress to cut Social Security and Medicare as a means of balancing the federal budget; and
- Peter Thiel—tech entrepreneur, billionaire, and right-wing political activist who was among the largest political donors to Republican campaigns in the 2022 election.

Christian nationalism—roughly, the notion that the laws and official customs of the United States should reflect the prevailing cultural norms of conservative, white evangelicals—was a prominent theme of the EBF's 2022 National Conservatism Conference.[10]

The Statement of Principles presents itself as a commentary on the state of "Western nations" generally, and its principles aren't tailored to the institutional arrangements or political conventions of any particular nation-state. Nonetheless, the statement addresses itself at various points to specific features of US history, legal tradition, and polity.

The document's preamble complains that "traditional beliefs, institutions, and liberties underpinning life in the countries we love have been progressively undermined and overthrown." One might expect the statement that follows to express the authors' dismay over the growing menace of far-right political movements across the West—movements that are openly antagonistic to classical liberal values such as the rule of law, the independent judiciary, free and fair elections, civil liberties, and respect for the rights of vulnerable minorities. One would be disappointed.

Instead, the statement presents a cocktail-napkin sketch of a strategy for franchising culture war politics across the West—which isn't altogether surprising, given that a couple of the statement's contributing authors are on the payroll of the Danube Institute.

The Danube Institute is a think tank headquartered in Budapest and bankrolled by Hungary's government. At the direction of Hungarian Prime Minister Viktor Orbán, the institute was founded in 2013 by John O'Sullivan, a conservative British pundit and journalist who is listed among the coauthors of the EBF's Statement of Principles. O'Sullivan, who succeeded William F. Buckley as editor in chief of the *National Review*, served as a top adviser to conservative Prime Minister Margaret Thatcher and later assisted her in the writing of her two-volume memoir.[11] Andrew Marantz reports that "in 2020, the Danube Institute started hosting fellows—writers and scholars from abroad who were invited to Budapest for a few weeks or months, given a stipend and a comfortable apartment, and asked to work on articles or books that might help the cause."[12] The cause in question is marketing Orbán-style competitive authoritarianism to like-minded conservatives across the West, most notably in the United States and United Kingdom.

Political scientists define *competitive authoritarianism* as a political regime that features regular elections that are free but distinctly unfair. Thus competitive authoritarianism is a form of soft authoritarianism, in the sense that it's technically possible—though exceedingly unlikely—that any given election might bring about a change in political leadership. Indeed, at least superficially, a competitive authoritarian regime might look more democratic than authoritarian. Steven Levitsky and Lucan A. Way observe that in competitive authoritarian regimes, "although elections are regularly held and are generally free of massive fraud, incumbents routinely abuse state resources, deny the opposition adequate media coverage, harass opposition candidates and their supporters, and in some cases manipulate electoral results."[13] In their book *How Democracies Die*, Levitsky and Daniel Ziblatt explain that

> this is how democracies now die. Blatant dictatorship—in the form of fascism, communism, or military rule—has disappeared across much of the world. Military coups and other violent sei-

zures of power are rare. Most countries hold regular elections. Democracies still die, but by different means. Since the end of the Cold War, most democratic breakdowns have been caused not by generals and soldiers but by elected governments themselves.[14]

Established liberal democracies give way to competitive authoritarianism through a process that political theorists call *democratic backsliding*, wherein a political party gains power by legitimate means and then uses that power to undermine democratic institutions and stack elections in its own favor. In Hungary, such tactics have enabled Orbán's Fidesz Party "to convert vote totals of forty-four per cent and forty-eight per cent in the past two parliamentary elections into legislative supermajorities."[15]

*Hungary for Power*

Viktor Orbán has been elected prime minister of Hungary five times—once in 1998, and in each of the last four elections since 2010. As Marantz recounts,

> During his first term as Prime Minister, starting in 1998, Orbán, who still identified as a liberal democrat, vowed to build up the country's civic infrastructure. President Bill Clinton hosted him at the White House, extolling Orbán's "youthful and vigorous and progressive leadership." Then, in 2002, Orbán lost a reelection campaign to a Socialist coalition and, according to the biographer József Debreczeni, resolved to return to power and change "the rules of the game" so that he would never lose again.[16]

Between 2002 and 2010, Orbán served as the leader of Hungary's political opposition. In 2008, through fellow traveler Benjamin Netanyahu, the Israeli prime minister, Orbán made the acquaintance of Arthur Finkelstein—the very Arthur Finkelstein who, in 1970, advised Richard Nixon to "polarize the election around that issue which cuts best in your direction, i.e., drugs, crime, race, etc." (see Chapter 5). According to Marantz,

Finkelstein became so indispensable that Orbán reportedly came to refer to him, dotingly, as Finkie. One of Finkelstein's protégés later told the Swiss journalist Hannes Grassegger, "Arthur always said that you did not fight against the Nazis but against Adolf Hitler." Orbán had been running against globalism, multiculturalism, bureaucracy in Brussels. These were abstractions. By 2013, Finkelstein had an epiphany: the face of the enemy should be George Soros.[17]

After eight years in the Hungarian opposition, Orbán returned to the seat of power in 2010. Orbán's victory was quickened by the leaked recording of a now infamous speech given by Orbán's political rival, Prime Minister Ferenc Gyurcsány, at a closed party meeting in 2006: a twenty-seven-minute, profanity-laced rant in which Gyurcsány castigates his own administration for lying about Hungary's economic outlook in order to win the 2006 election. With the onset of the global financial crisis in 2008, Hungary's economy only worsened over the course of Gyurcsány's administration.

Outrage over the contents of Gyurcsány's 2006 speech, prevailing dissatisfaction with Hungary's faltering economy, and the popular appeal of Orbán's culture war rhetoric all contributed to a landslide victory in 2010: Orbán regained the prime minister's office, and his Fidesz Party won a supermajority in Parliament. This enabled Orbán and his political allies to amend Hungary's constitution. Orbán and his colleagues wasted no time instituting antidemocratic reforms and illiberal policies. Within a year of their 2010 victory, Orbán's party had made a dozen amendments to Hungary's constitution. When that didn't achieve the desired results, they discarded the constitution altogether and drafted a new one in 2012. Orbán packed the constitutional court and forced hundreds of unsympathetic judges into retirement. He gerrymandered voting districts so that his party can maintain a parliamentary supermajority with less than half the vote, which they've done twice.[18]

Nor have Orbán's reforms been limited to the mechanics of government. Orbán has also seized control of the centers of cultural production in media and education. Media outlets that criticize Orbán's agenda are routinely purchased by Orbán's allies, who promptly close them down. Outlets that aren't purchased and shuttered have been massively curtailed: one radio station known for voicing dissent against Orbán's government lost its broadcast signal, and newspapers critical of Orbán have lost all revenue from government advertising—a major source of funding in the Hungarian media ecosystem. Notably, Orbán has achieved all of this without engaging in explicit media censorship. Dissent isn't prohibited; it's merely economically crippled or deplatformed by means of policies that appear unrelated to disfavored content. One of Hungary's leading universities, Central European University—which was founded by George Soros—has been exiled to Vienna. The field of gender studies has effectively been banned within Hungarian institutions of higher learning. Meanwhile, on the popular front, Orbán's government sponsors an advertising campaign that encourages women to think of themselves primarily as mothers and homemakers. And as Elisabeth Zerofsky reports, the Hungarian government now offers an array of pronatalist financial incentives: "There are subsidies for family cars; women who have four or more children will never pay income tax again; and some older citizens who leave their jobs to take care of grandchildren are compensated by the government."[19] Notably, these subsidies are reserved exclusively for Hungarian natives: Orbán has publicly decried "race mixing" and has expressed anxieties associated with white replacement theory.[20]

Stripped of their racist and xenophobic elements, we know that Hungarian-style subsidies for children would improve the circumstances of many American children and their families. We know this because we know that the temporary expansion of the child tax credit in 2021 cut child poverty by 46 percent, lifting 3.7 million children out of poverty.[21] And yet, curiously, this appears to be one aspect of Orbán's regime that American conservatives have little interest in imitating. Despite their "family values" rhetoric, when it comes to economic policy, conservatives don't appear to value families. As we noted in chapter 5, every single Senate Republican voted to end the expanded child tax credit in December 2021. Still, anemic attempts to simulate Hungary's family subsidies are already underway. On February 28, 2023, citing Hungary's pronatalist policies as inspiration, Texas State Representative Bryan Slaton announced his intention to propose a bill (HB 2889) that would provide a 40 percent reduction in property tax to married Texas parents with at least four children, and up to 100 percent relief from property taxes to families with ten or more children.

### Rod Dreher

The Danube Institute is essentially a state-sponsored marketing firm, tasked with selling Orbán's Hungary to sympathetic conservatives around the West. As part of its fellowship program, the institute recruits "fellows" from established liberal democracies, primarily in the North Atlantic region. The institute provides fellows with a stipend, privileged access to high-level Hungarian officials, and a tastefully appointed timeshare in Hungary's picturesque capital of Budapest. In return, the institute's fellows market Orbán's cultural and political agenda to conservatives back home.

The most prolific fellow of the Danube Institute is Rod Dreher. Along with the institute's president, John O'Sullivan, Dreher is listed among the coauthors of the EBF's Statement of Principles. Dreher is perhaps best known for his 2017 bestseller *The Benedict Option*, which argues that conservative Christians should accept that they've lost the culture war, retreat from national politics, and focus instead on shaping local communities. However, as Andrew Marantz reports,

> after his Danube Institute fellowship . . . he retreated from his retreatism: actually, conservatives could win real power, and Hungary could show the way. "Orbán was so unafraid, so unapologetic about using his political power to push back on the liberal elites in business and media and culture," Dreher told me. "It was so inspiring: this is what a vigorous conservative government can do if it's serious about stemming this horrible global tide of wokeness."[22]

In April 2021, Dreher invited his friend and Fox News host Tucker Carlson to visit Budapest. According to Dreher, if someone like

Orbán "has all the right enemies, if the liberal establishment is obsessed with treating them as a hate object, then it's natural for a right-populist like me or Tucker to react by going, Huh, maybe there's something interesting there."[23] He assured Carlson that "Hungary is a normal country, not a perfect one. Still, there are plenty of good things going on here, and lessons that American conservatives can learn and should learn from the way Prime Minister Viktor Orbán and the Fidesz party govern their country."[24] A few months later, Carlson hosted his Fox News program from Hungary for an entire week. One night's broadcast featured a fifteen-minute interview with Orbán himself, in which the subject of Orbán's antidemocratic agenda didn't come up.

Carlson and Dreher are hardly the only American conservatives to have shown an interest in Orbán's Hungary. Marantz reports that

> in recent years, Orbán or institutions affiliated with his government have hosted, among others, Mike Pence, the former Vice-President; new-media agitators including Steve Bannon, Dennis Prager, and Milo Yiannopoulos; and Jeff Sessions, the former Attorney General, who told a Hungarian newspaper that, in the struggle to "return to our Christian roots based on reason and law, which have made Western civilization great, . . . the Hungarians have a solid stand."[25]

In 2022, the Conservative Political Action Coalition hosted a Conservative Political Action Conference in Budapest—"CPAC Hungary"—its first outside the US. Orbán's address to CPAC Hungary consisted of a twelve-point plan for conservative success, including the imperative to "play by our own rules." A few months later, Orbán was a featured speaker at CPAC's conference in Dallas, Texas. And CPAC returned to Budapest in May 2023 for its second annual CPAC Hungary conference.

According to Dreher, what attracts American conservatives like himself to the Hungarian model is Orbán's use of state power to stem the perceived tide of progressivism. Dreher alleges that "we all seem to be barreling towards a future that is not liberal and democratic but is going to be either left illiberalism, or right illiberalism. If that's true, then I know which side I'm on: the side that isn't going to persecute me and my people."[26]

Notably, Dreher appears to be genuinely unconcerned with the details of how his favored political regime deals with progressive rivals. His indifference is palpable in an interview with the Hungarian news outlet Klubrádió in August 2021 (translated by David Baer):

DREHER.    You're telling me the media is in government hands, but then how is it possible I'm talking to you? You belong to the opposition media.

KLUBRÁDIÓ.    Maybe you're not aware that Klubrádió no longer has a radio frequency and can only be heard on the internet.

DREHER.    I did not know that.

KLUBRÁDIÓ.    Orbán secured a two-thirds majority in Parliament with only 50 percent of the popular vote because of how he changed the election law. In 2014 he got a two-thirds majority with only 45 percent of the popular vote.

DREHER.    I have to be honest with you, I don't know about Orbán's modification of the election law.

KLUBRÁDIÓ.    What do you say about the fact that there are no independent regional newspapers?

DREHER.    I was told the paper with the largest circulation in the country belongs to the opposition. Is that true?

KLUBRÁDIÓ.    Yes, but Orbán supports this paper to prove there's an opposition media.

DREHER.    Is that the only opposition paper in the whole country?

KLUBRÁDIÓ.    Yes.

DREHER.    Okay, well you're telling me something I didn't know.[27]

Dreher's blend of culture war rhetoric, authoritarian sympathies, and generalized disinterest in specifics is characteristic of the national conservative movement as a whole. And the EBF's Statement of Principles—which lists Dreher and Danube Institute President John O'Sullivan among its coauthors—is no exception.[28]

Consider, for example, the statement's article on religious nationalism, according to which "the Bible should be read as the first among the sources of a shared Western civilization in schools and universities." The article gives no indication of *which version* of the Bible is to be considered authoritative, or whose interpretation of the text should be regarded as definitive. (The Bible *according to whose understanding*: Those who claim that the Bible commands us to seek justice on behalf of the oppressed? Those who claim that the Bible commands us to practice racial segregation? Those who say that our political community should impose the death penalty on anyone who transgresses sexual norms found in the Hebrew Bible, as those norms are understood by conservative evangelicals? The statement fails even to acknowledge these questions.) The Bible, as Jerome Copulsky points out, is not a "self-glossing document."[29]

The statement's article on "Public Research" is equally light on substantive details that admit of no obvious or uncontroversial solution. According to the statement's authors,

> At a time when China is rapidly overtaking America and the Western nations in fields crucial for security and defense, a Cold War-type program modeled on DARPA, the "moon-shot," and SDI is needed to focus large-scale public resources on scientific and technological research with military applications. . . . Most universities are at this point partisan and globalist in orientation and vehemently opposed to nationalist and conservative ideas. Such institutions do not deserve taxpayer support unless they rededicate themselves to the national interest. Education policy should serve manifest national needs.

Apart from providing "large-scale public resources" to subsidize whatever the military-industrial complex happens to be geeking out on at the moment, the statement offers no indication of what constitutes the national interest. The statement doesn't even coun-

tenance the possibility that our nation's interests might be served by
a college-educated citizenry that refuses to uncritically accept the
proposition that our nation's interests are served by reserving "large-
scale public resources" for "research with military applications."

### Rule of Law and Religious Nationalism

In keeping with the national conservatives' prevailing enthusiasm for
Orbán's politics, the EBF's Statement of Principles suggests a willingness to repress political dissent. Consider the statement's article
on the rule of law:

> 5. The Rule of Law. We believe in the rule of law. By this we mean
> that citizens and foreigners alike, and both the government and
> the people, must accept and abide by the laws of the nation. In
> America, this means accepting and living in accordance with the
> Constitution of 1787, the amendments to it, duly enacted statu-
> tory law, and the great common law inheritance. All agree that the
> repair and improvement of national legal traditions and institu-
> tions is at times necessary. But necessary change must take place
> through the law. This is how we preserve our national traditions
> and our nation itself. Rioting, looting, and other unacceptable
> public disorder should be swiftly put to an end.

This is transparent law and order propaganda. The tell is in the last
sentence, which eviscerates every principle invoked in the lines that
precede it. "Rioting, looting, and other unacceptable public disorder
should be swiftly put to an end." The phrase *put to an end* suggests coercion—presumably at the hands of law enforcement. (If not agents
of law enforcement, then who? Vigilantes? Neighborhood Watch
volunteers? Law enforcement is the best-case scenario. So, absent
specifics, we'll assume that the authors have formal law enforcement
in mind.) And what kind of activity, exactly, is law enforcement put-
ting to an end?

The beginning of the sentence specifies "rioting" and "looting."
So far, so good: rioting and looting are illegal—by definition, this is

the sort of conduct that invites official intervention. Indeed, we might stipulate that (proportionate) official intervention is a warranted response to *any* illegal conduct. Notably, the statement doesn't say this. Instead, the last sentence of article 5 drifts almost imperceptibly from the subject of conduct that's *illegal*—rioting and looting—to the subject of conduct deemed *unacceptable* (by whom, it doesn't say). Whatever is meant by "other unacceptable public disorder," it's a third type of conduct that isn't captured by "rioting" or "looting." Presumably, whatever this third type of conduct is, if it rose to the level of illegality, the authors would say so. But they don't. Instead, they allege that this third type of conduct, whatever it may be, involves some form of "public disorder" that is "unacceptable," and they call for official intervention to ensure that it is "swiftly put to an end." In so doing, this principle that sets out to affirm the rule of law actually militates against the very ideal it purports to celebrate.

In a society that is governed by the rule of law, agents of law enforcement are tasked with *enforcing law*. If and insofar as agents of law enforcement (as such) intervene in the affairs of private citizens to enforce norms that have no basis in law—for example, to enforce parochial opinions about which forms of "public disorder" are "unacceptable"—we are ruled not by law but by some other standard that is by definition nonlegal.[30] Thus the final sentence of the statement's article on the rule of law provides a standard for official intervention that is itself an exemplary violation of the rule of law. It's propaganda.

Some might worry that my treatment of the statement's article on the rule of law is uncharitable. Not so. We're not talking about a term paper composed by an undergraduate who might be excused for an unfortunate choice of words. Nor is it a single sentence cherry-picked from a five-hundred-page tome on political economy, the overall thrust of which would suggest that my reading is at odds with authorial intent. Indeed, as far as intent is concerned, several of the statement's authors and signatories have expressed sympathy for and a desire to emulate the authoritarian tactics of Viktor Orbán—which is entirely in keeping with the account of laws and law enforcement I glean from the text. Moreover, although most of its authors and signatories possess little or no expertise in political theory or related fields, a few of the statement's contributors have earned advanced degrees in political science. I assume that those with the relevant training have the wherewithal to produce a short paragraph that accurately reflects their considered views on the rule of law. Any assumption to the contrary would, in my judgment, be truly uncharitable. So when the statement's authors invite official intervention to stifle conduct that is lawful yet somehow "unacceptable," I take them at their word.

Having clarified the substance of article 5, the time has come to acknowledge that this conception of the rule of law suggests an alarming posture toward the First Amendment right of oppressed minorities to present the public with their grievances against the established order. The authors don't tell us exactly what they mean by "unacceptable public disorder," but the text contains a few highly suggestive cues that frame its innuendo with crystal clarity. The article's reference to "repair and improvement of national legal traditions" that "must take place through the law" indicates political dissent. And the political dissidents that the right most associates with "rioting" and "looting" are those who engage in public protests over racialized oppression. So make no mistake: when the statement's authors speak of "unacceptable public disorder" that "should be swiftly put to an end," they are calling upon law enforcement to suppress public protests over racialized oppression.

In case there's any doubt about who the statement's authors have in mind when they speak of political dissidents who engender unacceptable (though not illegal) public disorder that's vaguely related (though not identical) to "rioting" and "looting," consider Rod Dreher's remarks in an October 2020 interview with Albert Mohler.

MOHLER. I have to wonder if, between the time you set out this argument [in the book *Live Not by Lies*] and when we're having this conversation, you've had further thoughts about the distinction between hard and soft totalitarianism. Play that out a bit for us.

DREHER. [*chuckling*] Well you know, I conceived the idea of the book back in 2015. . . . I finally sold the book pro-

posal in early 2019, turned the manuscript in at the
end of February, and thought, "You know, how am
I gonna sell this book to my fellow Christians?" I believe the argument is solid that we're on the verge of
a soft totalitarianism. But I remember with *The Benedict Option*, I got a lot of Christians saying, "You're
being alarmist. Things really aren't that bad." Well
then, since I turned the final manuscript in, here
comes COVID and here comes George Floyd and
race riots and the militant wokeness now within institutions—within college campuses, within journal-
ism, within big business—that's really transforming
these environments. I don't think now that I have
nearly as much of a challenge selling the argument
to Christians who are the least bit observant as I
would have just six, seven months ago.[31]

Mohler appears to have caught Dreher midway through a personal
ideological whirlwind. Roughly six months prior, Dreher was reflecting on the challenge of "selling the argument to Christians" that we
should fear the looming threat of soft totalitarianism; six months
hence, in April 2021, he was in Budapest, selling the argument to
Tucker Carlson that the soft authoritarianism of Viktor Orbán offers
hope for the future of American conservatism. And in September
2022, Dreher announced his intention to relocate to Hungary in order
to help build networks between American conservatives and Orbán's
authoritarian regime.[32] More on authoritarianism in a moment.

Notably, any policy that calls upon agents of law enforcement
to suppress otherwise legal public protest is irreconcilable with the
right to freedom of expression guaranteed by the First Amendment—
at least as that right has been understood by judges throughout the
American legal tradition. So it's worth observing that the statement's
article on the rule of law is inconsistent with its own claim to embrace "the Constitution of 1787, the amendments to it, duly enacted
statutory law, and the great common law inheritance." Nor is this
inconsistency limited to the statement's article on the rule of law.

The statement's fourth article, "God and Public Religion," likewise appears to be in some tension with the statement's claim to embrace "the Constitution of 1787."

> 4. God and Public Religion. No nation can long endure without humility and gratitude before God and fear of his judgment that are found in authentic religious tradition. For millennia, the Bible has been our surest guide, nourishing a fitting orientation toward God, to the political traditions of the nation, to public morals, to the defense of the weak, and to the recognition of things rightly regarded as sacred. The Bible should be read as the first among the sources of a shared Western civilization in schools and universities, and as the rightful inheritance of believers and non-believers alike. Where a Christian majority exists, public life should be rooted in Christianity and its moral vision, which should be honored by the state and other institutions both public and private. At the same time, Jews and other religious minorities are to be protected in the observance of their own traditions, in the free governance of their communal institutions, and in all matters pertaining to the rearing and education of their children. Adult individuals should be protected from religious or ideological coercion in their private lives and in their homes.

As Jerome Copulsky observed in his panel discussion at the Yale conference on "White Christian Nationalism and the Midterm Elections," this call for the establishment of Christianity as a national religion contradicts the establishment clause in the First Amendment. (The *establishment* clause prohibits government from establishing an official religion; the *free exercise* clause prohibits government from restricting religious practice. Together, the establishment clause and the free exercise clause of the First Amendment form the basis of religious liberty within the US legal tradition.) In light of this tension between the US Constitution and the policies put forward by national conservatives, it's difficult to escape the conclusion that national conservatism's ultimate objective is not the recovery of an American identity that has been lost, but rather a refounding of the United

States based on the imposition of a cultural and religious identity that has never, in fact, defined the American population as a whole.[33]

*Mythic Past*

In 2021, the "Freedom Sunday" homily at First Baptist Church of Dallas was delivered by guest speaker David Barton. Pastor Robert Jeffress introduced Barton to the congregation as a "patriot and a prophet of God" who would "declare that historical reality that this nation was founded as a Christian nation."[34] Barton is an influential activist, self-taught historian, and conservative political advisor whose clients include George W. Bush, Newt Gingrich, and Michele Bachmann. Former Arkansas governor Mike Huckabee regards Barton as "maybe the greatest living historian on the spiritual nature of America's early days."[35] In 2012, Mr. Barton published *The Jefferson Lies: Exposing the Myths You've Always Believed about Thomas Jefferson*, in which he argues that Jefferson was a conservative Christian who in fact opposed the separation of church and state. Readers of the History News Network voted it the least credible history book in print. Despite the fact that it was a *New York Times* bestseller, the book's publisher ended publication and distribution, citing "loss of confidence in the book's details."[36]

Historian Kathleen Wellman observes that conservative evangelicals hoping to establish America's Christian founding are particularly eager to demonstrate that Jefferson, as the author of the Declaration of Independence, was an orthodox Christian. "They often cite . . . Jefferson's statement that 'the God who gave us life gave us liberty at the same time; the hand of force may destroy but cannot disjoin them.'"[37] As Wellman points out, this statement is far less compelling an example of Jefferson's Christian faith when considered in the fuller context of *A Summary View of the Rights of British America*, protesting British taxation:

> But let them not think to exclude us from going to other markets
> to dispose of those commodities which they cannot use, or to
> supply those wants which they cannot supply. Still less let it be

proposed that our properties within our own territories shall be taxed or regulated by any other power on earth but our own. *The God who gave us life gave us liberty at the same time; the hand of force may destroy but cannot disjoin them.*[38]

(Wellman adds the emphasis to indicate the passage that's taken out of context.) Wellman notes that this method of prooftexting is used to establish "a deeply religious Franklin, Jefferson, and Washington [who] feature in popular works such as those of Peter Marshall and Michael Novak. The chief founders then become staunch Christians through selective citation, as we briefly saw with Jefferson's quotation." Thus we see that the hermeneutics of legitimization isn't limited to Scripture: it also informs how white evangelicals read our nation's founding documents and the words of the founders more generally.

This selective reading of American history forms the basis of a Christian nationalist mythology that is foundational to white evangelicals' self-understanding as founder-victims. As the ideological descendants of America's founders, white evangelicals are the "real Americans." They are therefore the aggrieved victims of efforts by overzealous bureaucrats and activist judges to make laws and alter the Constitution, effectively reshaping the United States against the will of "real Americans" (for more on this point, see the article on "National Government" in the EBF's Statement of Principles).[39] Historians who warn against this mischaracterization—who point to the fact that the founders considered and explicitly rejected proposals to officially declare the United States a "Christian nation"—are drowned out by the evangelical culture war machine: the fact that Jeffress and Dreher know as much about US history as MacArthur and Mohler know about paleontology is perfectly irrelevant. Note the parallel. Creation science isn't about scientific insight: it's about facilitating social control through a "biblical" narrative that legitimizes race and gender hierarchy and delegitimizes "secular" sources of authority. Similarly, the notion of America's Christian founding isn't about history: it's a mythology that confers privileged status on white evangelical claims to political and economic power. Rival ac-

counts of politics and economics, including demands for justice on
behalf of marginalized groups, are by definition illegitimate, foreign,
and other.

This is the impetus behind much hysteria surrounding the pur-
ported influence of critical race theory (CRT) in the sphere of education, particularly in the area of history. On the surface, such disputes
appear to center on competing versions of America's history. But the
real disagreement revolves around competing visions of history as
an enterprise. Cultural conservatives wish to approach history as an
exercise in corporate nostalgia, meant to reinforce their preferred
understanding of who we are as a nation. Whether this nostalgia has
any basis in our nation's actual past is beside the point. And insofar
as genuine insights into the people, events, or material conditions
that have shaped our nation threaten to undermine conservative legitimizing narratives, the work of professional historians is at cross-
purposes with the function that many conservatives call upon history to perform—namely, promoting a national myth that confers
legitimacy on their understanding of America as *their* nation, rooted
in *their* values. In other words, conservatives reject the consensus
of professional historians *not* because they prefer one version of
American history over another but because they prefer mythology
over history.

For example, conservatives are generally reluctant to discuss our
nation's history of racial discrimination in housing, because they
refuse to acknowledge that the racial wealth gap has nothing to do
with merit (see chapter 2). But another reason they don't want to talk
about housing discrimination is that doing so would require them
to acknowledge the role of the Federal Housing Administration in
creating the white middle class. And that, in turn, would require us to
recognize that the single greatest era of wealth creation and upward
mobility in our nation's history was predicated not on the character of
men who pulled themselves up by their own bootstraps, but on massive government subsidies funded by a steeply progressive income
tax. This reality threatens to expose the myth of meritocracy as the
fantasy that it is, and post-Reagan conservatives must obscure that
reality at any cost.[40]

The moment we begin to interrogate claims about a special relationship between God and the United States, the entire facade of American exceptionalism begins to crumble, exposing the fact that America's power and wealth are not a mark of divine favor but merely a by-product of empire building. What if, by mistaking the fruits of empire for God's blessing, Christian nationalists have gotten confused about what sorts of things God favors—confused about the features of our civilization that followers of Christ should make an effort to cultivate and amplify into the future? What if, far from being an unfortunate but necessary means to some consecrated destiny, it's just a very bad thing that the US government systematically slaughtered and dispossessed Indigenous peoples and desecrated their holy places? And what if there's nothing redeeming about the fact that much of America's early wealth issued from the fruits of labor that was straightforwardly stolen from people who were kidnapped and sold into bondage? What if that's just evil, full stop?

White Christian nationalists tend to perceive an analogy between God's relationship to the United States and God's relationship to ancient Israel. They read the Exodus narrative and see themselves reflected in the plight of Israel rather than the privilege of Egypt. This is nothing short of biblical illiteracy, engendered by an evangelical intellectual class that is so preoccupied with the bidding of their political masters—so fixated on alerting Christian voters to the infirmities of secular American culture—that they seem to have forgotten that judgment begins in the house of God. More on this in the chapter to follow.

## Authoritarianism

We've now established two distinct but related dimensions along which the ideology of the religious right qualifies as a species of authoritarianism—one social and intellectual, the other explicitly political. On the social and intellectual dimension, we've traced the contours of an ideology that uses the resources of Christian theology—via propaganda, prooftexting, and dubious, self-serving methods of biblical exegesis—to legitimize social hierarchies that assign power and privilege to white evangelical men at every level of human society: marriage, church, political community, and so on. In laying out this ideology, we've documented all the classic criteria that define the authoritarian cast of mind:

- a social identity rooted in nostalgia for a mythic past;
- propaganda that manipulates moral and intellectual ideals;
- conspiracy theories that delegitimize conventional sources of authority;
- anti-intellectualism;
- rigid commitment to social hierarchy as a source of moral order;
- a sense of victimhood that engenders populist resentment of "cultural elites";
- emphasis on "law and order" as a means of preserving the status quo; and
- sexual anxiety that finds expression in patriarchal masculinity and fetishization of racial or ethnic purity.[41]

Given these habits of mind and social practice, it's hardly surprising that the religious right, sensing that the culture war is lost, has found comfort in the prospect of imitating an authoritarian regime that has cemented its own minority rule for the foreseeable future.

On the political dimension, the religious right is perhaps the largest single faction of a conservative vanguard that actively seeks to imitate the authoritarian tactics that have transformed Hungary from a functioning democracy to an authoritarian state. Moreover, reliable evangelical support has enabled conservatives to consistently advance policies that perpetuate radical economic inequality. Such economic conditions invariably engender precisely the kind of populist reaction that confers political power on authoritarian leaders, which power they then use to undermine democratic institutions and guarantee the preservation of their own power.

# 7

## *Resisting Christo-Authoritarianism*

The time has come to suggest an alternative to Christo-authoritarianism. Ideology, propaganda, and motivated reasoning are powerful forces that afflict all human beings. But evangelicals can and should resist these forces by actively questioning the legitimacy of social hierarchies that privilege our own interests above those of our neighbors, which is precisely what Christians are called to do. When we divest ourselves of our own interests in defending the established order, we are free to abandon theological narratives that the religious right uses to legitimize that order—along with any antagonism toward expertise that poses a threat to those theological narratives. For example, when I am no longer invested in defending the way that resources are allocated in the United States, I am free to admit that racial disparities in wealth and income are wrought by centuries of racial injustice. When we focus on giving others their due instead of legitimizing our own privilege, flawed ideology loses its intellectual purchase and we can see propaganda for what it is. Thus evangelicals can subvert Christo-authoritarianism by pursuing justice rather than pouring their energy into maintaining social arrangements that work to their own advantage.

Below I'll argue that Christian morality provides resources for resisting Christo-authoritarianism. I hasten to add that this isn't a grand strategy for persuading evangelicals to abandon en masse the authoritarian movement that appears to have captured the religious right in the United States. I'm not at all confident that such a strategy exists. But I am hopeful that once they see Christo-authoritarianism for the nihilistic, self-serving, and anti-Christian ideology that it is, a critical mass of younger evangelicals—many of whom have already begun the painful process of disentangling their faith from the politics of their parents' generation—will have the courage to walk away from the religious right and never look back.

The aim of this chapter is fundamentally different from those that precede it. Up to this point, my object has been to *describe* the ideology of the religious right: insofar as I've offered a critique of propaganda, the purpose of that critique has been merely to expose the ways in which the ideology of the religious right manipulates moral, intellectual, and theological ideals to reinforce the anti-Christian social practices around which it revolves. By contrast, my goal in this chapter is to provide a *normative* account of moral knowledge—which is to say, an account of how Christian faith *should* inform our thinking about morality and related questions in the political sphere. I begin by arguing that the moral axioms of Christo-authoritarianism are inherently devoid of resources for claiming knowledge of objective moral truth.

## Moral Knowledge

The reason many conservative evangelicals appear to be moral relativists is that they are moral relativists. I'm confident they would deny this, but their denial doesn't make it any less true. (As we noted in connection with logically implicit white supremacy in chapter 2, people are capable of holding beliefs that are obviously false or mutually incoherent.) It's commonly supposed that the problem with religious fundamentalism is that its moral commitments are too rigid. In fact the opposite is true: morality based on the hermeneutics of legitimization is infinitely flexible. In the hands of ecclesial authorities who've insulated themselves from expert critique, sacred texts become a vehicle for legitimizing all manner of ungodliness, injustice, and abuse, in the name of an Authority that is transcendent and therefore unavailable for interrogation. Thus the moral and intellectual intransigence of religious fundamentalists is a product, not of immutable principles, but rather of the fact that fundamentalist techniques of knowledge furnish an unassailable pretext for maintaining social practices and habits of mind that are morally and intellectually bankrupt.

In the span of a few decades, conservative evangelicals who purport to embrace objective morality have claimed biblical sanction for totally contrary positions on such issues of moral salience as segregation and abortion (see chapter 1). The arc of that moral evolution wasn't drawn by objective moral truth or God's word; it was shaped by white evangelicals who remitted their collective conscience to the care of religious authorities tasked with deciding what constitutes the "biblical" view of gender, race, science, culture, and politics—which views tend to coalesce around whatever serves the interests of the evangelical culture war machine at a given moment. White evangelical religious authorities in the South didn't give up on racial segregation in the 1970s by virtue of some new interpretive insight that helped them better understand the biblical prooftexts that had been used for centuries to sanctify white supremacist ideology. Rather, their maniacal devotion to segregation became overwhelmingly unpopular in the wake of the civil rights movement, and financially untenable when the US Department of Justice threatened the tax-exempt status of religious institutions that openly practiced racial discrimination. Thus the culture war machine's about-face on issues of race was motivated by financial self-interest and broader shifts in social perception, not theology or moral principle. Objective moral truth cannot be underwritten by the hermeneutics of legitimization—if it could, those who practice the hermeneutics of legitimization wouldn't have such frequent occasion to revise their moral convictions.

It will be worthwhile here to say something about the intellectual conditions that allow the religious right to rely exclusively on the hermeneutics of legitimization as the arbiter of moral knowledge. We typically divide all assertions into two categories: *matters of fact* and *matters of opinion*. Matters of fact include propositions like:

1.   The freezing point of water ($H_2O$) is 32°F (at sea level).
2.   The distance between the earth and the sun is approximately 93 million miles (on average).
3.   Julius Caesar crossed the Rubicon in 49 BCE.
4.   There's an even number of trees on the campus of UNC–Chapel Hill.

Two elements of propositions 1–4 deserve special attention. The first is that they each make a claim about some feature of the world that is *observably true or false*. If I had the time and the inclination, I could easily take some water to sea level, cool it to 32°F or below, and watch it freeze. Observability is key, especially when it comes to resolving factual disputes. If I claim that the freezing point of water is 32°F and you disagree with me, there is a procedure for settling our disagreement: we take some water to sea level, cool it to 32°F, and wait for it to freeze. Having demonstrated that water freezes at 32°F, if you still disagree with me, I can reasonably accuse you of failing to think rationally about the claim at issue.

Estimating the distance from the earth to the sun is a bit more difficult than watching water freeze. But I know that the distance has been calculated by others, based on meticulous observations and basic principles of geometry. And they've communicated these observations, along with the details of their reasoning, in scientific literature. So although the distance from the earth to the sun isn't as straightforwardly observable as the freezing point of water, it is observable nonetheless. Similarly, I'm in no position to observe Caesar's crossing of the Rubicon. But the people around Caesar at the time were in such a position; and their observations inform the historical record of Caesar's whereabouts and actions, according to which he crossed the Rubicon in 49 BCE. Finally, consider proposition 4, which states that there's an even number of trees on the campus of UNC–Chapel Hill. I have no idea whether this proposition is true: I've never added up all the trees on UNC's campus and I don't know of anyone who has. So I don't know whether the total number of trees amounts to an even or an odd number. Nevertheless, I *could* add up all the trees on UNC's campus, if I so desired, and assess whether or not the sum is an even number. So proposition 4, just like propositions 1–3, is *observably true or false*.

The second notable feature of statements 1–4 is that they each make a claim that is *objectively true or false*. A claim is objectively true or false when its truth or falsity is mind-independent—that is, when the matter of its truth or falsity doesn't depend on what anyone thinks about it.[1] So, for example, although I have no idea how many trees there are on UNC's campus, the fact remains that the sum of all those trees is identical to a number, and either that number is even or it is odd. The same clearly applies to propositions 1–3: my beliefs and attitudes have no impact on the freezing point of water, the distance between the earth and the sun, or Caesar's having crossed the Rubicon at some or other point in time. Thus matters of fact are observably and objectively true or false.

By contrast, matters of opinion are *subjective*. An assertion is subjective when it's not objectively true or false—that is, when it's based on personal feeling, taste, or perspective. For example:

5. Blue is the best color.
6. Celery is a delicious snack.
7. The game of baseball is enjoyable to watch.

Suppose my friend John thinks that blue is the best color, while I prefer the color green. In that case, it's a fact that *John believes* blue to be the best color; and it's a fact that *I believe* green to be the best color. But there's no fact of the matter about which color is, objectively speaking, the best color. It's strictly a matter of preference—which is to say, it's subjective. (There may, of course, be a fact of the matter about which color most people prefer; but that would be a fact about which color is most popular, which is a different matter from which color is best.) Similarly, I'm aware of people who willingly choose to eat celery because they believe it to be delicious, whereas I find it totally repugnant. And while I enjoy watching baseball, others find it boring. As with color preference, there is no objective, mind-independent truth about whether celery is delicious or baseball is enjoyable to watch. Such things depend on personal taste—they are strictly matters of opinion.[2]

The distinction between facts and opinions is a helpful one. But it's potentially problematic to suppose that *all* assertions fit into one of these two categories. Consider the following moral claims:

8.   It is wrong to lie about one's age (for the sake of personal vanity, let's say).
9.   It is wrong to lie for any reason whatsoever.
10.  It is wrong to steal.

Do propositions 8–10 express facts or opinions? Recall that matters of fact are *observably true or false*, which means that there's a procedure for settling factual disagreements—some method for observing, to the satisfaction of any rational person, the truth or falsity of the claim in question.

Suppose you claim it's wrong to steal, and I disagree. If it's a fact that it is wrong to steal, then there should be some procedure for observing the wrongness of stealing. Is there such a procedure? Imagine that we have security camera footage of someone robbing a jewelry store in the middle of the night. We watch the thief break in the front door and move from one display case to the next, shoveling watches and necklaces and diamond rings into a duffle bag. Upon viewing the footage, you shake your head and lament the wrongness of the acts we've just witnessed. In response, I say, "I just don't see it—I've got no problem with anything the thief did." What procedure might we follow in order to resolve our disagreement? Should we watch the recording over and over again, until I'm struck by the wrongness of the thief's conduct? Would the wrongness stand out to me if we watched the video in slow motion? No, of course not. Moral wrongness isn't visible in that way. There's no method for *seeing* that stealing is morally wrong. And the same goes for lying. It follows that 8–10 aren't claims about matters of fact.

Here the reader might object that "stealing is *illegal*—as is lying, at least in certain contexts. And laws are observable, which means that there is a method for settling our disagreement: consulting the law. So it's a fact that stealing is wrong." While it's certainly true that stealing is illegal, and it's true that laws are observable, the problem with this objection is that law answers to morality, not the other way around. If moral disagreements could be decided by our laws, then we wouldn't have any *moral* reason to reform laws that are immoral—such as ending slavery, conferring voting rights on those previously disenfranchised, integrating public education, and so forth. So although laws are observable and our laws prohibit stealing and certain forms of lying, it simply doesn't follow that the moral wrongness of lying or stealing is observable.[3]

Let's distill our reasoning thus far. Factual claims are observably true or false, which moral claims are not. It follows that moral claims aren't factual. So if all assertions are either fact or opinion, we must place moral claims in the category of opinion. And since matters of opinion are subjective, this means that morality is subjective: there's no objective moral truth.

If the prospect of abandoning moral objectivity seems disconcerting but manageable in the case of lying and stealing, consider moral claims like:

11.   It is wrong to commit murder.
12.   It is wrong to commit serial murder.
13.   It is wrong to commit acts of genocide.

Are these merely opinions? Is there no objective truth about the wrongness of murder, serial killing, or genocide? If all declarative statements are either *facts* or *opinions*, then this result seems unavoidable, since the wrongness of genocide is no more observable than the wrongness of stealing. The same holds for normative claims about the wrongness of racial discrimination, the institution of slavery, school segregation, or denying women the right to vote.

In broad outline, there are two ways of resisting the modern tendency to relegate moral convictions to the category of *subjective opin-*

*ion.* One is to place moral claims in the category of *verifiable fact*; the other is to reject the premise that all objective truth is empirically verifiable—and thus reject the notion that moral claims must be either a matter of *verifiable fact* or a matter of *subjective opinion.*

Many conservative evangelicals have opted for the former approach: instead of rejecting modernity's premise that all objective truth is empirically verifiable, many evangelicals have attempted to shoehorn morality into the category of verifiable fact. And in keeping with common sensism, they purport to verify their moral truth claims with Scripture, which they regard as a divinely inspired encyclopedia—an archive of ethical and other facts, certified by their provenance in the testimony of an all-knowing God. (The literature on common sensism is rife with this sentiment—see chapter 1.) Problem solved: all truth claims are empirically verifiable; and moral truth claims are verified in Scripture.

This strategy is tempting, for two reasons. First, Scripture is entirely true; and much of that truth pertains to morality. Second, apart from special revelation, it's difficult to imagine where we might go to find empirical verification of moral truth—you can't just *see* moral properties the way you can see that the freezing point of water is 32°F.

The problem with this approach is that Scripture isn't a straightforward collection of facts. The Bible isn't an encyclopedia; it is a sacred text, composed in several languages, by dozens of authors spanning many centuries, vastly disparate cultural contexts, and different literary genres. History testifies that when we ignore these complexities and engage in facile prooftexting, the hermeneutics of legitimization can be used to justify all manner of wickedness—from slavery and holy war to Jim Crow and the subjugation of women. So whose understanding of Scripture is definitive? Whose prooftexts carry the day? Do we trust the guy who says that Scripture condones chattel slavery, or the guy who says that Scripture commands us to seek justice for the oppressed? In my lifetime, the religious right's answer has been, roughly, "We'll trust whoever uses Scripture to legitimize social arrangements that make America great for me." That's moral relativism—and a particularly vicious form of relativism at that, since it pegs moral truth to the arbitrary preferences of those who enjoy privileged status within the established order.

## Political Economy

The moral relativism of the religious right is not restricted to the domain of private morality: a rejection of intrinsic value is the very essence of the political economy that has come to define American "conservatism." The term *political economy* refers to the area of overlap between economics and public morality. In chapter 2 we observed that the religious right's neoliberal economic paradigm suffers from two glaring problems: first, it fails to appreciate the morally salient difference between choices and circumstances; and second, it involves a commitment to (logically) implicit white supremacy. A distinct but related problem with the religious right's approach to economics is that it's tied into a view of political economy that is logically incoherent. Observe the following three pillars of the religious right's approach to political economy:

1. *The good prosper.* In America, if you work hard and live a morally upright life, God will provide for your material needs. It follows that if you are poor, you have failed to work hard or failed to live uprightly, or both. So the poor are responsible for their own poverty, and providing public assistance to the poor only serves to encourage laziness and immorality.

2. *God favors free markets.* The allocation of resources should be determined entirely through free enterprise and market competition. It follows that we should allow market forces to decide the value of everything, including labor and access to medical care. Some people shouldn't earn a living wage or receive medical benefits, since some people's labor just isn't worth that much.

3. *America has fallen into moral degeneracy.* America was once a great nation, enjoying military and economic supremacy abroad, and law and order at home. But, under the influence of secular humanism, our nation has fallen into moral degeneracy. America will not reclaim its former glory unless we reject secular human-

ism and return to our Judeo-Christian roots. Therefore, we should
once again have prayer and Bible reading in our public schools,
and we must defend the traditional definition of *marriage* as "one
man and one woman," etc.

Notice that according to the second tenet of this paradigm, our society should allocate resources entirely on the basis of free enterprise and market competition. Generally speaking, the free market
rewards those who are willing and able to sell something that consumers value. Importantly, the free market does not discriminate between things that consumers value and things that consumers *should
value*. Thus, in assigning rewards to those who possess things that
consumers value, the free market does not discriminate between,
for example, those who sell life-saving medicines and those who
sell pornography. So, on the free market, one can make a fortune
in the pharmaceutical hustle or selling *Hustler*. The market cares
not which.

Now, according to the third tenet of the religious right's political economy, America has fallen into moral degeneracy. Note
that moral degenerates tend to value the wrong sorts of things—
that's what makes them morally degenerate. (For example, Bob
is behaving in a morally degenerate fashion if, say, Bob pawns all
of his daughter's possessions in order to obtain money for booze
and gambling. Bob's behavior is morally degenerate because he
should value his daughter's well-being far more than he values
booze and gambling: he values booze and gambling too highly,
and his daughter's well-being not highly enough.) So, given our
nation's overall state of moral degeneracy, Americans do not tend
to value the things they *should* value; and Americans do tend to
value things they *shouldn't* value.

Market forces and moral degeneracy conspire in distressing ways.
For example, since Americans tend to value the wrong things, such
as pornography, Larry Flynt and Hugh Hefner amassed fortunes by
producing and selling pornographic materials on the free market.
Meanwhile, Americans fail to devote sufficient resources to objectively important things like education. Predictably, the net result is

that Flynt and Hefner got rich while most schoolteachers have to live on instant ramen for five years to pull together a downpayment on a modest home. Here's the takeaway: when we combine an overall state of moral degeneracy with an unregulated free market, pornographers prosper more than teachers.

Finally, recall the first tenet of the religious right's political-economic paradigm: namely, that the good prosper. It should now be clear that the free market in a morally degenerate society does *not* allocate resources in a way that is sufficiently sensitive to moral worth. It is therefore incoherent to maintain *both* that our society is morally degenerate *and* that the free market in our society rewards those who work hard and live uprightly.

### Markets, Morals, and Nihilism

As of 2019, the highest paid state employees in twenty-eight out of fifty states were college football coaches. In twelve of the remaining thirty-two states, the highest paid state employees were college basketball coaches. So in forty states, or 80 percent of all the states in the US, the highest paid state employees are college football or basketball coaches.[4] Missouri is one of those forty states. The head football coach at the University of Missouri earns an annual salary of $2.8 million. That's a big number. Just to put it in perspective, $2.8 million is about twenty-one times the salary of the governor of Missouri ($133,800) and more than fifty-two times the annual income of an average Missouri household ($53,578). In other words, it would take the governor of Missouri about twenty-one years to earn as much money as the head football coach at the University of Missouri earns in a single year, and it would take the average Missouri household over half a century.

Now consider this. Public school teachers in Missouri are eligible to retire after thirty years of service. As of 2022, the average pay for a Missouri public school teacher was just under $52,000 per year.[5] The product of $52,000 and thirty is just under $1.6 million, which is about 57 percent of $2.8 million. So, according to the labor market, an entire career of teaching in a Missouri public school is approximately 60 percent as valuable as a single year of football coaching at the University of Missouri. (It's worth noting that this situation is far from exceptional. The salary of the football coach at the University of Missouri is about 75 percent *below* the average for a football coach in the Southeastern Conference. The University of Alabama pays its football coach $8.9 million per year, which is about 165 times the average salary of a public school teacher in the state of Alabama [$54,000] and 262 times the starting salary for an Alabama state trooper [$34,000].) [6]

These features of the labor market raise a number of important questions. For instance, is the labor performed by the head football coach at the University of Missouri in a single year equal in value to the labor performed by an average Missouri household over roughly half a century? In terms of work product, is the football coach at the University of Missouri worth twenty-one governors of Missouri? Is a whole career of teaching in Missouri worth less than eight months of coaching football at the University of Missouri?

In at least one sense, the answer to all of these questions is yes: whether it's a year of coaching football or a gallon of milk, the value of something *just is* what it costs to buy that thing. This kind of value is called *market value*, since it is determined by the price that is agreed upon when buyers and sellers meet in the market to buy and sell goods or services. Thus the market value of the labor performed by a Missouri public school teacher is equal to what it costs public schools in Missouri to buy teaching services. As it happens, that cost is about $1.5 million over thirty years. And $1.5 million is 60 percent of $2.8 million, which is what it costs the University of Missouri to purchase a year of head football coaching services. So in terms of market value, an entire career of public school teaching in Missouri is about 60 percent as valuable as a single year of coaching football at the University of Missouri.

Some people think that market value is the *only* objective truth about value. They reason as follows. "We all place different values on things, based on what's important to us. For instance, some people value nothing more than living in the biggest house they can afford; so they build a place in the suburbs, furnish it with whatever Ikea and Target are selling that year, and spend the rest of their professional lives sitting in traffic for two or three hours every weekday. Others prefer a midcentury bungalow in a crowded neighborhood that's only a few miles from the office. Some people don't care all that much about their house or their job, as long as they can remain in the community where they grew up. Others care very little about where they call home, provided that they can earn a decent living doing something they find meaningful. Some people value quiet; others want vibrant nightlife. Some people have dogs, some have cats, others have both, and some people prefer to have no pets at all. No one is in a position to judge the value of these or any other of the infinitely many preferences that find expression in the different choices people make. So the only objective truth about how valuable things are is the truth about how much things cost: the only truth about the value of a given house is the truth about how much someone is willing to pay for that house; the only truth about the value of a gallon of milk is the truth about how much people pay for a gallon of milk; and the only truth about the value of a teaching career is the truth about how much teachers are paid." Let's call this view *market realism*, since it asserts that the only real truth about value is the truth about market value.[7]

Notice that if market realism is correct, then there is no such thing as value that exists independently of the value people assign to things. According to market realism, value is constituted by what people are willing to pay. It follows that people decide how valuable things are; and there is no value apart from what people decide. So if market realism is correct, then there is no such thing as *intrinsic value*. The view that there is no such thing as intrinsic value is called *nihilism*. (The word *nihilism* comes from the Latin word *nihil*, which means "nothing." Hence, *nothing-ism*—as in, the worth of a thing is nothing unless humans say otherwise.) Thus a consequence of market realism is nihilism.

This underlying commitment to nihilism explains why the market realist isn't concerned about how much more the State of Missouri values the football coach at the University of Missouri than its public school teachers. Nor is the market realist likely to worry about potential links between inadequate funding for public education and the fact that the public school system in Kansas City went three decades without full accreditation.[8] (For thirty years, in other words, the public school system in Missouri's largest city was, in the judgment of those whose job it is to evaluate such things, failing to provide its students with an adequate education. Incidentally, I'm not suggesting that inadequate funding is the sole reason why this is the case. But it's undoubtedly part of the reason.)[9] According to the market realist, all of this is as it should be: the value of things is determined by how much we pay for them. So we pay our teachers exactly what they are worth, because the worth of teachers is determined by how much we pay them. The same goes for college football coaches, entire school districts, children's healthcare, professional sports arenas, roads, bridges, and so on.

I agree with the market realist that what we are willing to pay for something reveals how much we value that thing. No matter what we *say* we value, and no matter what we *think* we value, we direct our resources to that which we *actually* value.[10] Consumers demonstrate what they value as individuals in the way they spend their personal resources (e.g., spending on clothes or travel, investing in hobbies, donating to charity, saving for retirement, or what have you). And our political community demonstrates what we value as a society in the ways we use our collective resources (e.g., spending on law enforcement, national defense, public education, infrastructure, healthcare subsidies, and so forth).

I also agree with the market realist that, as far as it concerns *most* things, value is determined by the market: objectively speaking, things like cars, toasters, T-shirts, houses, couches, and college football coaching services are just as valuable as the price they command. But I disagree with the market realist's nihilism. In my view, *some* things have value independently of whether or how much we value them. In particular, I believe that all human beings are intrinsically valuable. So, in my view, it's not up to us to decide the value of certain things that are essential to human flourishing—like access to basic education, nourishment, or healthcare. As a political community, we are free to decide how valuable we *think* these things are; and what we decide will be reflected in the resources we devote to educating our children and caring for those who are sick. But we aren't free to decide how valuable those things *actually* are. So my disagreement with the market realist amounts to this. Since I'm not a nihilist, I think it's possible for the members of our political community to be mistaken about the value of things like public education and access to healthcare.

## Methodological Individualism

The evangelical culture war machine is heavily invested in the notion that morality is reducible to individual conduct—and thus that the systemic moral questions I just raised concerning the allocation of resources in our society are not, in fact, moral questions. We'll call this approach to ethics *methodological individualism*, since it involves a method of moral analysis that assumes that individual conduct is all that matters. In the power centers of conservative evangelicalism, Christians who raise concerns about systemic injustice—for example, systemic racism or economic oppression—are often dismissed as false teachers or theological liberals who don't take the Bible seriously.[11]

A further complication is that many conservative evangelicals in the last few years have come to conflate all concerns about systemic injustice with critical race theory (CRT). This is a mistake. One needn't endorse CRT—or care anything about CRT, really—in order to be concerned about systemic justice. CRT is just one among many academic approaches that deals with questions about systemic justice. And it is hardly the first or the most influential. For example, roughly 2,500 years before the inception of CRT, Plato discussed systemic justice in his *Republic* and *Laws*. A millennium before Plato, God inspired Moses to establish a legal system animated by God's hatred of institutional oppression. And God commanded his people to cherish and keep these laws in remembrance of their liberation from Egyptian oppression.

Systemic injustice is second only to idolatry among the occasions for God's wrath in the Hebrew Bible. And more often than not, when idolatry is at issue, the idols in question are implicated in efforts to secure wealth or power by participating in an oppressive system. So it's important to understand that a commitment to systemic justice in general, or racial justice in particular, isn't the same thing as fondness for CRT. The former is a foundational moral imperative for all who fear God, whatever one thinks of the latter. Yet the methodological individualists in conservative evangelicalism insist on conflating the two. We might assume, charitably, that this confusion derives from ignorance—of which the intellectual class of the religious right displays much, and with remarkable boldness. But the persisting myth that we should regard those who demand systemic justice as false teachers or theological liberals is more than mere error: it presents a false image of who God is and what God requires of us.

According to Scripture, false teachers dwell in the political or religious establishment, and they misrepresent God to the people of God in order to fortify their own position of power or influence. False teachers lie about God for their own personal gain.[12] So, in the logic of Christian theology, it doesn't even make sense to say that those who demand systemic justice *on behalf of others* are false teachers. Demanding justice for others isn't what false teachers do: Scripture provides not a single example of a false prophet demanding justice for the oppressed. By contrast, Scripture provides many examples of God's prophets decrying the political or religious establishment for perpetuating systemic injustice.

## Two Views of Justice

The term *justice* describes a family of related ideas. In its narrowest sense, justice is a quality of individual conduct: I behave justly when I accurately report and pay all the taxes owed on my earnings from the previous fiscal year, or when I return my shopping cart to a designated shopping-cart-return area in the grocery store parking lot. And I behave *unjustly* when I deceive my golfing companions about the number of putts I took on the eighth green, or when I decide not to inform my waiter that he omitted the extra side of French fries from my dinner bill. Thus, at the level of my own conduct, justice is achieved when I give all that I owe and take nothing beyond what I am owed.

In political contexts, justice describes a feature of institutions. An *institution* is basically a system of rules about who deserves what: who deserves what honor; who deserves what paycheck; who deserves this authority; who is entitled to that opportunity; who is allowed to do this or to say that, and so on. In other words, an institution is a set of norms or traditions that guide our understanding of what constitutes justice within a given sphere. Examples of institutions include the United States, families, contracts, the State of Missouri, Major League Baseball, the game of baseball, the US Senate, Christmas, the Constitution, and so forth.

Conflicts arise when an institution's rules are violated—when a spouse engages in an extramarital affair, when a Major League Baseball player uses a banned substance, when a building contractor fails to complete a project by an agreed-upon date. Some conflicts that arise within a given institution cannot be resolved inside the boundaries of the institution itself—when there is disagreement about how assets should be divided following a divorce, or when one firm sues another for breach of contract. On such occasions, an appeal is made to a higher institution that has sovereign rules for deciding what justice requires. We call this higher institution a court. The rules that guide the decisions of our courts are laws; and our laws are sovereign insofar as there are no rules or institutions above our laws within our political community.

Our courts also decide what justice demands in response to criminal conduct like fraud, burglary, or murder—conduct so unjust that it is prohibited in all contexts, without regard to an individual's status or institutional affiliation.[13] So our laws, as administered by our courts, are sovereign over all disputes about what is just, who is guilty of injustice, and what justice demands by way of compensation or punishment.[14] These laws are authored by elected officials in Congress; and enforcement of the law is supervised by elected officials in the executive branch of government. So justice in our society is administered by a network of public institutions that are subject, ultimately, to the will of the electorate. When I speak of institutional justice, I am referring to justice at the level of these public or political institutions.

Here we confront an ancient question that is central to politics: What does it mean for our political institutions to administer justice?[15] Put another way: What does it mean to say that a law passed by Congress is *a just law*? Here's one answer. "Since laws establish the rules about what is just, and Congress determines the law, it follows that Congress determines what is just. So a law passed by Congress is just by virtue of the fact that *what is just* is determined by the laws that Congress passes." In this view, justice is whatever our political institutions deem it to be. Apart from the law, in other words, there is no objective truth about what justice is. We will call this view *political realism*, since it holds that the only real truth about justice is political power.[16]

I disagree with political realism. In my view, there *is* objective truth about what people deserve and what we owe each other; and it is only by conforming to that objective truth that our laws achieve justice. We'll call this view *moral realism*, since it holds that moral truth is (or should be) the foundation of our politics.

I have two sets of reasons for affirming moral realism. One set of reasons is theological: Scripture expresses pointed views about what justice is and offers us a paradigm for political institutions that conform to the truth about justice. Since I affirm the truth of Scripture, I believe there is objective truth about what is just. And I believe this truth should be reflected in our own political institutions.

I also have philosophical reasons for believing that there is objective truth about justice—reasons that I believe appeal to everyone, not merely those who affirm the truth of Scripture. Here's a concrete example. In 1919, our political institutions didn't allow women to vote in federal elections. That was the law. So if justice were defined by our laws, then it wouldn't have made any sense to claim, in 1919, that it is unjust to deny voting rights to women. But it *did* make sense. Proponents of universal suffrage said, "Look, contrary to what the law says, women deserve to have an official voice in how our political community is governed—justice demands that women be allowed to vote. Our laws are denying women that right. So the law should be changed, in order to give women this thing that they are due." Moreover, I don't think the truth about *justice* changed between 1919 and 1920, when our political institutions finally recognized women's right to vote. Rather, I think justice was the same in 1920 as it was in 1919. By recognizing women's right to vote in 1920, our political institutions *became more just* than they were in 1919. Similarly, I don't believe that the truth about justice changed in 1954 when the Supreme Court outlawed segregation in our public schools. Rather, it is objectively true that segregation is unjust. In 1954, the Supreme Court's ruling in *Brown v. Board of Education* altered our political institutions to reflect that truth.

Because our political institutions answer to an electorate, advances like desegregation and women's suffrage are the product of negotiations about what is just. We all enter the political arena with concerns about what we are owed, and we defend our interests according to our vision of what justice demands. These negotiations are the point of contact between political institutions and every Christ follower's sacred calling to seek justice. When we, as Christians, enter into the political arena where rights are negotiated, we are called to use our influence to advocate for the rights of those who have no other advocate. *We are not called* to seek wealthy and powerful political allies who will help us defend our rights. God is our defender. And God calls us to defend the rights of orphans, widows, immigrants, and all who are poor and oppressed. There's nothing inherently wrong with being wealthy or having powerful friends. But we dishonor our calling and misrepresent Christ to the world when we advocate for political institutions that serve the interests of wealth and power *at the expense of the poor*, and then dispense charity as though it were a substitute for justice.

## Two Paradigms of Political Engagement

The purpose of government is to enforce the rule of law, and the purpose of politics is to decide how we are to be governed—and by extension, what our laws will be. There are two distinct views of what our political efforts should aim to achieve, each based on a different conception of what justice is. We've just noted that according to political realism, justice is determined by the law. In this view, there's no objective standard for what people deserve and what we owe each other. Thus, when Congress passes a law, Congress thereby decides what justice is. In this view, the aim of politics is to achieve laws and public policies that define *justice* in ways that accord with our own interests (or what we take to be our interests). We'll call this the *special-interest paradigm* of political engagement, since its object is to secure a special set of interests—namely, our own.

According to the view of justice that we're calling *moral realism*, there is objective truth about what people deserve and what we owe each other—which is to say, there's objective truth about justice. So a law passed by Congress is just only if, and only insofar as, that law conforms to the objective truth about justice. In this view, when we engage in politics, our aim should be to bring our laws and policies into conformity with the truth about what people deserve and what we owe each other. We'll call this the *justice-oriented paradigm* of political engagement, since it aims to establish laws and public policies that give everyone their due.

We should dwell for a moment on the affinity between these respective views of justice and the political paradigms corresponding to each. The special-interest paradigm is attractive to the political realist because he doesn't recognize any objective standard that our laws or public policies might fail to meet. In the absence of such a standard, the only guide to political engagement is self-interest; and the only reason to make concessions to competing interests would be enlightened self-interest. (So, for example, the political realist might capitulate to others' demands for recognition of their civil rights, but only in the interest of avoiding the social and economic turmoil associated with civic unrest.) Of course, if it's rhetorically convenient, the political realist might frame their position in terms of progress toward justice—but they don't actually *believe* in progress toward an objective standard of justice, since they don't believe that any such standard exists. By contrast, the moral realist believes that there is objective truth about what people are due. So their principal ambition in the political sphere must be the realization of laws and public policies that conform to the truth about justice. And since the special-interest paradigm favors laws and policies that further one's own interests, it would be inconsistent for the moral realist to adopt a special-interest approach to politics.

As documented throughout this book, the rhetoric of American evangelicals has openly embraced the special-interest paradigm of political engagement for at least fifty years—arguing, in effect, that the interests of white Christians should take priority over claims of other interest groups.[17] Consider, for example, Rod Dreher's testimony that "we all seem to be barreling towards a future that is not liberal and democratic but is going to be either left illiberalism, or right illiberalism. If that's true, then I know which side I'm on: the side that isn't going to persecute me and my people."[18] This is a classic example of a special-interest approach to politics, rooted in political realism. There's no mention of justice, or what people deserve, or what human beings owe one another. This outlook is totally incompatible with moral realism, and it is therefore an approach to political engagement that is unbefitting anyone who claims to have moral roots in the Christian tradition.

## Conclusion

On some level, the antidote to Christo-authoritarianism lies in the recognition that there is objective truth about what people deserve and what we owe each other, and our participation in politics should aim to bring about public institutions that conform to that truth. Notably, the matter of whether a given social arrangement suits my personal preferences or aligns with my self-interest is largely irrelevant. So we can resist the forces of ideology and motivated reasoning by actively interrogating the legitimacy of social arrangements that work to our own benefit, which is precisely what Christ calls us to do. When we are no longer concerned with legitimizing the established

order, we are free to abandon theological narratives that the religious
right uses to legitimize that order—along with any antagonism toward expertise that poses a threat to those theological narratives.
Thus the antidote to Christo-authoritarianism is the pursuit of justice
over and against the pursuit of social arrangements that reinforce my
own power and privilege.

# Acknowledgments

For better or for worse, my mom and dad are the people most responsible for my inclination toward philosophical inquiry. In countless conversations, dating back to my earliest memories, my mother and father have consistently nurtured my intellectual pursuits, invited thoughtful dissent, and encouraged disdain for institutional hypocrisy and abuse. I'm grateful to my parents for imparting the conviction that freedom is found in fearing God—which is to say, fearing God rather than human beings. Above all, I'm grateful to my mom and dad for their unconditional love and support. This book is the fruit of my own reflections on what it means to practice the moral and intellectual precepts I inherited from them. And although they may disagree with some of the conclusions I reach in this book, I know they will be proud of me for having written it anyway. I would also like to thank my sister, Caitlin, for her generous offer to publish a favorable Amazon review of this book.

I'm grateful to my friends and colleagues at Mount St. Mary's University for their encouragement and support throughout the writing of this book. Jack Dudley's insights have been especially helpful, both in conversation and in the seminar on theory that I had the pleasure of coteaching with him. The project has also benefited from Josh Hochschild's input, both in comments on early drafts and in many casual conversations I enjoyed when our offices were across the hall from one another—an arrangement I would not willingly have abandoned for anything less than the physical space and access to natural light afforded by my present accommodations.

Many conversations with my friend Ruben Rosario have shaped my understanding of race, gender, and social justice—and, by extension, several of the arguments presented in the pages that follow. I'm thankful for his leadership, his powers of perception, and his considerable gifts as a teacher.

My views on political economy, theory, and Christian ethics have benefited enormously from conversations with Matthew Arbo over the last couple of decades. Any deficiencies in these features of my account I blame on the fact that we don't talk as often as we should. I'm grateful for his friendship and his counsel.

I'd like to express my gratitude to the dozen or so faculty and administrators at various SBC seminaries who have offered personal encouragement, perspective on institutional dynamics, and insightful comments throughout the process of researching and writing this book. My reasons for omitting individual names from this acknowledgment are, if not immediately apparent to the reader, likely to come into sharp focus over the course of the book.

I'm grateful for the students it has been my good fortune to teach over the last fifteen years—first as a graduate instructor at Purdue University, and more recently as a member of the philosophy faculty at Mount St. Mary's. Many of the arguments in this book have been refined over years of conversation with students, in response to thoughtful objections and questions. I appreciate their patience with me as I've worked through these ideas. Apart from their contributions to my research, I'm also deeply grateful to my students for making my occupation as a teacher so enjoyable.

I'm grateful to a number of friends and family members for their interest in this project as it was in process. Their enthusiasm has been an encouragement, and the final product has been improved by their thoughtful questions, comments, and support. Some friends who stand out in this regard are Jonathan and Shannon, Scott and Christine, Brad and Haley, Mathew and Gina, Joe and Judy, Anton and Taylore, Garret and Christy, Brian and Amy, Roger G., Jeff P., Jessie H., Elana H., Chaquita M., Madeline B., and Ashley C. My uncle Dave was kind enough to read an early draft of the project and offer helpful feedback that improved subsequent drafts. My in-laws, Pastor and Mrs. Zetts, have been equally gracious in their support. I'd like to thank Mr. Zetts for lending me his copies of Boice's commentary on Genesis. He and my brother-in-law, Daniel, have offered thoughtful comments on a number of my arguments, for which I am grateful.

For reasons that are between me and my therapist, I began my undergraduate career at Liberty University. It was there that I attended my first philosophy class, taught by David Beck, and it was in the very first meeting of my first philosophy class that I decided to pursue the study of philosophy as a vocation. I'm grateful for this introduction to the perennial questions that have shaped my intellectual life and for the handful of lifelong friendships I forged in the philosophy department there. Nevertheless, due to the prevailing enthusiasm on Liberty's campus for an ideology now called "white Christian nationalism," after a couple of semesters I resolved to complete my undergraduate career elsewhere.

I applied to the University of North Carolina–Chapel Hill as a transfer student, and, for reasons I still don't understand, my application was accepted. Two professors at UNC were particularly generous to me. One was my thesis advisor, William G. Lycan, who observed that my writing "lacks the kind of ambiguity that one hopes for when one is slightly wrong"—a backhanded compliment so exquisite that it haunts me to this day. The other is Gregory Flaxman, whose teaching style was formative in shaping my own approach to the classroom. He also took the time to impress upon me the difference between conservative beliefs and the conservative cast of mind. The former involves social and intellectual commitments that are amenable to revision based on arguments or evidence; the latter involves militant resistance to arguments or evidence that threaten one's social and intellectual commitments. What stands out to me is the fact that Dr. Flaxman knew I held any number of illiberal views that (I strongly suspect) he found ethically and intellectually indefensible. But instead of dismissing me as a fascist, he evaluated my ideas and then explained to me (in so many words) why I wasn't a fascist. According to much of the religious right's rhetoric, college professors like this don't exist—and they certainly don't teach in places like Chapel Hill.

One of this book's subplots is the story of how the ideology of the religious right has obscured the Bible's emphases on justice and the moral salience of institutions. I became attuned to these biblical themes as a graduate student in systematic theology at the University of Notre Dame. My courses with Cyril O'Regan, Gary Anderson, Tzvi Novick, and Bradley Malkovsky were especially formative.

I owe a great deal to Paul Draper, my friend and mentor in the Department of Philosophy at Purdue University. I'm grateful to Paul for demanding that I express myself in language resembling English prose. Lamenting a particularly unreadable draft early in the dissertation process, Paul protested that "I've seen you teach! I wish you would just write like you teach!" This is one of the more meaningful compliments I've ever received as a teacher and the best advice I've ever received as a writer. I'm also grateful to Michael Bergmann for his generous contributions as a member of my dissertation committee. And I'm thankful to Dan Smith for his friendship, his insights on evangelical theology and ideology, and his brilliant seminars on Deleuze and the ethics of immanence.

The argument of this book is predicated on the understanding that strictly normative accounts of ethics, epistemology, and theology are inadequate for addressing American evangelicalism's moral and intellectual infirmities. In my case, this understanding was occasioned by the scholarship of Kristin Du Mez, Jemar Tisby, Beth Allison Barr, Anthea Butler, Andrew Whitehead, Samuel Perry, Philip Gorski, Sheila Gregoire, Gerardo Martí, Kevin Kruse, Aimee Byrd, Brian Sears, Robert P. Jones, Jesse Curtis, Jessica Johnson, Katherine Stewart, Julie Ingersoll, J. Russell Hawkins, Molly Worthen, Katherine Wellman, and Frances FitzGerald. Before encountering this body of work, I may have been tempted to suppose that white evangelicalism's moral and political degeneracy were simply a by-product of intellectual bankruptcy: corrupt practices engendered by corrupt thinking. I now understand that this picture is incomplete.

What these scholars have helped me see is that certain modes of corrupt thinking are equally a result of efforts to defend the legitimacy of corrupt practices. So, while it's true that corrupt thinking engenders corrupt practices, it's just as important to recognize that corrupt practices engender corrupt thinking. We cannot fully account for one set of problems or the other without explaining both. What follows is my attempt to offer such an explanation.

The arguments to follow are also informed by the work of scholars whose research focuses on distinct but related questions concerning ideology, propaganda, race, religion, gender, history, and US politics. These include Jason Stanley, Ian Hancy López, Robin Corey, Richard Rothstein, Garry Wills, Daniel Ziblatt, Steven Levitsky, Paul Pierson, Jacob S. Hacker, Rick Perlstein, Mark Noll, George M. Marsden, and Vanessa Williamson. And I am deeply indebted to the meticulous work of several historians of creationism and creation science—the late Ronald Numbers, David E. Long, Adam Laats, Benjamin J. Huskinson, and Christopher P. Toumey. Julie Ingersoll's analysis of creation science in *Building God's Kingdom* is also indispensable.

I'm grateful to several other scholars and friends who have shared generously from their experience and expertise in ways that have sharpened my understanding of power dynamics within white evangelical ideology and institutions. These include Trey Ferguson, John Onwuchekwa, Sam Won, Pastor Dwight McKissic, Pastor Ken Fentress, Susan Codone, Brynn Tannehill, Danté Stewart, Mark Satta, Matt Martens, Aaron Griffith, Stephen L. Young, Bradly Mason, Taylor Schumann, Charis Granger-Mbugua, Rachel Joy Welcher, Marty Duren, Todd Littleton, Russ Meek, Scott Camp, and Robert Downen.

Working with the folks at Eerdmans has been an absolute delight. Their enthusiasm for the project and commitment to excellence have been an inspiration. I'm grateful to Andrew, my acquisitions editor, for guiding the project from proposal to completed manuscript. I'd like to thank my copyeditor, Victoria, for thoughtful improvements to the manuscript that enhanced clarity, consistency, and readability. And I'm grateful to Jenny, my project editor, for guiding the project from completed manuscript to publication.

Finally, I'd like to acknowledge incalculable contributions to this project from my spouse, Melissa, to whom this book is dedicated and without whom it would not exist. I have no idea what path my vocation would have followed without the benefit of her discernment and general intolerance for idle theorizing. But I'm certain it would have been less interesting and enriching than our journey together. I should also mention that large sections of this book are filled with subtexts and turns of phrase designed principally to make Melissa laugh out loud.

# Notes

*Introduction*

1. Robert P. Jones et al., "Competing Visions of America: An Evolving Identity or a Culture under Attack? Findings from the 2021 American Values Survey," Public Religion Research Institute, November 1, 2021, https://tinyurl.com/3ryb276r.

2. Cary Funk and Becka A. Alper, "Religion and Science," Pew Research Center, October 22, 2015, https://tinyurl.com/bddfmk3v.

3. I'll use the term *slavery* to describe race-based chattel slavery—i.e., slavery as practiced in the United States prior to 1865. Thus nothing I say about slavery pertains to, e.g., the system of indentured servitude as described in the Pentateuch.

4. Consistent with the practice that Jemar Tisby commends in *How to Fight Racism*, and following his rationale, I'll use the word *Black* in reference to "the people group descended of people from Africa. This is because naming is a political act, a demonstration of power. For generations, Black people have been denied the power of naming themselves, of self-identifying according to their history, heritage, and personality. Capitalizing the *B* in *Black* is an act of reclamation and dignity. *Black* also refers to a racial and ethnic group, and capitalizing it coheres with other capitalization standards as in *Native American* or *Asian*. Finally, *Black* is the preferred term over *African American* because *Black* is inclusive of all people in the African diaspora regardless of their affiliation with the United States and connotes the global phenomenon of anti-Black racism." *How to Fight Racism: Courageous*

*Christianity and the Journey toward Racial Justice* (Grand Rapids: Zondervan, 2021), 1.

5. See Jemar Tisby, *The Color of Compromise: The Truth about the American Church's Complicity in Racism* (Grand Rapids: Zondervan, 2019), 76–80.

6. This list of prooftexts is gathered from Mark A. Noll, *The Civil War as a Theological Crisis* (Chapel Hill: University of North Carolina Press, 2006), 33–35.

7. Alexander McLeod (1774–1833), a Presbyterian minister in New York City, wrote, "In order to justify Negro slavery from this prophecy [in Genesis 9], it will be necessary to prove four things. (1) That all posterity of Canaan were to suffer slavery. (2) That African Negroes are really descended of Canaan. (3) That each of the descendants of Shem and Japheth has a moral right to reduce any of them to servitude. (4) That every slaveholder is really descended from Shem or Japheth. Want of proof in any of these particulars will invalidate the whole objection. In a practice so contrary to the general principles of the divine law, a very express grant from the supreme authority is the only sanction to us. But not one of the four facts specified as necessary can be supported with unquestionable documents." Quoted in Wongi Park, "The Blessing of Whiteness in the Curse of Ham: Reading Gen 9:18–29 in the Antebellum South," *Religions*, October 25, 2021.

8. Iveson L. Brookes, *A Defence of the South Against the Reproaches and Incroachments of the North: In Which Slavery is Shown to be an Institution of God Intended to Form the Basis of the Best Social State and the Only Safeguard to the Permanence of a Republican Government* (Hamburg, SC: The Republican Office, 1850), 8–9.

9. Robert L. Dabney, *A Defence of Virginia and Through Her, of the South, in Recent and Pending Contests Against the Sectional Party* (New York: E. J. Hale & Son, 1867), 102.

10. Southern Baptist Theological Seminary, "Report on Slavery and Racism in the History of the Southern Baptist Theological Seminary," December 12, 2018, https://tinyurl.com/6k24y5wy.

11. Three clarifying notes. First, I'm not asserting bad faith on the part of evangelicals who used biblical prooftexts to legitimize slavery in the antebellum South. Nor will I allege bad faith on the part of modern evangelicals who use theology to justify contemporary social arrangements that are unjust. No doubt some such appeals are disingenuous, but that's not my immediate concern. On the contrary, my purpose in tracing the contours of white supremacy in the antebellum South is to expose the conditions that make it possible for evangelicals to sincerely embrace theological narratives that legitimize regressive social practices and anti-intellectual habits of mind. Second, I hasten to add that I don't mean to suggest that white evangelicals raised in the antebellum South weren't morally culpable for defending or participat-

ing in the institution of slavery. As I'll argue, the practice of Christian faith requires us to place the interests of others—particularly the marginalized—before our own. Thus the failure of antebellum southerners to interrogate an established order that so clearly failed to contemplate the humanity of enslaved persons is inexcusable, especially for those who claimed to follow the teachings of Christ. And third, having cited the Southern Baptist Theological Seminary's account of its own involvement in defending slavery and racism, I should note the following. In addition to their guilt in perpetuating racism and slavery, *theologians and clergy* who furnished biblical justifications for slavery were also guilty of rank exegetical and homiletical malpractice. So I find it alarming that an evangelical seminary in the twenty-first century would insist that its current mission is sufficiently aligned with the vision of its founders all of whom stridently maintained biblical sanction for white supremacy and slavery—that the names of those founders should adorn its buildings and colleges. I find it incredible that an institution that exists to train pastors and advance theological understanding would celebrate its association with theologians and ministers who were so incompetent that they sincerely believed race-based chattel slavery to be justified in light of Genesis 9—or so corrupt that they proffered their arguments disingenuously.

12. For John MacArthur's remarkable take on why Jesus doesn't really intend for his followers to "do likewise," see John MacArthur, "The Good Samaritan," Grace to You, September 14, 2003, https://tinyurl.com/3fadxrub.

13. Given the way that many evangelical institutions function, those who occupy positions of practical authority also exercise authority over biblical interpretation. So practical authority and interpretive authority form a feedback loop in which interpretive authority is wielded to legitimize practical authority, which reinforces interpretive authority, and so on. Thus the prevailing order within evangelical institutions tends to remain the prevailing order.

14. National Association of Evangelicals, "What Is an Evangelical?," https://tinyurl.com/49x6t97y.

15. Kristin Kobes Du Mez, *Jesus and John Wayne* (New York: Liveright, 2020); Tisby, *The Color of Compromise*; Andrew L. Whitehead and Samuel L. Perry, *Taking America Back for God: Christian Nationalism in the United States* (New York: Oxford University Press, 2020); Philip S. Gorski and Samuel L. Perry, *The Flag and the Cross: White Christian Nationalism and the Threat to American Democracy* (New York: Oxford University Press, 2022).

16. Three further notes about why I'm not concerned to provide a precise definition of *evangelical*. First, in the case of marginal beliefs or practices, it might be important to give *evangelical* a precise definition. I intend to pull from *prevalent* beliefs and practices—i.e., beliefs and practices about which there is no controversy on the subject of whether those beliefs and practices

are common among evangelicals (regardless of how the term is defined). Second, my analysis doesn't stand or fall on the matter of whether everyone who counts as an evangelical endorses every single aspect of the religious right's ideology: being enmeshed in an ideology isn't like embracing a conspiracy theory, in the sense that one needn't affirm each and every element of a given ideology in order to fall under its sway. Third, according to Michele F. Margolis, *From Politics to the Pews: How Partisanship and the Political Environment Shape Religious Identity*, Chicago Studies in American Politics (Chicago: University of Chicago Press, 2018), 11, the moral and political conservatism of a given evangelical Christian correlates more strongly to the theological conservatism of her congregation (or religious group) than to her own theological convictions. For example, if young-earth creationism is the prevailing view among the members of my church, then I'm likely to embrace the political commitments that flow from young-earth creationism even if I do not personally affirm young-earth creationism (cf. Kenneth D. Wald, Dennis E. Owen, and Samuel S. Hill Jr., "Churches as Political Communities," *American Political Science Review* 82, no. 2 [June 1988]: 531–48). So what matters for my purposes isn't whether this or that evangelical endorses young-earth creationism, or whether evangelicals themselves regard creationism as a central tenet of evangelicalism. What matters is that a majority of evangelicals endorse young-earth creationism, which has an impact on the moral and political conservatism of evangelicals more broadly—beyond, i.e., just those who personally affirm young-earth creationism.

17. For example, the Southern Baptist Convention, the Presbyterian Church in America, the Southern Baptist Theological Seminary, Reformed Theological Seminary, the Acts 29 church-planting network, Desiring God ministries, and the Gospel Coalition are all evangelical institutions with an established record of theological positions taken on various matters of social or political concern. We might say that areas of general overlap in those positions among organizations like these represent prevailing evangelical norms.

18. For the record: unless I explicitly indicate otherwise, nothing in my account should be taken as a comment on the theology or politics of individuals or institutions affiliated with Roman Catholic, Eastern Orthodox, or mainline Protestant traditions.

19. Jason Stanley, *How Fascism Works: The Politics of Us and Them* (New York: Random House, 2018), 6. Arguably, these conditions are jointly sufficient for Christo-authoritarianism to constitute a form of fascism in particular. Some scholars argue that fascism, properly so-called, requires the prevalence of certain economic conditions that engender anxieties about downward mobility. Though I think the case could be made that these conditions do, in fact, hold true as of this writing, I wish to avoid those complications. So I'm content to make the weaker, more general claim that Amer-

ican evangelicals are under the sway of Christo-authoritarianism. But since fascism is a species of authoritarianism, my account is entirely consistent with the claim that what I'm calling Christo-authoritarianism is in fact a form of fascism.

20. Ronald L. Numbers, *The Creationists: From Scientific Creationism to Intelligent Design*, expanded ed. (Cambridge, MA: Harvard University Press, 2006), 1.

21. Pew Research Center, "Evolution and Perceptions of Scientific Consensus," *Americans, Politics and Science Issues*, July 1, 2014, chap. 4, https://tinyurl.com/2yam8sbu.

22. John MacArthur, "History in the New World," Grace to You, July 1, 2001, https://tinyurl.com/57eyx52z; John MacArthur, "If Adam and Eve Were the First Two People, How Did We Get So Many Races?," September 26, 2010, https://tinyurl.com/343vmcuf.

23. Whitehead and Perry, *Taking America Back*, 16.

*Chapter 1*

1. Historians seem to agree that (1) the commonsense realism of the Scottish Enlightenment had an important and lasting impact on Protestant evangelical theology in the United States (though the exact nature of said impact is contested); and (2) evangelical Protestants adapted commonsense realism in important ways (though the exact nature of these adaptations is a matter of debate). So note that I use the term *common sensism* to describe the relevant disjunction of American adaptations of commonsense realism. The relationship between (American) common sensism and (Scottish) commonsense realism is, for the purposes of my argument, irrelevant (except insofar as that relationship is relevant to the substance of common sensism).

2. George M. Marsden, *Fundamentalism and American Culture* (New York: Oxford University Press, 2022), 16.

3. Marsden, *Fundamentalism and American Culture*, 15.

4. Mark Noll, "Common Sense Traditions and American Evangelical Thought," *American Quarterly* 37, no. 2 (1985): 221.

5. For now we can safely ignore the complicated relationship between common sensism and empirical science.

6. Regarding background assumptions: it's not uncommon for prominent Southern Baptist or Presbyterian ministers or seminary faculty to cite white supremacist theologians in support of some theological principle or point of biblical interpretation. It's impossible to overstate the degree to which the theological background assumptions of many contemporary evangel-

icals overlap with the views of theologians who used the Bible to defend American slavery.

7. Tom Strode, "Southern Baptists Transformed as U.S. Grappled with Roe v. Wade," *Baptist Press*, January 22, 2003, https://tinyurl.com/mr4xetxj. In case the reader is inclined to think that this is a symptom of the SBC's "liberalism" in the era preceding the conservative resurgence, note that no less than W. A. Criswell favored legal access to abortion in the 1970s. See Randall Balmer, *Thy Kingdom Come: How the Religious Right Distorts the Faith and Threatens America* (New York: Basic Books, 2006), 12; Frances FitzGerald, *The Evangelicals: The Struggle to Shape America* (New York: Simon & Schuster, 2017), 255–56.

8. Jonathan Haidt, *The Righteous Mind: Why Good People Are Divided by Politics and Religion* (New York: Pantheon Books, 2012), 15–27. My reason for omitting some examples that Haidt cites here is that the omitted examples are obviously cases in which apparent moral disagreement derives from factual disagreement (e.g., Indian and American respondents disagreed on the moral value of a widow eating fish, due to divergent beliefs about the effects of eating fish on romantic appetites and the permissibility of pursuing romantic attachments subsequent to the death of one's spouse). Ethicists regard such cases as something other than genuine moral disagreement, since it's possible that the disagreement would dissolve in the event that everyone agreed on all the morally salient facts.

9. Moreover, examples of moral disagreement multiply once we begin looking across time *and* culture. For instance, women were prohibited from operating motor vehicles in Saudi Arabia until 2018 (and Saudi "guardianship" laws still require women to secure the consent of a male family member to carry out basic tasks). South Africa officially repealed the apartheid regime in 1991 and first held an election that permitted people of all races to run for public office in 1994. Informal surveys of my college students (at two universities over roughly ten years) suggest that most Americans roughly my age and younger regard these legal regimes as morally unacceptable.

10. This isn't to say that morality can't be both objective and *sensitive* to social context—e.g., inviolable moral principles that might be articulated very differently across disparate social contexts.

11. For the record—and contrary to the caricature of philosophy circulating in some evangelical circles—most philosophers regard moral relativism as wildly implausible.

12. A variant of this reply would be the claim that Christians have "redeemed reason," while unbelievers do not. But this doesn't solve the problem: the prevalence of moral disagreement even among Christians of the same denomination suggests that someone is mistaken.

13. In fact, it's easy to imagine some evangelicals claiming that moral

disagreement is to be expected—especially moral disagreement between believers and unbelievers, respectively. They might argue that our moral perception is corrupted by the fall, and that some part of sanctification involves repairing the believer's moral cognition (perhaps through spiritual practices such as prayer, Scripture reading, and church attendance).

14. Noll, "Common Sense Traditions," 224–25.

15. Noll, "Common Sense Traditions," 225.

16. Word of Life, *Segregation or Integration: Which?* (pamphlet), 1958, quoted in Kathryn Legg, "Equal in His Sight: An Examination of the Evolving Opinions on Race in the Life of Jerry Falwell, Sr." (senior honors thesis, Liberty University, 2019), 11. See also Katherine Stewart, *The Power Worshippers: Inside the Dangerous Rise of Religious Nationalism* (New York: Bloomsbury, 2022), 60; FitzGerald, *The Evangelicals*, 284–85.

17. Thomas Road Baptist Church, *Ministers and Marches* (pamphlet), 1965, quoted in Legg, "Equal in His Sight," 12; FitzGerald, *The Evangelicals*, 285.

18. Quoted in Legg, "Equal in His Sight," 13. See also Balmer, *Thy Kingdom Come*, 17; FitzGerald, *The Evangelicals*, 285–87.

19. Quoted in Legg, "Equal in His Sight," 14.

20. Quoted in Legg, "Equal in His Sight," 22. See also FitzGerald, *The Evangelicals*, 285–87.

21. Quoted in Legg, "Equal in His Sight," 15–16.

22. Jerry Falwell, *Listen, America!* (Garden City, NY: Doubleday, 1980), 221.

23. FitzGerald, *The Evangelicals*, 300.

24. Randall Balmer, "The Religious Right and the Abortion Myth," *Politico*, May 10, 2022, https://tinyurl.com/mrynr2ut.

25. "A Protestant Affirmation on the Control of Human Reproduction," originally published in *Christianity Today* (November 1968) and reprinted in the *Journal of the American Scientific Affiliation*, June 1970, 46–47.

26. Note that that account of moral intuitions doesn't apply to moral beliefs more generally—only to those moral beliefs that arise from what common sensism regards as the direct perception of moral truth (i.e., prereflective, noninferential belief states arising from direct observation).

27. Some of complementarianism's defenders characterize the association of complementarianism with patriarchy as a straw man. But in the spring 2012 issue of the *Journal for Biblical Manhood and Womanhood*, a former president of the Council on Biblical Manhood and Womanhood states that what used to be called patriarchy is now called complementarianism. So, in the view of at least one strident complementarian, patriarchy and complementarianism are two different names for the same set of views. See also Kevin DeYoung, "Death to Patriarchy?," Desiring God, July 19, 2022, https://tinyurl.com/ybwxw7ea.

28. Two notes. First, in case it isn't obvious, nothing in my argument applies to Roman Catholic teaching on complementarianism, which is quite different from that of evangelical Protestants. Second, a standard (evangelical Protestant) complementarian disclaimer is that according to their view, men and women are *ontologically* equal, despite their having been assigned very different roles in this life (or for all eternity, depending on which complementarian one asks). Nothing in my account requires me to comment on whether that particular claim is plausible or even intelligible.

29. J. Ligon Duncan, "Why 'Together for the Gospel' Embraces Complementarianism," *Journal for Biblical Manhood and Womanhood* 13, no. 1 (Spring 2008): 25. (An endnote indicates that an earlier version of Duncan's essay appeared on T4G's official website, www.T4G.com.) Duncan describes T4G as "a consortium of Reformed evangelicals who are committed to a comprehensive recovery and reaffirmation of the biblical Gospel." The purpose of the essay is to explain why an organization devoted to recovering and reaffirming the gospel would include in its *mission* a secondary (at best) doctrine such as complementarianism.

30. Duncan, "Complementarianism," 25.

31. Duncan, "Complementarianism," 26.

32. At the SBC's annual meeting in June of 2023, Albert Mohler rehearsed both of these reasons in his remarks on the subject of gender roles in SBC churches—declaring that the SBC's prevailing commitment to gender hierarchy "is *not* just a matter of church polity. It is *not* just a matter of hermeneutics. It's a matter of biblical commitment—a commitment to the scripture that unequivocally, we believe, limits the office of pastor to men. It is an issue of biblical authority." See John Fea, "Rick Warren vs. Al Mohler on the floor of the Southern Baptist Convention meeting in New Orleans" (video), *Current*, June 13, 2023, https://tinyurl.com/2p83ap9m.

33. Complementarians disagree among themselves about whether this hierarchy is to be maintained in church, in the home, or both. Some, like John Piper, hold that gender hierarchy should be the norm even beyond the church and the home. (More on Piper below.) For present purposes, this intramural debate is irrelevant.

34. Two notes. First, I'm not suggesting that the Bible contradicts itself. That would be inconsistent with my commitment to biblicism, since it would imply that the Bible says something false (i.e., given that one or more of the claims in a contradictory set must be false). Second, the notion that egalitarians must engage in exegetical gymnastics in order to make certain complementarian prooftexts mean the opposite of what they say is, I think, a diversion. Some egalitarians may torture the text in order to conjure their desired meaning. Others might claim that Scripture contains errors, or that certain biblical commands should be ignored. But egalitarianism, as such,

doesn't entail any of that. One of the egalitarian's options, e.g., is to say, "Yes, Paul wrote those sentences, and those sentences mean what complementarians say they mean. But complementarians have missed something in the context, and that has led them to misunderstand what Paul is up to and how it applies to us now."

35. I hasten to emphasize that my purpose in laying out a potential egalitarian line of thinking is *not* to furnish an argument for egalitarianism. I only mean to offer a plausible story that's consistent with an egalitarian reading of Scripture. The point isn't to persuade a complementarian that egalitarianism is true, only to demonstrate that egalitarianism doesn't entail the low view of Scripture that complementarians like Duncan and Mohler say it does. No doubt the story I lay out includes any number of claims that a complementarian would likely reject. That's fine. What matters is that the perspective I lay out doesn't entail a low view of Scripture, and it doesn't involve any assertions that it would be unreasonable for an egalitarian to accept.

36. Beth Allison Barr, *The Making of Biblical Womanhood: How the Subjugation of Women Became Gospel Truth* (Grand Rapids: Brazos, 2021), 33.

37. In and of itself, the fact that the Gospels don't report Jesus promoting gender hierarchy doesn't entail that complementarians are reading the Bible incorrectly. But it does suggest that complementarians who claim that gender hierarchy is *really important* are badly mistaken: if gender hierarchy is really important, it seems like Jesus might have indicated this at some point. And if the gospel writers were at all competent (not to mention divinely inspired), it seems plausible to expect that they would have made note. But the Gospels contain no such record. So even if complementarianism is true, it doesn't seem as though Jesus was all that concerned to emphasize it.

38. For example: Paul shows a lot of concern for avoiding the appearance of disorder. Perhaps that's his reason for restricting positions of visible leadership to men: a woman preaching an extemporaneous sermon to men would have been totally beyond the pale in a first-century context, and therefore so off-putting to potential converts that it would be a detriment to the church's witness. Arguably, in the context of the modern West, the total absence of women from visible leadership is equally off-putting. So, for the very same reason that Paul restricts leadership roles to men in the first century, modern Christians ought to encourage women to serve in leadership.

39. In at least one instance, there's good reason to think that Paul is citing conventional wisdom in order to refute it—a kind of dialectic mode of argument that Paul is known to employ elsewhere.

40. Al Mohler, "Getting It Right, Getting It Wrong, Getting It Fixed, Getting It Done: Learning Ministry from Apollos" (chapel address at the Southern Baptist Theological Seminary, Louisville, September 14, 2010), quoted in

Trevin Wax, "Al Mohler on Why He Changed His Mind on Women Pastors," Gospel Coalition, September 28, 2010, https://tinyurl.com/4vst33z9.

41. Al Mohler, "Al Mohler: A Spirited Q&A with Students in 1993," video, accessed April 16, 2023, https://tinyurl.com/k97mu6se.

42. Owen Strachan, "Authority and Submission," Ligonier Ministries, August 15, 2015, https://tinyurl.com/2p8na5y5.

43. John MacArthur, "Does the Bible Permit a Woman to Preach?," Grace to You, November 3, 2019, https://tinyurl.com/44t2bfnx. A few sentences later, MacArthur despairs that "in a survey conducted in 2017, about eighty percent of Americans are comfortable with a female pastor.... The women's movement has basically just erupted in the church. And the last frontier for the movement is the evangelical church, the last frontier to fall victim to the rebellion of feminism along with cultural Marxism."

44. John MacArthur, "Slavery and True Liberty (John MacArthur)," video interview, Grace to You, July 17, 2012, https://tinyurl.com/4kab92mf. MacArthur goes on to explain that he, personally, would be eager to serve as a slave to a master like God (omnibenevolent, omnipotent, omniscient, etc.) and reiterates his bewilderment at the modern aversion to slavery. MacArthur doesn't comment on the many ways in which being a slave to a human master would obviously differ from being a slave to God. Nor does he offer a single example of a human master that he, John MacArthur, would willingly serve as a slave. He simply notes his opinion that slavery would be a good option for people who have no other opportunity—people unlike himself, presumably. Though the provenance of the interview isn't entirely clear, it is produced by Grace to You, John MacArthur's media organization. The purpose statement on the Grace to You website reads: "As believers committed to God and walking in obedience to Him, we affirm the purpose of Grace to You, which is to teach biblical truth with clarity, taking advantage of various means of mass communications to expand the sphere of John MacArthur's teaching ministry" (https://tinyurl.com/yc4ft7ph).

45. MacArthur, "History in the New World." It's worth noting that MacArthur has served on the board of the Council on Biblical Manhood and Womanhood since the 1990s.

46. John MacArthur, "If Adam and Eve Were the First Two People, How Did We Get So Many Races?," September 26, 2010, https://tinyurl.com/343vmcuf.

47. MacArthur was instrumental in organizing the 2018 *Statement on Social Justice and the Gospel*, and his name appears first on the list of that document's original signers. It must be noted that if the statement has anything to do with the gospel, it has essentially nothing to do with social justice. The supplement to the statement's article on justice, "Article 3—Justice: Expla-

nation by Phil Johnson," includes the following reflection on the nature of social justice:

> There is no single authoritative definition of "social justice." Definitions abound from those who are promoting the terminology. But there are common themes that run through virtually all of them. Here are a couple of typical samples: "Social justice is a political and philosophical concept which holds that all people should have equal access to wealth, health, well-being, justice and opportunity." And "Social justice is the equal access to wealth, opportunities, and privileges within a society." (November 30, 2018, https://tinyurl.com/27t8r2xm)

Johnson doesn't cite any sources for the examples he places in quotes—examples that appear designed less to illuminate the concept of social justice than to fortify the statement's suggestion that social justice is a lightly revised form of Marxism. A Google search suggests that these characterizations of social justice—ostensibly one of the statement's two main subjects—are borrowed from an Investopedia.com entry (Daniel Thomas Mollenkamp, "Social Justice Meaning and Main Principles Explained," n.d., https://tinyurl.com/mux6dsr). Johnson appears to have amended the definitions slightly in an effort to emphasize absolute equality—though it's hard to say for sure, since the entry was updated in July 2022. It must be said that the Investopedia.com entry on social justice, at least in its current form, reflects greater familiarity with the subject than Johnson's offering.

48. Broward Liston, "Interview: Missionary Work in Iraq," *Time*, April 15, 2003, https://tinyurl.com/3k58m9d9. There's a gap in the online archive of the *Journal for Biblical Manhood and Womanhood* between winter 1998 and fall 2000. The winter 1998 issue lists Mohler as a member of the board of reference (alongside John MacArthur, who was still listed on the board as of 2021). The fall 2000 issue lists Mohler as a council member (alongside J. Ligon Duncan III).

49. Jonathan Merritt, "Al Mohler, Southern Baptist Leader, Says He Was 'Stupid' to Defend Slavery in 1998 Interview," Religion News Service, May 15, 2020, https://tinyurl.com/2vsan583. Two days before Mohler's appearance on *Larry King Live*, the Southern Baptist Convention, having just elected Paige Patterson SBC president, voted overwhelmingly to approve an amendment to the *Baptist Faith and Message* declaring that "a woman should 'submit herself graciously' to her husband's leadership and that a husband should 'provide for, protect and lead his family.'" Gustav Niebuhr, "Southern Baptists Declare Wife Should 'Submit' to Her Husband," *New York Times*, June 10, 1998, https://tinyurl.com/mthf6xfx.

50. Quoted in Merritt, "Al Mohler."

51. Quoted by Albert Mohler (@albertmohler), "This is John A. Broadus warning against the practice of women preaching in church worship. This is NOT a new belief or doctrine. Broadus wrote this in 1880." Twitter, May 9, 2021, 5:06 p.m., https://tinyurl.com/37j3m6ru. I'm consistently amazed by appeals to the theological acumen of men who were absolutely convinced that the Bible clearly and unambiguously blesses the institution of race-based chattel slavery.

52. Douglas Wilson, *Black and Tan: A Collection of Essays and Excursions on Slavery, Culture War, and Scripture in America* (Moscow, ID: Canon, 2005), 14. For the record, Wilson denies that he is a racist.

53. Wilson, *Black and Tan*, 33.

54. Wilson, *Black and Tan*, 19, 52.

55. Douglas Wilson, "Smash the Complementarity," *Blog & Mablog*, October 7, 2014, https://tinyurl.com/mrxzkuz9.

56. Douglas Wilson, "The Kill Switch and the Steering Wheel," *Blog & Mablog*, August 24, 2022, https://tinyurl.com/4wme42ey.

57. Du Mez, *Jesus and John Wayne*, 202. Du Mez documents the ways in which influential complementarians vouch for one another within evangelical networks, effectively encouraging those within their spheres of influence to ignore red flags (e.g., Wilson's defenses of slavery). Du Mez notes that

> John Piper helped smooth Wilson's path from the outer edges into more respectable circles. In 2009, Piper invited Wilson to speak at his Desiring God Conference. Suppressing a bit of a chuckle, Piper noted that Wilson had a way with language, that he was a "risk taker," but Wilson got the gospel right.... When controversy surfaced around Wilson's views on race, Piper again came to his defense. In a video that was at times almost flippant, Piper pushed back against those who had "perceived" Wilson to have minimized the horrors of slavery. He assured viewers that "Doug hates racism from the core of his gospel soul," and declared his readiness "to stand with him even if there are differences in historical judgments" concerning the Civil War and the best way to end slavery. (203)

58. See Jason Stanley, *How Propaganda Works* (Princeton: Princeton University Press, 2015), 134–40.

59. Given that "evangelicalism" subsists, at an institutional level, in an informal patchwork of church and parachurch organizations—which is to say, *not* in a formal, explicitly hierarchical system of institutions—I'd expect some to take issue with my use of the phrase *ecclesial authorities*. (Southern Baptists, in particular, emphasize the autonomy of local churches across a

number of domains, theological and otherwise, even within their own convention.) So note that *ecclesial authorities* refers to those who, (1) by virtue of their institutional affiliation, have the power to influence the doctrinal commitments of other evangelicals or evangelical institutions, and (2) by virtue of their rank within an evangelical institution, hold the power to silence dissenting viewpoints through coercion. Prime examples of ecclesial authority in this sense would be presidents of evangelical seminaries (e.g., Mohler, Duncan) or pastors of large evangelical churches that commit substantial resources to media that promote their pastors' theological viewpoints (e.g., John MacArthur, Mark Driscoll).

60. Notably, the title of the book's first chapter, "A Vision of Biblical Complementarity: Manhood and Womanhood Defined according to the Bible," foretells an account of gender that is both biblical and defined according to the Bible.

61. John Piper, "Manhood and Womanhood in Parachurch Ministry," June 26, 2023, https://tinyurl.com/4v5fyx4j.

62. Wayne Grudem, interview by Marvin Olasky, "The Case for Donald Trump: A Positive Assessment of Trump's Tenure and Future Outlook," *World*, September 24, 2020, https://tinyurl.com/3dyys5pa.

63. John Piper and Wayne Grudem, eds., *Recovering Biblical Manhood and Womanhood: A Response to Evangelical Feminism* (Wheaton, IL: Crossway Books, 1991), xv. See also DeYoung, "Death to Patriarchy?" DeYoung's defense of Piper and Grudem employs a common tactic among conservative evangelical gatekeepers: since Grudem and Piper deny that complementarianism oppresses women in ways associated with patriarchy, he concludes that it's wrong to claim that complementarianism oppresses women in ways associated with patriarchy. Of course, we can debate whether complementarian social arrangements oppress women (in ways associated with patriarchy or otherwise). But it's absurd to cite Piper and Grudem's denial that complementarianism oppresses women as a good reason for concluding that complementarianism doesn't oppress women. Consider a parallel line of argument: Marxists deny that Marxist policies inevitably lead to untold human misery, therefore it's dishonest to claim that Marxist policies inevitably lead to untold human misery. We can debate whether Marxist policies inevitably lead to human misery. But it's absurd to claim that Marxist policies don't lead to human misery simply because Marxists deny that their policies lead to human misery. Of course they deny it—they're Marxists. The point is whether the substantive claim is true.

64. Susan Douglas and Meredith Michaels, *The Mommy Myth: The Idealization of Motherhood and How It Has Undermined Women* (New York: Free Press, 2004), 15.

65. US Bureau of Labor Statistics, "Labor Force Statistics from the Cur-

rent Population Survey," 2019, https://tinyurl.com/ycknrfw8. Presumably, by virtue of advances in technology, some number of "labor force participants" work from home.

Chapter 2

1. Billy Graham, quoted in Kevin Kruse, *One Nation under God* (New York: Basic Books, 2015), 53.

2. Billy Graham, "God before Gold," *Nation's Business*, September 1954, 34, quoted in Kruse, *One Nation under God*, 37.

3. Kruse, *One Nation under God*, 31–32, quoting an unnamed Lutheran minister.

4. Rev. Kenneth W. Sollitt, "Freedom under God: We Can Go on Making a God of Government, or We Can Return Again to the Government of God" (sermon), *Faith and Freedom*, September 1951, quoted in Kruse, *One Nation under God*, 32.

5. Jerry Falwell, "Conditions Corrupting America" (sermon, May 16, 1976), LU-Archives, OTGH–192, Liberty University, Lynchburg, VA, quoted in Michael Sean Winters, *God's Right Hand: How Jerry Falwell Made God a Republican and Baptized the American Right* (New York: HarperCollins, 2012), 106–7.

6. Ralph Reed, *Awakening: How America Can Turn from Economic and Moral Destruction Back to Greatness* (Brentwood, TN: Worthy Books, 2014), 2. Ralph Reed is founder of the Faith and Freedom Coalition, former executive director of the Christian Coalition, and a perennial evangelical thought leader. He garnered fame for leveraging his coalition connections to lobby for stricter casino regulations *on behalf of the casino industry*. Specifically, by his own admission, Reed accepted payments of no less than $1.23 million from a consortium of casino operations. (In 2006, a bipartisan Senate investigation found that Reed had accepted payments in excess of $5.3 million—cf. chapter 5.) In return, Reed unleashed scores of evangelical ministers and political activists to lobby for new casino regulations. Reed failed to inform his evangelical friends that their lobbying efforts served the interests of Reed's clients in the casino industry, in that the regulations at issue would bar new competitors from entering the casino market. Among the "alarming social trends" outlined in the first chapter of his book, Reed has the temerity to list *legalized gambling*. Notwithstanding Reed's stated fondness for liberty, regulatory capture didn't make the list.

7. Reed, *Awakening*, 12.

8. Gerardo Martí, *American Blindspot: Race, Class, Religion, and the Trump*

*Presidency* (London: Rowman & Littlefield, 2020), 116. See also Kruse, *One Nation under God*, 16–21.

9. This is an oversimplification: sometimes circumstances are a by-product of our own choices; and our choices are always limited by our circumstances. We'll account for this in due course.

10. So it's one thing to say, as some libertarians do, that people like Frank shouldn't receive public assistance because no one should ever receive public assistance. This position is entirely consistent with an acknowledgment that Frank has done nothing blameworthy. But it's another matter entirely to suggest, as the rhetoric of the meritocracy does, that someone in Frank's situation is to blame for his inability to earn a living. Setting aside related but different questions about public assistance, it's just not appropriate to fault people for aspects of their lives over which they have no control.

11. Jason Stanley, *How Propaganda Works* (Princeton: Princeton University Press, 2015), 195.

12. Richard Rothstein, *The Color of Law: A Forgotten History of How Our Government Segregated America* (New York: Liveright, 2017), 64–65.

13. In addition to denying minorities access to FHA-backed mortgages, federal overseers deemed minorities a "credit risk," making it difficult for private banks to issue mortgages to qualified minorities—even at higher interest rates, without the benefit of FHA insurance.

14. The quality of local schools, in turn, impacts property value—so there's a feedback system between real estate values and the quality of local schools.

15. Rothstein, *The Color of Law*, 55.

16. Rothstein, *The Color of Law*, 181. Further complicating matters, wages began to stagnate around the same time that housing prices began their steep ascent.

17. Rothstein, *The Color of Law*, 182. Additionally, renters cannot benefit from the mortgage-interest tax deduction.

18. As with other contentious legal reforms (cf. *Brown v. Board*), there were pockets of open resistance to the Fair Housing Act. Racially discriminatory zoning persisted until as late as 1987 via "spot zoning" in places like Austin, Atlanta, Kansas City, and Norfolk. See Rothstein, *The Color of Law*, 47–48.

19. Rothstein, *The Color of Law*, 187. A "poor neighborhood" is one in which at least 20 percent of residents live at or below the poverty line.

20. Benjamin Harris and Sydney Schreiner Wertz, "Racial Differences in Economic Security: The Racial Wealth Gap," US Department of the Treasury, September 15, 2022, https://tinyurl.com/bnpnbbfw.

21. Artificial intelligence is still subject to bias, though in a narrower sense than humans. We can safely ignore this complication.

22. We might imagine some strategies for making the contest fair; but this would take us far afield from present concerns and, frankly, from reality. In the context of an athletic competition, it seems likely that the game would simply be canceled or rescheduled. Of course, the purpose of the analogy is to highlight the inadequacy of merely instituting neutral rules as a means of compensating for many generations of injustice.

23. Perhaps a better (though far more complicated) analogy would involve a track meet in which individual contestants are organized into teams (almost like families) that compete with any number of other teams to amass points.

24. J. Russell Hawkins, *The Bible Told Them So: How Southern Evangelicals Fought to Preserve White Supremacy* (New York: Oxford University Press, 2021), 47.

25. Carey Daniel, *God the Original Segregationist*, pamphlet reprint found in Right Wing Collection of the University of Iowa Libraries, roll 26, frame C28, 4, quoted in Hawkins, *Bible Told Them So*, 47.

26. A. C. Lawton Sr., "Christianity vs. Integration," *Councilor*, October 20, 1963, quoted in Hawkins, *Bible Told Them So*, 47.

27. Maylon D. Watkins, "Segregation of the Races Is Biblical and Therefore Christlike," article reprint found in box 457, folder 3, Thomas R. Waring Jr. Papers, South Carolina Historical Society, quoted in Hawkins, *Bible Told Them So*, 48.

28. Montague Cook, *Racial Segregation Is Christian*, pamphlet found in box 59, folder "Race," Clifton J. Allen Papers, Southern Baptist Historical Library and Archives, quoted in Hawkins, *Bible Told Them So*, 50.

29. Hawkins, *Bible Told Them So*, 52.

30. J. Elwood Welsh, "Is Racial Segregation Right and Christian?," sermon reprint found in box 436, folder 6, Thomas R. Waring Jr. Papers, quoted in Hawkins, *Bible Told Them So*, 53.

31. See Jeremy Schipper, "Religion, Race, and the Wife of Ham," *Journal of Religion*, July 1, 2020, 386–401.

32. Hawkins, *Bible Told Them So*, 62.

33. Jesse Curtis, *The Myth of Colorblind Christians: Evangelicals and White Supremacy in the Civil Rights Era* (New York: New York University Press, 2021), 84.

34. Martí, *American Blindspot*, 149–50.

35. Diana Orcés, "Changes in Views over Racial Injustice during Summer 2020 Short-Lived," Public Religion Research Institute (PRRI), June 20, 2022, https://tinyurl.com/3scpr2e4. The same survey found that 65 percent of white evangelicals affirm the proposition that "today discrimination against whites has become as big a problem as discrimination against Black Americans and other minorities."

36. No doubt there are racists in our society who actively engage in efforts to perpetuate racial inequality. This is important—it's just not important to the present point concerning systemic racism.

### Chapter 3

1. Benjamin J. Huskinson, *American Creationism, Creation Science, and Intelligent Design in the Evangelical Market*, Christianities in the Trans-Atlantic World (Cham, Switzerland: Palgrave Macmillan, 2020), 17–18. Huskinson's list also includes *Revelational Day Theory*, according to which "the six days described in the Genesis narrative are not days of creation, but days during which the progressive acts were revealed to the author of Genesis. In this interpretation, the process of creation was revealed to the author over the course of six days, with each day's revelation recorded as a separate act." For present purposes, we can safely ignore this view.

2. Young-earth creationists disagree among themselves about how young the earth is. Some say less than seven thousand years, some say fifteen thousand years. This intramural dispute among young-earth creationists is immaterial to my account.

3. Quoted in Christopher P. Toumey, *God's Own Scientists: Creationists in a Secular World* (New Brunswick, NJ: Rutgers University Press, 1994), 101.

4. "Modern science" in this context is shorthand for the overwhelming consensus of scientists in the fields of geology, geophysics, physics, paleontology, biology, anthropology, and archaeology, among others.

5. "The Top 25 Most Influential Preachers of the Past 50 Years," *Christianity Today*, 2006, https://tinyurl.com/26s2ahvu.

6. John MacArthur, "Creation: Believe It or Not," *Master's Seminary Journal* 33, no. 1 (Spring 2002): 12, 14.

7. Albert Mohler, "Why Does the Universe Look So Old?" (presentation, Ligonier Ministries National Conference, Orlando, FL, June 19, 2010). Transcript published in *Credo*, June 25, 2013, https://tinyurl.com/yc85msu8.

8. Ronald L. Numbers, *The Creationists: From Scientific Creationism to Intelligent Design*, expanded ed. (Cambridge, MA: Harvard University Press, 2006), 90.

9. MacArthur, "Creation."

10. Mohler, "Why Does the Universe Look So Old?"

11. The result would be a hermeneutic that allows us to pick and choose those parts of the Bible we wish to take seriously and those we prefer to dismiss as figurative or allegorical. Ironically, they seem to be describing what I've called *motivated literalism* in the hermeneutics of legitimization.

12. I don't see how a theological conservative might reject either of the

two claims involved in principled literalism (unless it's on the grounds that the second claim is *too* conservative—i.e., because there are cases where a nonliteral reading is appropriate even though Scripture doesn't indicate this). The first claim is merely a *ceteris paribus* commitment to the mode of interpretation preferred by theological conservatives—namely, literalism. The second claim holds that we must defer to the authority of Scripture on matters concerning the interpretation of Scripture.

13. Ken Ham, ed., *The New Answers Book 1* (Green Forest, AR: Master Books, 2006), chap. 8: "Could God Really Have Created Everything in Six Days?" Available online at https://tinyurl.com/2s8fu2cb.

14. Ham, *New Answers Book 1*, chap. 8.

15. John MacArthur, "The Creation of Woman," Grace to You, November 28, 1999, https://tinyurl.com/nhhxve6u.

16. Even Wayne Grudem rejects young-earth creationism—see Wayne Grudem, "Our Old Earth," Desiring God, July 7, 2022, https://tinyurl.com/5n83548v.

17. Ligon Duncan, "The First Things (Creation) (3): The Days of Creation," LigonDuncan.com, May 10, 1998, https://tinyurl.com/4e84xnd6.

18. Mohler, "Why Does the Universe Look So Old?"

19. MacArthur, "Creation."

20. Some young-earthers might object that Augustine believed in a "young" earth. This is true but potentially misleading. Yes, Augustine believed that the earth was a few thousand years old—but not because he believed that the creation narratives in Genesis offer a historical account of the earth's origins: manifestly, he did not.

21. Ewald M. Plass, *What Martin Luther Says: A Practical In-Home Anthology for the Active Christian* (St. Louis: Concordia, 1959), 1523.

22. Perhaps Duncan and Mohler only intend to make a broader observation about the prevalence of young-earth views among *Christians in general* prior to the nineteenth century. Perhaps, but neither offers any evidence to support such a claim. And even if we stipulate that a majority of all Christians prior to the nineteenth century were young-earthers, it's far from obvious that a consensus among pre-nineteenth-century Christians—many of whom never held a copy of Genesis and would have been unable to read it if they had—should carry more weight than the considered views of, say, Origen, Augustine, or Jerome.

23. Numbers, *The Creationists*, 7.

24. Megan Brenan, "40% of Americans Believe in Creationism," Gallup, July 26, 2019, https://tinyurl.com/yjaspsmc. Admittedly, these polls aren't sufficiently fine-grained to contradict MacArthur's claim directly: they're not limited to evangelicals, and the view that God created humans within the last ten thousand years is consistent with a version of old-earth creationism.

But that claim is the signature of young-earth creationism, and evangelicals constitute a significant majority of young-earth creationists. So, absent some reason for thinking otherwise—which reason MacArthur doesn't provide—the picture painted by the data isn't consistent with what we would expect to see if "large numbers of evangelicals" were defecting from young-earth creationism.

25. Adam Laats, *Creationism USA: Bridging the Impasse on Teaching Evolution* (New York: Oxford University Press, 2021), 23–24.

26. James Montgomery Boice, *Genesis: An Expositional Commentary*, vol. 1, *Genesis 1–11* (Grand Rapids: Zondervan, 1982), 56–62.

27. See MacArthur's comments on theological liberalism, quoted on pages 87–88. Similarly, Mohler names higher criticism as one of the four factors that contributed to the rise of old-earth creationism in the nineteenth century.

*Chapter 4*

1. "Bill Nye Tours the Ark Encounter with Ken Ham," Answers in Genesis, July 8, 2016 (uploaded March 13, 2017), https://tinyurl.com/wvxm2tce.

2. Ice cores are cylinders of ice up to two miles long, drilled out of massive glaciers in places like Antarctica and Greenland. The National Science Foundation describes them as "essentially time capsules that allow scientists to reconstruct climate far into the past. Layers in ice cores correspond to years and seasons.... By drilling down into the ice sheet or glacier and recovering ice from ancient times, scientists are able to determine the past composition and behavior of the atmosphere, what the climate was like when the snow fell, and how the size of ice sheets and glaciers have changed in the past in response to different climate conditions." US Geological Survey, "About Ice Cores," National Science Foundation, accessed April 16, 2023, https://tinyurl.com/3jre7eau.

3. Another assumption of conventional science that creation scientists question, sometimes called *uniformitarianism*, is the belief that the earth's geological record is a result of continuous and uniform processes. I won't indulge the creation scientist's skepticism on this point, except to say this. It would be within God's power to disrupt the normal progress of nature and reorganize the geological record in ways that would make it appear uniform even though it isn't. But if we assume that this is the sort of thing God would do, or has done, then dwelling on the details of empirical science is probably a misuse of our time.

4. In 2017, scientists recovered an ice core from Antarctica with ice estimated to be 2.7 million years old (Paul Voosen, "Record-Shattering

2.7-Million-Year-Old Ice Core Reveals Start of the Ice Ages," *Science*, August 15, 2017, https://tinyurl.com/3ee2krb6). As this is an outlier, and it's not integral to the point at hand (namely, that basic scientific observation reveals the earth to be much older than creation scientists would have it), I've omitted this example from my analysis.

5. This presents a dilemma vis-à-vis archaeologists who believe themselves to be excavating human structures that are more than four thousand years old. Either manmade structures somehow survived a global catastrophic flood that completely remade the geological record below, or we must add archaeologists to the list of scientists who badly misunderstand their evidence. I assume that creation scientists would claim the latter, since archaeology is another field in which scientists study things that they take to be more than six thousand years old—which would be older than the earth, according to the "biblical view."

6. Paolo Gabrielli and Paul Vallelonga, "Contaminant Records in Ice Cores," in *Environmental Contaminants*, ed. J. M. Blais et al., Developments in Paleoenvironmental Research 18 (Dordrecht: Springer, 2015), chap. 14.

7. C. Barbante et al., "Greenland Ice Core Evidence of 79 AD Vesuvius Eruption," *Climate of the Past*, June 13, 2013.

8. This evidence is, of course, also consistent with the earth's being far more than hundreds of thousands of years old. Also note: some distortions in layering occur due to compression or ice flows, which makes manually counting layers more difficult and less reliable farther down the core. Thus results are confirmed or improved with the help of computer modeling and cross-referencing with data from other ice cores in various locations.

9. T. A. Frail, "Meet the 100 Most Significant Americans of All Time," *Smithsonian Magazine*, November 17, 2014, https://tinyurl.com/2e4tfura.

10. Biblical Research Institute of the General Conference of Seventh-day Adventists, "The Inspiration and Authority of the Ellen G. White Writings: Ten Affirmations and Ten Denials on Ellen White's Authority," *Adventist Review*, December 23, 1982.

11. Ellen G. White, *The Spirit of Prophecy*, vol. 1 (Battle Creek, MI: Seventh-day Adventist Publishing Association, 1870), chap. 8, quoted in Ronald L. Numbers, *The Creationists: From Scientific Creationism to Intelligent Design*, expanded ed. (Cambridge, MA: Harvard University Press, 2006), 90.

12. Ellen G. White, *Spiritual Gifts*, vol. 3 (Battle Creek, MI: Seventh-day Adventist Publishing Association, 1864), chap. 8, quoted in Numbers, *The Creationists*, 90.

13. White, *Spiritual Gifts*, chap. 7, quoted in Numbers, *The Creationists*, 101.

14. Adam Laats, *Creationism USA: Bridging the Impasse on Teaching Evolution* (New York: Oxford University Press, 2021), 32.

15. Numbers, *The Creationists*, 92.

16. Quoted in Numbers, *The Creationists*, 91.

17. Quoted in Numbers, *The Creationists*, 92.

18. Quoted in Numbers, *The Creationists*, 100.

19. While the difference between Price's view of evolution and the conventional view may appear subtle at first glance, the two are roughly as similar as a "Secret Santa" gift exchange with a $50 minimum versus a "white elephant" gift exchange with a $5 maximum. In the first scenario—analogous to Price's view—your gift might reflect a modicum of intentionality, and you may end up with something immediately useful. In the "white elephant" scenario—analogous to the conventional view of evolution—your gift will be random and in all likelihood useless to you.

20. Numbers, *The Creationists*, 101.

21. Quoted in Numbers, *The Creationists*, 101.

22. Numbers, *The Creationists*, 101–2.

23. Numbers, *The Creationists*, 117.

24. Numbers, *The Creationists*, 117.

25. Quoted in Numbers, *The Creationists*, 116.

26. Numbers, *The Creationists*, 234; see also Paul Sharf, "The Genesis Flood, Tidal Wave of Change," *Baptist Bulletin*, July 9, 2010, https://tinyurl.com/2p9kwvzh.

27. Numbers, *The Creationists*, 223.

28. Henry M. Morris and John C. Whitcomb, *The Genesis Flood: The Biblical Record and Its Scientific Implications* (Phillipsburg, NJ: Reformed Publishing, 1961), xii.

29. Henry Morris, *The Beginning of the World: A Scientific Study of Genesis 1–11* (Green Forest, AR: Master Books, 1991), 132–34.

30. Ken Ham, "Ark Encounter & Creation Museum Welcome 10 Millionth Guest," Answers in Genesis, April 14, 2022, https://tinyurl.com/3bz4xx2v.

31. "Meet the Ladies in Noah's Family," Ark Encounter, July 12, 2018, https://tinyurl.com/22m6z4x8.

32. Numbers, *The Creationists*, 238.

33. Numbers, *The Creationists*, 238.

34. Quoted in Numbers, *The Creationists*, 238.

35. Quoted in Jesse Curtis, *The Myth of Colorblind Christians: Evangelicals and White Supremacy in the Civil Rights Era* (New York: New York University Press, 2021), 57; John Fea, "Tim LaHaye Had Some Choice Words for Wheaton College When the Evangelical School Hosted a Memorial Service for Martin Luther King Jr.," *Current*, January 17, 2022, https://tinyurl.com/k9c6kpac.

36. David A. DeWitt, "Missing Dr. Falwell," Answers in Genesis, May 19, 2007, https://tinyurl.com/yn9s3hvd.

37. Numbers, *The Creationists*, 351–72.

38. Julie J. Ingersoll, *Building God's Kingdom: Inside the World of Christian Reconstruction* (New York: Oxford University Press, 2015), 127.

39. Ingersoll, *Building God's Kingdom*, 130.

40. Quoted in Ingersoll, *Building God's Kingdom*, 133.

41. Creation Ministries International, "Jerry Bergman, Ph.D., Biology," accessed April 17, 2023, https://tinyurl.com/3r9b747b. Ingersoll cites a slightly older biography on the Answers in Genesis website that appears to have been removed. That biography listed only six hundred publications, so it seems that Bergman's productivity hasn't declined in the last several years. On the split between Answers in Genesis and Creation Ministries International, see National Center for Science Education, "Answers in Genesis in Legal Turmoil," June 21, 2007, https://tinyurl.com/4bycrj3z.

42. Wayne State University College of Education, "Doctor of Education and Doctor of Philosophy in Educational Evaluation and Research," accessed April 17, 2023, https://tinyurl.com/38cb3tur. See also Ingersoll, *Building God's Kingdom*, 133.

43. State of California, "California Supreme Court Upholds Denial of Columbia Pacific University's Approval to Operate" (press release), December 1, 2000, https://tinyurl.com/536cjp82.

44. Ingersoll, *Building God's Kingdom*, 133–34.

45. Laats, *Creationism USA*, 48.

46. David E. Long, *Evolution and Religion in American Education: An Ethnography*, Cultural Studies of Science Education 4 (Dordrecht: Springer, 2011), 19, quoted in Laats, *Creationism USA*, 65.

47. Laats, *Creationism USA*, 66.

48. Jerry Falwell, *Listen, America!* (Garden City, NY: Doubleday, 1980), 179, quoted in Laats, *Creationism USA*, 66.

49. Albert Mohler, "Why Does the Universe Look So Old?" (presentation, Ligonier Ministries National Conference, Orlando, FL, June 19, 2010). Transcript published in *Credo*, June 25, 2013, https://tinyurl.com/yc85msu8. Mohler's sense of creationism's popularity presents a sharp contrast to MacArthur's alarm over evangelicals abandoning Scripture for science.

50. Christopher Hitchens, "Is There an Afterlife?" moderated discussion between Hitchens, Sam Harris, Rabbi Bradley Artson Shavit, and Rabbi David Wolpe, February 15, 2011, Wadsworth Theatre, Los Angeles, https://tinyurl.com/uyf4dtbs.

51. Henry Morris, *The Long War against God: The History and Impact of the Creation/Evolution Conflict* (Green Forest, AR: Master Books, 2008), 132, quoted in Laats, *Creationism USA*, 67. Laats refers to this as Morris's "scattershot get-off-my-lawn polemic" (67).

52. Ken Ham, *Evolution, Creation, and the Culture Wars* (pamphlet) (Cincinnati, OH: Answers in Genesis, 2005), 2.

53. Laats, *Creationism USA*, 91.

54. Laats, *Creationism USA*, 93.

55. Tim LaHaye, *The Battle for the Public Schools: Humanism's Threat to Our Children* (Old Tappan, NJ: Revell, 1983), 196, quoted in Laats, *Creationism USA*, 93.

56. I hasten to qualify: *mis*information, not necessarily *dis*information. Disinformation involves intentional deception—at least at the point of origin—while misinformation is just demonstrably false.

57. George M. Marsden, *Fundamentalism and American Culture* (New York: Oxford University Press, 2022); Mark A. Noll, *The Scandal of the Evangelical Mind* (Grand Rapids: Eerdmans, 1994).

58. "Science News: World's Oldest Living Tree—9550 Years Old—Discovered in Sweden," *Science Daily*, April 16, 2008, https://tinyurl.com/5xtjb2e5.

59. Albert Mohler, "Why Does the Universe Look So Old?"

60. Propagandistic appeals to biblical authority involve a paradox for those who sincerely disagree with the position of those making the appeal. The only way to satisfy the demand to submit to "Scripture" (as they understand it) is to submit to the authority of men over and against what one actually believes to be the teaching of Scripture—which is precisely what the objection insists that we mustn't do.

61. Kevin Leman, *Sheet Music: Uncovering the Secrets of Sexual Intimacy in Marriage* (Carol Stream, IL: Tyndale House, 2002), 206. "There are times for whatever reason that a wife may choose to make use of 'hand jobs.' A woman . . . who has just gotten through a pregnancy . . . may genuinely feel that sex is more than she can handle. But with a minimum of effort, she can help her husband who feels like he's about ready to climb the walls because it's been so long." Quoted in Sheila Wray Gregoire, "We Need a More Nuanced Conversation about Post-Partum Sex," *Bare Marriage*, June 11, 2021, https://tinyurl.com/2p86k6yv.

62. *The Great Sex Rescue* documents—with empirical evidence—the sexual trauma and marital dysfunction in the wake of this and other pernicious evangelical myths around marriage and sexuality. See Sheila Wray Gregoire, Rebecca Gregoire Lindenbach, and Joanna Sawatsky, *The Great Sex Rescue: The Lies You've Been Taught and How to Recover What God Intended* (Grand Rapids: Baker Books, 2021). Sawatsky, Lindenbach, and Gregoire also provide an alternative paradigm that is biblically informed and, where factual claims are concerned, based on factual evidence.

*Chapter 5*

1. Daniel Ziblatt, *Conservative Parties and the Birth of Democracy* (Cambridge: Cambridge University Press, 2017).

2. Quoted in Anthea Butler, *White Evangelical Racism: The Politics of Mo-*

*rality in America* (Chapel Hill: University of North Carolina Press, 2021), 73. See also Philip S. Gorski and Samuel L. Perry, *The Flag and the Cross: White Christian Nationalism and the Threat to American Democracy* (New York: Oxford University Press, 2022), 97.

3. Phyllis Schlafly, "North Carolina Embraces Honest Elections," *WorldNetDaily*, August 19, 2013, quoted in Gorski and Perry, *Flag and the Cross*, 96.

4. Andrew Kaczynski, "Mike Huckabee Says He Doesn't Want 'Stupid' People to Vote," *Buzzfeed News*, September 22, 2015, quoted in Gorski and Perry, *Flag and the Cross*, 96–97.

5. Vanessa Williamson, "The Austerity Politics of White Supremacy," *Dissent*, Winter 2021, https://tinyurl.com/m6wx7sbp.

6. Williamson, "Austerity Politics."

7. Quoted in Williamson, "Austerity Politics."

8. Williamson, "Austerity Politics."

9. *Discussions of Robert Lewis Dabney*, ed. C. R. Vaughan, vol. 4 (Harrisonburg, VA: Sprinkle Publications, 1994), 177–78.

10. John MacArthur, "The Consequences of Non-expositional Preaching, Part 1," Grace to You, February 22, 2009, https://tinyurl.com/pmewz7up. It's worth noting that this sermon on the consequences of nonexpositional preaching is, as its title suggests, *topical*—which is to say, completely nonexpositional. For an extensive treatment of John MacArthur's relationship to the work of R. L. Dabney, see Daniel Kleven, "John MacArthur on Robert Lewis Dabney," *Biblioskolex*, August 26, 2018, https://tinyurl.com/sb556nfw. As Kleven documents, Dabney's acolytes also include prominent complementarians John Piper and Douglas Wilson. (See Kleven, "John Piper, Desiring God, and Robert Lewis Dabney," *Biblioskolex*, December 16, 2021, https://tinyurl.com/yc2f572v; Kleven, "Douglas Wilson on Robert Lewis Dabney," November 18, 2018, https://tinyurl.com/yxakw8e3.) See chapters 1 and 2 of this book for more on Wilson, Piper, MacArthur, and the connections among white supremacist legitimizing narratives, proslavery hermeneutics, and arguments for "biblical" patriarchy.

11. Jemar Tisby, *The Color of Compromise: The Truth about the American Church's Complicity in Racism* (Grand Rapids: Zondervan, 2019), 105–6.

12. Tisby, *The Color of Compromise*, 103–4.

13. Inaugural address of Governor George C. Wallace, Montgomery, Alabama, January 14, 1963, https://tinyurl.com/ytp3z4xp.

14. Ian Haney López, *Dog Whistle Politics: How Coded Racial Appeals Have Reinvented Racism and Wrecked the Middle Class* (New York: Oxford University Press, 2014), 13–14.

15. Dan T. Carter, *The Politics of Rage: George Wallace, the Origins of the*

*New Conservatism, and the Transformation of American Politics* (Baton Rouge: Louisiana State University Press, 1995), 109, quoted in López, *Dog Whistle Politics*, 14.

16. Carter, *The Politics of Rage*, 95, quoted in López, *Dog Whistle Politics*, 14.

17. Carter, *The Politics of Rage*, 95, quoted in López, *Dog Whistle Politics*, 14.

18. López, *Dog Whistle Politics*, 14.

19. López, *Dog Whistle Politics*, 14.

20. López, *Dog Whistle Politics*, 15.

21. López, *Dog Whistle Politics*, 15.

22. López, *Dog Whistle Politics*, 22–23.

23. López, *Dog Whistle Politics*, 17.

24. Jack Bass and Walter De Vries, *The Transformation of Southern Politics: Social Change and Political Consequences since 1945* (Athens: University of Georgia Press, 1995), 27, quoted in López, *Dog Whistle Politics*, 17.

25. Rick Perlstein, *Before the Storm: Barry Goldwater and the Unmaking of the American Consensus* (New York: Nation Books, 2009), 430–31, quoted in López, *Dog Whistle Politics*, 20.

26. Kevin P. Phillips, *The Emerging Republican Majority* (New Rochelle, NY: Arlington House, 1969), 232, quoted in Jacob S. Hacker and Paul Pierson, *Let Them Eat Tweets: How the Right Rules in an Age of Extreme Inequality* (New York: Liveright, 2020), 44.

27. Hacker and Pierson, *Let Them Eat Tweets*, 43.

28. Corey Robin, *The Reactionary Mind: Conservatism from Edmund Burke to Donald Trump* (New York: Oxford University Press, 2018), 47.

29. Quoted in Joe McGinniss, *The Selling of the President, 1968* (New York: Trident Books, 1969), 23.

30. John Ehrlichman, *Witness to Power: The Nixon Years* (New York: Simon & Schuster, 1970), 233, quoted in López, *Dog Whistle Politics*, 24.

31. Phillips, *The Emerging Republican Majority*, quoted in López, *Dog Whistle Politics*, 25.

32. Quoted in Andrew Marantz, "Does Hungary Offer a Glimpse of Our Authoritarian Future?," *New Yorker*, June 27, 2022, https://tinyurl.com/2s9yfneu.

33. Richard Nixon, "Transcript of David Frost's Interview with Richard Nixon," ed. Jeremy D. Bailey, May 19, 1977, https://tinyurl.com/yf3hchu9.

34. "'Welfare Queen' Becomes Issue in Reagan Campaign," *New York Times*, February 15, 1976, quoted in López, *Dog Whistle Politics*, 58.

35. Quoted in López, *Dog Whistle Politics*, 58.

36. López, *Dog Whistle Politics*, 58.

37. López, *Dog Whistle Politics*, 30.

38. Indeed, it seems that the success of Reagan's enterprise was contingent on the pitch of his dog whistle. Perlstein recounts one instance in which the racial resentment passed into audible range and the backlash that ensued. Reagan opened his 1980 campaign at the Neshoba County Fair outside Philadelphia, Mississippi.

> In 1964, the fair opened as planned on August 8 even though six days earlier, the bodies of three SNCC voter-registration workers were discovered buried in an earthen dam a few miles away. They had been assassinated by the Ku Klux Klan, with the assistance of the local sheriff, Lawrence Rainey. And now Ronald Reagan was raising the curtain on his campaign there. Which raised more than a few eyebrows. . . . Later, a defensive state party official insisted it was [Mississippi Congressman Trent] Lott—and certainly not *them*—who suggested that if Reagan really wanted to win this crowd over, he need only fold a certain two-word phrase into his speech: *states' rights*.
>
> These were the most reliable code words southern demagogues could deploy to activate their audiences' most feral rage against Black civil rights. Ronald Reagan, whose unshakable belief in his own purity of motivation was his defining trait, surely got to immediate work persuading himself that in uttering them, he was referring to *all* federal intrusion into local affairs, from the Occupational Safety and Health Administration to the Department of Ed—the same thing he *always* excoriated. He seemed anxious about taking the suggestion all the same. For, as Reagan speeches went, this was a strange one. . . . He began reciting his familiar litany of federal government failure, though a little more wobbly than was customary. . . . He had started rushing, like he was nervous, far shy of his usual level of energy, when he delivered the payload: "I believe in states' rights; I believe in people doing as much as they can for themselves at the community level and at the private level, and I believe that we've *distorted* the balance of government." Then, he returned to his usual boilerplate. Far from the usual Neshoba County Fair demagoguery, the way he carried out Trent Lott's suggestion doused the enthusiasm of a previously energetic crowd. . . . And it was hardly worth it. The backlash was immediate and caustic. . . . Many white Mississippians who might have once been proud of their state's reputation as the most fearsome bastion of resistance were now ashamed to find the nation pointing it out. Which was why, claimed an embarrassed Mississippi Reagan fan in a let-

ter . . . , "Three weeks ago Reagan had a landslide victory in Mississippi. Today it is a tossup." Rick Perlstein, *Reaganland: America's Right Turn, 1976–1980* (New York: Simon & Schuster, 2020), 829–33.

39. Lee Atwater, quoted in Robin, *The Reactionary Mind*, 47, from an interview by Alexander P. Lamis, a political scientist at Case Western Reserve University. See also Butler, *White Evangelical Racism*, 73; López, *Dog Whistle Politics*, 56; Tisby, *The Color of Compromise*, 152–53.

40. In August 2018, Manafort was convicted of tax fraud and bank fraud. He later pled guilty to witness tampering and conspiracy to defraud the United States. In November 2019, Stone was convicted of making false statements, witness tampering, and obstructing an official proceeding. Both men received presidential pardons.

41. Quoted in Sidney Blumenthal, *Pledging Allegiance: The Last Campaign of the Cold War* (New York: HarperCollins, 1990), 264–65.

42. López, *Dog Whistle Politics*, 66.

43. Dan T. Carter, *From George Wallace to Newt Gingrich: Race in the Conservative Counterrevolution, 1963–1994*, Walter Lynwood Fleming Lectures in Southern History (Baton Rouge: Louisiana State University Press, 1996), 79, quoted in López, *Dog Whistle Politics*, 106–7.

44. Hacker and Pierson, *Let Them Eat Tweets*, 65.

45. Hacker and Pierson, *Let Them Eat Tweets*, 62.

46. Hacker and Pierson, *Let Them Eat Tweets*, 52.

47. "Max Heller: 1919–2011," *Greenville (SC) Journal*, June 16, 2011, https://tinyurl.com/yc6mvvaz.

48. Richard Gooding, "The Trashing of John McCain," *Vanity Fair*, November 2004.

49. Gooding, "Trashing of John McCain."

50. Gooding, "Trashing of John McCain."

51. Gooding, "Trashing of John McCain."

52. Gooding, "Trashing of John McCain."

53. United States Senate Committee on Indian Affairs, "Exhibits to the 2005-06-22 Hearing of the Senate Committee on Indian Affairs" (PDF), June 22, 2005, 31–34.

54. See "Reed Confirms Fees from Indian Casino Lobbyists," *Washington Post*, August 30, 2004.

55. Bob Jones III, interview by Larry King, "Dr. Bob Jones III Discusses the Controversy Swirling around Bob Jones University," *Larry King Live*, March 3, 2000.

56. Eric Pooley, "Read My Knuckles," CNN, February 21, 2000, https://tinyurl.com/47e3brp4.

57. Jennifer Steinhauer, "Confronting Ghosts of 2000 in South Carolina," *New York Times*, October 19, 2007, https://tinyurl.com/yc654p6w.

58. Gooding, "Trashing of John McCain."

59. Pooley, "Read My Knuckles."

60. United States Senate Committee on Indian Affairs, "Exhibits," 31–34. See also Alex Gibney, "The Deceptions of Ralph Reed," *Atlantic*, September 26, 2010, https://tinyurl.com/2p9cwh8w.

61. Hedrick Smith, *Who Stole the American Dream?* (New York: Random House, 2012), 107–8, quoted in Hacker and Pierson, *Let Them Eat Tweets*, 106.

62. Hacker and Pierson, *Let Them Eat Tweets*, 44–46.

63. Hacker and Pierson, *Let Them Eat Tweets*, 56. See also López, *Dog Whistle Politics*, 66.

64. Kalee Burns, Liana Fox, and Danielle Wilson, "Child Poverty Fell to Record Low 5.2% in 2021," United States Census Bureau, September 13, 2022, https://tinyurl.com/2myejfn7.

65. Leah Hamilton et al., "The Impacts of the 2021 Expanded Child Tax Credit on Family Employment, Nutrition, and Financial Well-Being: Findings from the Social Policy Institute's Child Tax Credit Panel (Wave 2)," Brookings Institution, April 13, 2022, https://tinyurl.com/466k3mv7.

66. "Absence of Monthly Child Tax Credit Leads to 3.7 Million More Children in Poverty in January 2022," Center on Poverty and Social Policy at Columbia University, February 17, 2022, https://tinyurl.com/m7eppc48.

67. "Santorum Singles out Blacks for Entitlement Reform," CBS News, January 2, 2012, https://tinyurl.com/2jfwm288.

68. In an interview on CNN, Santorum claimed: "I've looked at that quote. In fact, I've looked at the video. And I don't . . . in fact I'm pretty confident I didn't say *Black*. What I think . . . I started to say a word, and sort of, *bleaugh*, sort of mumbled it and changed my thought."

69. "Santorum Addresses Answer of Black's Entitlement Reform," CBS News, January 2, 2012, https://tinyurl.com/4y4mb9ab.

*Chapter 6*

1. In states where the authority hasn't been delegated to an independent body, congressional district lines are drawn by state legislatures over the two years following each US census—which is to say, once every ten years. The composition of state legislatures in 2011–2012 was decided by the 2010 midterm election. In keeping with an established pattern in US politics—namely, that the first midterm election following the inauguration of a new presi-

dent favors the opposing party—the 2010 midterm election following the inauguration of President Barack Obama heavily favored Republicans. Thus Republicans dominated the redistricting process in 2011–2012. What made this redistricting process different from any that had come before is that advances in the speed of computing made it possible to gerrymander with significant help from computer modeling. Computing speed is key because gerrymandering is essentially a complex optimization problem: "Within certain (legal) parameters, given past and likely future voting patterns, which way of drawing the lines will produce the most seats for my party?" Generally speaking, a computer doesn't actually "solve" complex optimization problems—it runs thousands and thousands of "guess and test"-type calculations and selects the most optimal solution from those it has tried. (In the parlance of computer science, complex optimization problems fall into the "NP" category—which, for our purposes, means we don't know of a formula or algorithm that guarantees the single best answer to the problem at hand.) Republicans in many states leveraged this technology to draw maps that would allow them to achieve far more representation in Congress than the percentage of the votes they managed to win.

2. J. Michael Luttig, "The Republican Blueprint to Steal the 2024 Election," CNN, April 27, 2022, https://tinyurl.com/ycyy6wsz.

3. Lauren R. Kerby, *Saving History: How White Evangelicals Tour the Nation's Capital and Redeem a Christian America* (Chapel Hill: University of North Carolina Press, 2020), 6. Kerby notes two other identities—exiles and saviors—that do not factor in my account.

4. Michael J. Mooney, "How First Baptist's Robert Jeffress Ordained Himself to Lead America," *D Magazine*, December 21, 2011, https://tinyurl.com/3k27txxc.

5. Quoted in Andrew L. Whitehead and Samuel L. Perry, *Taking America Back for God: Christian Nationalism in the United States* (New York: Oxford University Press, 2020), 56.

6. Quoted in Whitehead and Perry, *Taking America Back*, 56.

7. Quoted in Whitehead and Perry, *Taking America Back*, 57.

8. The statement was drafted by Will Chamberlain, Christopher DeMuth, Rod Dreher, Yoram Hazony, Daniel McCarthy, Joshua Mitchell, N. S. Lyons, John O'Sullivan, and R. R. Reno. https://tinyurl.com/5apa3fjj.

9. "Conservatism, Religion, Nationalism, and the Current Cultural Crisis—a Conversation with Yoram Hazony," June 15, 2022, https://tinyurl.com/2b5x6nxr.

10. Two of the "National Conservatism" statement's authors, Rod Dreher and EBF president Yoram Hazony, discussed their shared enthusiasm for religious nationalism in a May 2022 episode of Dreher's podcast. Hazony's

understanding of American history appears to be indebted to the work of David Barton.

DREHER. I was in Israel recently, right there in Jerusalem, where you [Hazony] live, and I noticed that it's possible in this robustly secular state of Israel, that religion can be talked about, religion seems to be much more respected in public life, than it is even here, in the United States. Am I wrong about that? And if I'm not, what can the United States learn from Israel on this point?

HAZONY. I do think you're right, but I don't want to idealize the picture too much. All of the democratic nations are suffering from pretty much the same disease. It's at different stages in different countries. The importation of liberalism into Israel as a public philosophy is basically . . . it pretty much becomes something serious in the 1970s, 1980s, when the Israeli Supreme Court and other institutions begin to challenge the idea that there's anything legitimate about Israel as a Jewish state. So Israel has an explicit founding character and identity as the state of a particular nation with a particular inheritance, and that's responsible for a lot of what you're seeing there in Israel, Rod, is that the public life of Israel does in fact, to some significant degree, honor the traditional Sabbath and the traditional holidays. . . . And the reason for these things is not because there's a religious majority that supports it, but because even people who are themselves not so observant, see it as part of the national heritage, part of the national inheritance. This began with Herzl in the 1890s. He himself was not a very observant man, but from the First Zionist Congress he made respect for the Sabbath and various other elements of Jewish tradition an integral part of the Zionist movement. I don't think it's so far from, in many respects, what America was like at the time of the American founding, when George Washington and his party—the national conservatives of the Federalist Party, who wrote the American Constitution—they also saw religion as something that was an intrinsic part of their inheritance, an intrinsic part of what America was. . . . So I think that Americans can certainly learn from Israel and from other countries. But if you dig into America's past, you find something very similar. (Interview with Yoram Hazony by Rod Dreher and Kale

Zelden, "Yoram Hazony and the Next Conservatism," *American Conservative*, May 23, 2022, https://tinyurl.com/2kb3rfju)

11. For the uninitiated: Thatcher is to British conservatism what Reagan is to American conservatism. And William F. Buckley was perhaps the most significant conservative public intellectual in the United States during the second half of the twentieth century. In addition to founding the *National Review*, which helped to define the conservative movement and promote the fusion of social conservatism and fiscal libertarianism, Buckley hosted the television show *Firing Line* for over thirty years.

12. Andrew Marantz, "Does Hungary Offer a Glimpse of Our Authoritarian Future?," *New Yorker*, June 27, 2022, https://tinyurl.com/2s9yfneu.

13. Steven Levitsky and Lucan A. Way, "The Rise of Competitive Authoritarianism," *Journal of Democracy*, April 2002.

14. Steven Levitsky and Daniel Ziblatt, *How Democracies Die* (New York: Broadway Books, 2018), 5.

15. Benjamin Wallace-Wells, "What American Conservatives See in Hungary's Leader," *New Yorker*, September 13, 2021, https://tinyurl.com/45wfwrnk.

16. Marantz, "Does Hungary Offer a Glimpse?"

17. Marantz, "Does Hungary Offer a Glimpse?"

18. Elisabeth Zerofsky, "How the American Right Fell in Love with Hungary," *New York Times Magazine*, October 19, 2021, https://tinyurl.com/ym3zejct; Marantz, "Does Hungary Offer a Glimpse?"; Wallace-Wells, "What American Conservatives See"; Lydia Gall, "Hungary's Latest Assault on the Judiciary," Human Rights Watch, December 14, 2018, https://tinyurl.com/yzyufh93.

19. Zerofsky, "How the American Right."

20. H. David Baer, "What Viktor Orbán Revealed This Weekend," *Bulwark*, July 26, 2022, https://tinyurl.com/mr2ww2bt.

21. Kalee Burns, Liana Fox, and Danielle Wilson, "Child Poverty Fell to Record Low 5.2% in 2021," United States Census Bureau, September 13, 2022, https://tinyurl.com/2myejfn7.

22. Marantz, "Does Hungary Offer a Glimpse?"

23. Marantz, "Does Hungary Offer a Glimpse?"

24. Rod Dreher, "What Conservatives Must Learn from Orban's Hungary" (plenary address at the National Conservatism Conference, November 2, 2021), https://tinyurl.com/ymvwjjfs.

25. Marantz, "Does Hungary Offer a Glimpse?"

26. Wallace-Wells, "What American Conservatives See."

27. Rod Dreher, interview by Judit Csernyanszky, "Elferdíti az igazságot

az ellenzék Magyarországon, erről kell ma beszélnünk!," Klubrádió, August 7, 2021, https://tinyurl.com/24ay7w9r; translated into English by David Baer, August 29, 2021, at https://tinyurl.com/3rxh9vhz.

28. There are books to be written on the web of connections between the national conservative movement, particularly the Edmund Burke Foundation, and Viktor Orbán's government. Both Dreher and O'Sullivan were among the featured speakers at the EBF's 2022 National Conservatism Conference in Miami, as was Viktor Orbán's political director, Balázs Orbán (no relation). These are just a few of the most prominent examples.

29. Jerome Copulsky, "Panel 1: Ideologies," "White Christian Nationalism and the Midterm Elections" webinar conference, Yale Sociology Department, September 30, 2022, https://tinyurl.com/5xyp6329.

30. This isn't to say that the rule of law cannot tolerate any normative standard apart from the law in its current form. For example, natural law theorists hold that good systems of law conform to certain moral truths about what people deserve and what we owe each other. The point is that a society that is governed by the rule of law is one in which agents of law enforcement are not, as a matter of official policy, called upon to enforce nonlegal norms.

31. "Live Not by Lies: A Conversation with Author Rod Dreher about Moral Resistance in a Secular Age," October 28, 2020, https://tinyurl.com/bdhs4rf8.

32. Rod Dreher, "Büszke vagyok arra, amit Magyarország tesz Európában és a világszínpadon, ezért ide költözöm," interview on Kossuth Rádió, September 18, 2022.

33. Copulsky, "Panel 1: Ideologies."

34. "America's Godly Heritage," Freedom Sunday, First Baptist Church of Dallas, June 27, 2021, https://tinyurl.com/3dhmrn8h. See also Jack Jenkins, "The Activist behind Opposition to the Separation of Church and State," Religion News Service, July 18, 2022, https://tinyurl.com/2mum7dmn.

35. Erik Eckholm, "Using History to Mold Ideas on the Right," *New York Times*, May 4, 2011, https://tinyurl.com/2ubfrx8t.

36. Elise Hu, "Publisher Pulls Controversial Thomas Jefferson Book, Citing Loss of Confidence," NPR, August 9, 2012, https://tinyurl.com/n632kdj8.

37. Kathleen Wellman, *Hijacking History: How the Christian Right Teaches History and Why It Matters* (New York: Oxford University Press, 2021), 179.

38. Thomas Jefferson, quoted in Wellman, *Hijacking History*, 180.

39. The third article of the EBF's Statement of Principles reads: "3. National Government. The independent nation-state is instituted to establish a more perfect union among the diverse communities, parties, and regions of a given nation, to provide for their common defense and justice among them, and to secure the general welfare and the blessings of liberty for this time and for future generations. We believe in a strong but limited state, subject to constitutional restraints and a division of powers. We recommend

a drastic reduction in the scope of the administrative state and the policy-making judiciary that displace legislatures representing the full range of a nation's interests and values. We recommend the federalist principle, which prescribes a delegation of power to the respective states or subdivisions of the nation so as to allow greater variation, experimentation, and freedom. However, in those states or subdivisions in which law and justice have been manifestly corrupted, or in which lawlessness, immorality, and dissolution reign, national government must intervene energetically to restore order."

40. As we noted in chapter 5, one factor that contributed to Barry Goldwater's dismal failure in the 1964 US presidential election was proximity to the Great Depression and the New Deal. Much of the electorate had lived through these epochs in American history, and they weren't going to buy the notion that government spending on social welfare was the source of their problems.

41. Jason Stanley, *How Fascism Works: The Politics of Us and Them* (New York: Random House, 2018), 6.

### Chapter 7

1. I should acknowledge a small complication on this point. Obviously, facts regarding human cognition *are* contingent on the thoughts or feelings of a given cognizer. Thus, e.g., facts about the substance of Smith's beliefs at time *t* are entirely dependent on Smith's beliefs at time *t*. That said, the factual details of Smith's cognition at *t* are not contingent on what anyone, including Smith, believes about those facts. Of course, Smith's beliefs and attitudes may change or develop over time, due to outside influence or Smith's own metacognition. Be that as it may, details concerning the state of Smith's cognition at *t* are not contingent on anything other than Smith's cognition at *t*.

2. There's a distinct sense of the word *opinion* that we should highlight and set aside. The word *opinion* is sometimes used to describe a belief for which the believer lacks sufficient evidence or inferential support. In this sense, what makes a given belief an opinion is a matter of epistemic credence. Thus one might hold an "opinion" about a matter of fact—e.g., whether Caesar crossed the Rubicon in 49 BCE. So note that when I describe a given statement as a *matter of opinion*, I'm not referring to its epistemic status in the mind of some or other cognizer. Rather, I'm referring to a feature of the belief itself—namely, that the belief concerns something that is strictly subjective.

3. A related objection appeals to observable cultural mores that discourage lying and stealing. But cultural mores are no more reliable a guide to moral truth than our laws—often less so.

4. Charlotte Gibson, "Who's Highest-Paid in Your State?," ESPN, 2019, https://tinyurl.com/4ejf5jz8.

5. National Education Association, "Educator Pay and Student Spending: How Does Your State Rank?," April 26, 2022, https://tinyurl.com/5fwm22as.

6. Alabama State Personnel Department, "State of Alabama Trooper Candidate Information Guide," accessed April 18, 2023, https://tinyurl.com/2euyv9yn.

7. For technical reasons that are irrelevant to present concerns, economists call this view *marginalism*. See Mariana Mazzucato, *The Value of Everything: Making and Taking in the Global Economy* (New York: Public Affairs, 2018), for a secular critique of marginalism by an influential economist.

8. Associated Press, "Kansas City School District Doesn't Make Full Accreditation," KTVI FOX 2 News St. Louis, November 16, 2017, https://tinyurl.com/2pz23b3d.

9. See Bruce Baker and Kevin Welner, "School Finance and Courts: Does Reform Matter, and How Can We Tell?," *Teachers College Record* 113, no. 11 (November 2011): 2374–2414.

10. See Matt. 6:21. See also the economic theory of revealed preferences (versus expressed or stated preferences).

11. For historical perspective on methodological individualism among evangelicals, see Frances FitzGerald, *The Evangelicals: The Struggle to Shape America* (New York: Simon & Schuster, 2017), 16, 21, 54, 202. For a recent example, see Albert Mohler, "Systemic Racism, God's Grace, and the Human Heart: What the Bible Teaches about Structural Sin," *Public Discourse*, June 25, 2020, https://tinyurl.com/ajzs24mr.

12. The biblical picture of false prophets bears a striking resemblance to some of the more strident proponents of "biblical" patriarchy—most of whom are or were at one time associated with the Council on Biblical Manhood and Womanhood—whose dalliances with the doctrine of the "eternal subordination of the Son" have redounded to their own professional benefit. These men went so far as to misrepresent the very nature of the Trinity in an effort to legitimate a niche research agenda that they were well positioned to lead (largely because the most fertile theological minds of our era simply have no interest in advancing male headship). They spend their days stirring up controversy, insisting that God's people break fellowship over the secondary effects of tertiary issues that are a matter of grave importance only to men whose professional advancement depends on it—e.g., whether a church that allows a woman to speak on a Sunday morning is in compliance with the *Baptist Faith and Message*. It's clever in a strictly Machiavellian sense: find a subject that none of the really talented people in your field care about, create a journal for it, publish in your own journal, and then leverage politics and personal connections to demand that it be taken seriously.

13. It's worth observing that the vast majority of criminal law enforcement takes place at the state and local level—though state and local laws and the conduct of state and local law enforcement are subject to federal oversight, particularly where questions of due process are concerned.

14. Even when an arbitration agreement is in place, courts have the authority to rule on whether that agreement is legally binding.

15. See Plato's *Republic*, especially books 1–2.

16. See *Republic*, book 1, where this view is defended by Thrasymachus—and subsequently by Glaucon and Adeimantus, who defend roughly Thrasymachus's position for the sake of argument following the latter's departure. Machiavelli's *The Prince* is also an elaboration of political realism.

17. The ideological origins of the modern religious right go at least as far back as the middle of the twentieth century. I refer here to the political mobilization that coalesced around Ronald Reagan's 1980 presidential campaign and remained largely in force as of the 2020 presidential election. See Kristin Kobes Du Mez, *Jesus and John Wayne* (New York: Liveright, 2020); Kevin Kruse, *One Nation under God* (New York: Basic Books, 2015); Andrew L. Whitehead and Samuel L. Perry, *Taking America Back for God: Christian Nationalism in the United States* (New York: Oxford University Press, 2020).

18. Benjamin Wallace-Wells, "What American Conservatives See in Hungary's Leader," *New Yorker*, September 13, 2021, https://tinyurl.com/45wfwrnk.

# Bibliography

Balmer, Randall. *Thy Kingdom Come: How the Religious Right Distorts the Faith and Threatens America*. New York: Basic Books, 2006.

Barr, Beth Allison. *The Making of Biblical Womanhood: How the Subjugation of Women Became Gospel Truth*. Grand Rapids: Brazos, 2021.

Bass, Jack, and Walter De Vries. *The Transformation of Southern Politics: Social Change and Political Consequences Since 1945*. Athens: University of Georgia Press, 1995.

Blumenthal, Sidney. *Pledging Allegiance: The Last Campaign of the Cold War*. New York: HarperCollins, 1990.

Boice, James Montgomery. *Genesis: An Expositional Commentary*. Vol. 1, *Genesis 1–11*. Grand Rapids: Zondervan, 1982.

Brookes, Iveson L. *A Defence of the South Against the Reproaches and Incroachments of the North: In Which Slavery is Shown to be an Institution of God Intended to Form the Basis of the Best Social State and the Only Safeguard to the Permanence of a Republican Government*. Hamburg, SC: The Republican Office, 1850.

Butler, Anthea. *White Evangelical Racism: The Politics of Morality in America*. Chapel Hill: University of North Carolina Press, 2021.

Carter, Dan T. *From George Wallace to Newt Gingrich: Race in the Conservative Counterrevolution, 1963-1994*. Walter Lynwood Fleming Lectures in Southern History. Baton Rouge: Louisiana State University Press, 1996.

———. *The Politics of Rage: George Wallace, the Origins of the New Conservatism, and the Transformation of American Politics*. Baton Rouge: Louisiana State University Press, 1995.

Curtis, Jesse. *The Myth of Colorblind Christians: Evangelicals and White Supremacy in the Civil Rights Era*. New York: New York University Press, 2021.

Dabney, Robert L. *A Defence of Virginia and Through Her, of the South, in Recent and Pending Contests Against the Sectional Party*. New York: E. J. Hale & Son, 1867.

———. *Discussions of Robert Lewis Dabney*. Edited by C. R. Vaughan. Vol. 4. Harrisonburg, VA: Sprinkle Publications, 1994.

Douglas, Susan, and Meredith Michaels. *The Mommy Myth: The Idealization of Motherhood and How It Has Undermined Women*. New York: Free Press, 2004.

Du Mez, Kristin Kobes. *Jesus and John Wayne*. New York: Liveright, 2020.

———. *A New Gospel for Women: Katherine Bushnell and the Challenge of Christian Feminism*. New York: Oxford University Press, 2015.

Ehrlichman, John. *Witness to Power: The Nixon Years*. New York: Simon & Schuster, 1970.

Falwell, Jerry. *Listen, America!* Garden City, NY: Doubleday, 1980.

FitzGerald, Frances. *The Evangelicals: The Struggle to Shape America*. New York: Simon & Schuster, 2017.

Gorski, Philip S., and Samuel L. Perry. *The Flag and the Cross: White Christian Nationalism and the Threat to American Democracy*. New York: Oxford University Press, 2022.

Gregoire, Sheila Wray, Rebecca Gregoire Lindenbach, and Joanna Sawatsky. *The Great Sex Rescue: The Lies You've Been Taught and How to Recover What God Intended*. Grand Rapids: Baker Books, 2021.

Gribben, Crawford. *Survival and Resistance in Evangelical America: Christian Reconstruction in the Pacific Northwest*. New York: Oxford University Press, 2021.

Hacker, Jacob S., and Paul Pierson. *Let Them Eat Tweets: How the Right Rules in an Age of Extreme Inequality*. New York: Liveright, 2020.

Haidt, Jonathan. *The Righteous Mind: Why Good People Are Divided by Politics and Religion*. New York: Pantheon Books, 2012.

Ham, Ken, ed. *The New Answers Book 1*. Green Forest, AR: Master Books, 2006. Available online at https://tinyurl.com/2s8fu2cb.

Hawkins, J. Russell. *The Bible Told Them So: How Southern Evangelicals Fought to Preserve White Supremacy*. New York: Oxford University Press, 2021.

Huskinson, Benjamin J. *American Creationism, Creation Science, and Intelligent Design in the Evangelical Market*. Christianities in the Trans-Atlantic World. Cham, Switzerland: Palgrave Macmillan, 2020.

Ingersoll, Julie J. *Building God's Kingdom: Inside the World of Christian Reconstruction*. New York: Oxford University Press, 2015.

Johnson, Jessica. *Biblical Porn: Affect, Labor, and Pastor Mark Driscoll's Evangelical Empire*. Durham, NC: Duke University Press, 2018.

Kerby, Lauren R. *Saving History: How White Evangelicals Tour the Nation's Capital and Redeem a Christian America*. Chapel Hill: University of North Carolina Press, 2020.

Kruse, Kevin. *One Nation under God*. New York: Basic Books, 2015.

Laats, Adam. *Creationism USA: Bridging the Impasse on Teaching Evolution*. New York: Oxford University Press, 2021.

LaHaye, Tim. *The Battle for the Public Schools: Humanism's Threat to Our Children*. Old Tappan, NJ: Revell, 1983.

Legg, Kathryn. "Equal in His Sight: An Examination of the Evolving Opinions on Race in the Life of Jerry Falwell, Sr." Senior honors thesis, Liberty University, 2019.

Leman, Kevin. *Sheet Music: Uncovering the Secrets of Sexual Intimacy in Marriage*. Carol Stream, IL: Tyndale House, 2002.

Levitsky, Steven, and Daniel Ziblatt. *How Democracies Die*. New York: Broadway Books, 2018.

Long, David E. *Evolution and Religion in American Education: An Ethnography*. Cultural Studies of Science Education 4. Dordrecht: Springer, 2011.

López, Ian Haney. *Dog Whistle Politics: How Coded Racial Appeals Have Reinvented Racism and Wrecked the Middle Class*. New York: Oxford University Press, 2014.

Margolis, Michele F. *From Politics to the Pews: How Partisanship and the Political Environment Shape Religious Identity*. Chicago Studies in American Politics. Chicago: University of Chicago Press, 2018.

Marsden, George M. *Fundamentalism and American Culture*. New York: Oxford University Press, 2022.

Martí, Gerardo. *American Blindspot: Race, Class, Religion, and the Trump Presidency*. London: Rowman & Littlefield, 2020.

Mazzucato, Mariana. *The Value of Everything: Making and Taking in the Global Economy*. New York: Public Affairs, 2018.

McGinniss, Joe. *The Selling of the President, 1968*. New York: Trident Books, 1969.

Morris, Henry. *The Beginning of the World: A Scientific Study of Genesis 1–11*. Green Forest, AR: Master Books, 1991.

———. *The Long War against God: The History and Impact of the Creation/Evolution Conflict*. Green Forest, AR: Master Books, 2008.

Morris, Henry M., and John C. Whitcomb. *The Genesis Flood: The Biblical Record and Its Scientific Implications*. Phillipsburg, NJ: Reformed Publishing, 1961.

Noll, Mark A. *The Civil War as a Theological Crisis*. Chapel Hill: University of North Carolina Press, 2006.

———. *The Scandal of the Evangelical Mind*. Grand Rapids: Eerdmans, 1994.

Numbers, Ronald L. *The Creationists: From Scientific Creationism to Intelligent Design*. Expanded ed. Cambridge, MA: Harvard University Press, 2006.

Perlstein, Rick. *Before the Storm: Barry Goldwater and the Unmaking of the American Consensus*. New York: Nation Books, 2009.

———. *Reaganland: America's Right Turn, 1976–1980*. New York: Simon & Schuster, 2020.

Phillips, Kevin P. *The Emerging Republican Majority*. New Rochelle, NY: Arlington House, 1969.

Piper, John, and Wayne Grudem, eds. *Recovering Biblical Manhood and Womanhood: A Response to Evangelical Feminism*. Wheaton, IL: Crossway Books, 1991.

Plass, Ewald M. *What Martin Luther Says: A Practical In-Home Anthology for the Active Christian*. St. Louis: Concordia, 1959.

Reed, Ralph. *Awakening: How America Can Turn from Economic and Moral Destruction Back to Greatness*. Brentwood, TN: Worthy Books, 2014.

Robin, Corey. *The Reactionary Mind: Conservatism from Edmund Burke to Donald Trump*. New York: Oxford University Press, 2018.

Rothstein, Richard. *The Color of Law: A Forgotten History of How Our Government Segregated America*. New York: Liveright, 2017.

Smith, Hedrick. *Who Stole the American Dream?* New York: Random House, 2012.

Stanley, Jason. *How Fascism Works: The Politics of Us and Them*. New York: Random House, 2018.

———. *How Propaganda Works*. Princeton: Princeton University Press, 2015.

Stewart, Katherine. *The Power Worshippers: Inside the Dangerous Rise of Religious Nationalism*. New York: Bloomsbury, 2022.

Tannehill, Brynn. *American Fascism: How the GOP Is Subverting Democracy*. N.p.: Transgress Press, 2021.

Tisby, Jemar. *The Color of Compromise: The Truth about the American Church's Complicity in Racism*. Grand Rapids: Zondervan, 2019.

———. *How to Fight Racism: Courageous Christianity and the Journey toward Racial Justice*. Grand Rapids: Zondervan, 2021.

Toumey, Christopher P. *God's Own Scientists: Creationists in a Secular World*. New Brunswick, NJ: Rutgers University Press, 1994.

Wellman, Katherine. *Hijacking History: How the Christian Right Teaches History and Why It Matters*. New York: Oxford University Press, 2021.

White, Ellen G. *The Spirit of Prophecy*. Vol. 1. Battle Creek, MI: Seventh-day Adventist Publishing Association, 1870.

———. *Spiritual Gifts*. Vol. 3. Battle Creek, MI: Seventh-day Adventist Publishing Association, 1864.

Whitehead, Andrew L., and Samuel L. Perry. *Taking America Back for God: Christian Nationalism in the United States*. New York: Oxford University Press, 2020.

Wills, Garry. *Nixon Agonistes: The Crisis of the Self-Made Man*. New York: Open Road Integrated Media, 1969.

Wilson, Douglas. *Black and Tan: A Collection of Essays and Excursions on Slavery, Culture War, and Scripture in America*. Moscow, ID: Canon, 2005.

Winters, Michael Sean. *God's Right Hand: How Jerry Falwell Made God a Republican and Baptized the American Right*. New York: HarperCollins, 2012.

Worthen, Molly. *Apostles of Reason: The Crisis of Authority in American Evangelicalism*. New York: Oxford University Press, 2016.

Ziblatt, Daniel. *Conservative Parties and the Birth of Democracy*. Cambridge: Cambridge University Press, 2017.

# Index

*Note: "Evangelical" in the index refers specifically to white American evangelicals.*